Semantics of Statebuilding

This volume examines international statebuilding in terms of language and meanings, rather than focusing narrowly on current policy practices.

After two decades of evolution towards more 'integrated', 'multi-faceted' or, simply stated, more intrusive statebuilding and peacebuilding operations, a critical literature has slowly emerged on the economic, social and political impacts of these interventions. Scholars have started to analyse the 'unintended consequences' of peacebuilding missions, analysing all aspects of interventions.

Central to the book is the understanding that language is both the most important tool for building anything of social significance, and the primary repository of meanings in any social setting. Hence, this volume exemplifies how the multiple realities of state, state fragility and statebuilding are being conceptualised in mainstream literature, by highlighting the repercussions this conceptualisation has on 'good practices' for statebuilding. Drawing together leading scholars in the field, this project provides a meeting point between constructivism in international relations and the critical perspective on liberal peacebuilding, shedding new light on the commonly accepted meanings and concepts underlying the international (or world) order, as well as the semantics of contemporary statebuilding practices.

This book will be of much interest to students of statebuilding and intervention, war and conflict studies, security studies and international relations.

Nicolas Lemay-Hébert is a senior lecturer at the University of Birmingham.

Nicholas Onuf is Professor Emeritus of International Relations at Florida International University.

Vojin Rakić is Professor of Political Science at the University of Belgrade.

Petar Bojanić is a researcher at the Institute for Philosophy and Social Theory, Belgrade.

Routledge Studies in Intervention and Statebuilding

Series Editor: David Chandler

Statebuilding and Intervention
Policies, practices and paradigms
Edited by David Chandler

Reintegration of Armed Groups After Conflict
Politics, violence and transition
Edited by Mats Berdal and David H. Ucko

Security, Development, and the Fragile State
Bridging the gap between theory and policy
David Carment, Stewart Prest, and Yiagadeesen Samy

Kosovo, Intervention and Statebuilding
The international community and the transition to independence
Edited by Aidan Hehir

Critical Perspectives on the Responsibility to Protect
Interrogating theory and practice
Edited by Philip Cunliffe

Statebuilding and Police Reform
The freedom of security
Barry J. Ryan

Violence in Post-Conflict Societies
Remarginalisation, remobilisers and relationships
Anders Themnér

Statebuilding in Afghanistan
Multinational contributions to reconstruction
Edited by Nik Hynek and Péter Marton

The International Community and Statebuilding
Getting its act together?
Edited by Patrice C. McMahon and Jon Western

Statebuilding and State-Formation
The political sociology of intervention
Edited by Berit Bliesemann de Guevara

Political Economy of Statebuilding
Power after peace
Edited by Mats Berdal and Dominik Zaum

New Agendas in Statebuilding
Hybridity, contingency and history
Edited by Robert Egnell and Peter Haldén

Mediation and Liberal Peacebuilding
Peace from the ashes of war?
Edited by Mikael Eriksson and Roland Kostić

Semantics of Statebuilding
Language, meanings and sovereignty
Edited by Nicolas Lemay-Hébert, Nicholas Onuf, Vojin Rakić and Petar Bojanić

Semantics of Statebuilding

Language, meanings and sovereignty

Edited by Nicolas Lemay-Hébert, Nicholas Onuf, Vojin Rakić and Petar Bojanić

LONDON AND NEW YORK

First published 2014
by Routledge
2 Park Square, Milton Park, Abingdon, Oxfordshire OX14 4RN

and by Routledge
711 Third Avenue, New York, NY 10017

First issued in paperback 2016

Routledge is an imprint of the Taylor & Francis Group, an informa business

British Library Cataloguing in Publication Data
A catalogue record for this book is available from the British Library

Library of Congress Cataloging in Publication Data
Semantics of statebulding: language, meanings and sovereignty/edited by Nicolas Lemay-Hébert, Nicholas Onuf, Vojin Rakić and Petar Bojanić.
pages cm. – (Routledge studies in intervention and statebuilding)
Includes bibliographical references and index.
1. Nation-building. 2. Semantics. I. Lemay-Hébert, Nicolas.
JZ6300.S457 2014
327.1–dc23

2013015401

ISBN 13: 978-1-138-65025-1 (pbk)
ISBN 13: 978-0-415-81729-5 (hbk)

Typeset in Times
by Wearset Ltd, Boldon, Tyne and Wear

Contents

Contributors

Albena Azmanova is a senior lecturer at the University of Kent's Brussels School of International Studies. Her writing in social theory and political philosophy focuses on democratic transition and consolidation, social justice, and the transformation of political ideologies. Her latest book is *The Scandal of Reason: A Critical Theory of Political Judgment*, (2012).

Petar Bojanić is the Director of the Institute for Philosophy and Social Theory, Belgrade University, at which he is also a Senior Research Fellow. He also heads the Center for Ethics, Law and Applied Philosophy. His research interests include political philosophy, continental philosophy, German idealism and Marx, bioethics, phenomenology, Jewish philosophy, philosophy of law, ethics of war. After having completed his PhD, "The War (Last) and the Institution of Philosophy", under the supervision of Jacques Derrida and Etienne Balibar, he taught at the University of Cornell (USA), Aberdeen (UK) and the University of Belgrade (SRB). He is the author of numerous books, which include: *Carl Schmitt and Jacques Derrida* (1995), *Figures of sovereignty* (2007), *Provocations* (2008), and *World Governance* (with J. Babic) (2010).

Kenneth Chan is a doctoral researcher at the Leuven Centre for Global Governance Studies and Institute for International Law, University of Leuven. He has a background in law, receiving an LLB (Hons) from the University of Auckland, New Zealand (2009), and read for his LLM (Adv) in Public International Law at the University of Leiden (2010). He has interned at the ICTY and the Coalition for the ICC, acting as an independent legal observer for the Lubanga and Katanga/Ngudjolo trials. His main interests are in international criminal law, international humanitarian law and transitional justice

David Chandler is Professor of International Relations and Director of the Centre for the Study of Democracy at the Department of Politics and International Relations, University of Westminster. He is the founding editor of the *Journal of Intervention and Statebuilding* and the editor of a new journal *Resilience: International Policies, Practices and Discourses*. Recent books include *Freedom vs Necessity in International Relations* (2013) and *The*

Routledge Handbook on International Statebuilding (co-edited with Tim Sisk) (2013).

Friedrich Kratochwil studied philosophy and classics at Munich and received a PhD in political science from Princeton University. He has published widely on international relations social theory and international law. He taught at the universities of Maryland, Columbia, Denver and Penn before returning to Europe and becoming chair of international relations at the LMU in Munich and at the European University Institute in Florence. His latest book (*The Puzzles of Politics*) was published by Routledge in 2011. Presently he is international scholar at Kyung Hee University in Seoul and visiting Professor at the CEU Budapest, working on a book on the status of law in international society (*Meditations on the Status of Law in World Society*, Cambridge University Press).

Nicolas Lemay-Hébert is a senior lecturer at the International Development Department, University of Birmingham. His research interests include development and security sector reform debates surrounding local ownership and local participation, peace missions and the local narratives of resistance and contestation to international structures, and the political economy of international interventions. He has published various scientific articles in top refereed journals, including *International Studies Perspectives*, *Third World Quarterly*, *International Peacekeeping* and the *Journal of Intervention and Statebuilding*.

Iver B. Neumann, D. Phil. (Oxon, Politics 1992), Dr. Philos. (Oslo, Social Anthropology, 2009) is Montague Burton Professor of International Relations at the London School of Economics, but wrote this piece when he was Director of Research at the Norwegian Institute of International Affairs. He was the editor of *Cooperation and Conflict. Nordic Journal of International Relations* 1999–2001 and Professor in Russian Studies, Oslo University, 2005–2010. Among his fourteen books are *Russia and Europe. A Study in Identity and International Relations* (1996), *Uses of the Other: 'The East' in European Identity Formation* (1999), with Ole Jacob Sending, *Governing the Global Polity* (2010) and *At Home with the Diplomats: Inside A European Foreign Ministry* (2012).

Nicholas Onuf is Professor Emeritus, Florida International University, Miami, and Professor Associado, Instituto de Relações Internationais, Pontifica Universidade Católica do Rio de Janeiro. His latest book is *Making Sense, Making Worlds: Constructivism in Social Theory and International Relations*, which Routledge has published in conjunction with the republication of *World of Our Making* (1989).

Vojin Rakić is a Full Professor and Principal Research Fellow at the Institute for Philosophy and Social Theory of the University of Belgrade. He has a PhD in Political Science from Rutgers University (1998). Rakić worked as a senior research fellow at the Center for Higher Education Policy Studies at the University of Twente in the Netherlands (1999–2000). Between 2001 and 2003 he was a UN Special Adviser to the Government of Serbia, primarily in charge of public administration reform. Since 2003 he has worked as a university professor in Belgrade. Ha has published six books and a variety of articles in international scientific journals, mainly from the domain of political philosophy, comparative politics and bioethics.

Julian Reid is Professor of International Politics at the University of Lapland in Finland. Prior to that he taught at King's College London, the University of Sussex and SOAS, University of London. He studied for his BA at King's College London, his MA at the University of Amsterdam and took his PhD at the University of Lancaster. He has written extensively on the biopolitics of war and security in the modern age, and is the author of two books, *The Biopolitics of the War on Terror* (2006) and *The Liberal Way of War* (with Michael Dillon) (2009). He has also co-edited (with Brad Evans) a new book on *Deleuze and Fascism*, published by Routledge in 2013.

Jan Wouters is Professor of International Law and International Organizations, Jean Monnet Chair *Ad Personam* EU and Global Governance and Director of the Leuven Centre for Global Governance Studies and Institute for International Law at the University of Leuven. He is Visiting Professor at the College of Europe (Bruges), President of the Flemish Foreign Affairs Council, Member of the Royal Flemish Academy of Belgium for Sciences and Arts and practises law as *Of Counsel* at Linklaters, Brussels. He has published widely (around 450 publications, including 40 books and 80 international journal articles) on international and EU law.

Acknowledgements

Chapter 3 was first published as ‘Politics, law, and the sacred: a conceptual analysis’ in *Journal of International Relations and Development*, vol. 16, pp. 1–24, 2013, and is reprinted here with kind permission of Palgrave Macmillian.

An extended version of Chapter 9 was published as ‘The “Empty-Shell” Approach: The Setup Process of International Administrations in Timor-Leste and Kosovo, Its Consequences and Lessons’ in *International Studies Perspectives*, vol. 12, no. 2, 2011, pp. 190–211. The material is republished with kind permission.

1 Introduction

Disputing Weberian semantics

Nicolas Lemay-Hébert, Nicholas Onuf and Vojin Rakić

After two decades of evolution towards more 'integrated', 'multi-faceted' or, simply stated, more intrusive statebuilding and peacebuilding operations, a critical literature has slowly emerged on the economic, social and political impacts of these interventions. Scholars have started to analyse the 'unintended consequences' of peacebuilding missions, analysing all aspects of interventions, and not only those traditionally accounted for by the peacebuilding actors themselves (Aoi *et al.* 2007; Paris and Sisk 2009). Others have developed a critique of the liberal peace framework, questioning the wider normative framework of interventions and the values promoted by these interventions (Campbell *et al.* 2011; Chandler 2006 and 2010; Pugh *et al.* 2008; Richmond 2005, 2011; Tadjbakhsh 2011). To a certain extent, the debate has revolved around the Coxian dichotomy of 'critical scholars' and 'problem solvers' (Cox 1981, based on Horkheimer 1976), where 'problem solvers' are believed to focus on performance issues, while 'critical scholars' are more inclined to question the inherent assumptions underpinning the liberal peace (for a book bringing together the two strands, see Newman *et al.* 2009). These theoretical and empirical debates have been extremely fecund, and can be credited, for the most part, for a bona fide renewal of the broader field of peace studies (Mac Ginty 2011: 22–25).

While building on this burgeoning critical literature, this volume aims to take the discussion outside the strict confines of peace studies and political science, to fully engage with philosophical, sociological, historical and economic perspectives. In the process, contributors shed a new light on the 'bundle of practices and meanings' (Chandler 2010: viii) that statebuilding is, shifting attention from statebuilding as a professional practice to meanings associated with it. Central to the process is our understanding that language is both the most important tool for building anything of social significance and the primary repository of meanings in any social setting. Hence, this volume contributes in its own way to exemplify how the multiple realities of state, state fragility and statebuilding are being conceptualised in the mainstream literature, by highlighting the repercussions this conceptualisation has on 'good practices' for statebuilding, demonstrating how the semantics of statebuilding 'construct, reproduce and maintain particular visions of order' (Bellamy 2005: 33). But additionally – and this is perhaps one of the defining features of this collective volume – we do so by striving to emancipate ourselves from the normative straitjacket that has been imposed by the orthodoxy in the literature, broadening the scope of the debate to reach theoretical dimensions often left unexplored by preceding works on the subject.

A specific focus will be placed on language and meaning associated with statebuilding. In this volume, language is understood as a medium, a way to store and convey information about the world as we experience it. Language and other media are means to exchange information with others, in the process altering and rearranging the common stock of information, and language impacts what people do with the information conveyed to them. Using language is a complicated undertaking, dependent on rules to assure mutual intelligibility (grammar, syntax) and to convey our wishes (pragmatics). Yet language is not just a fancy storage locker, conveyor belt and sorting device. It bestows meaning, but only insofar as we give meaning to what we say and find meaning in what we hear. In the study of language, meaning is the province of *semantics*.

Linguists have developed a formidably technical language to talk about semantics – to harness meaning's meaning. In everyday usage, semantics is the study of how and why language users bring together sundry, relatively meaningless or apparently unrelated bits of information so as to give them meaning, both as a whole and as parts of a whole. To focus fully on meanings – on what goes on inside people's heads to the exclusion of all else – is to take a phenomenological stance. To focus just as fully on language as a more or less reliable medium – a thing outside minds with fixed properties and ascertainable content – is a positivist and perhaps (depending on meaning) materialist stance. The contributors to this volume go to neither extreme.

Instead we look for the meaning that social practices and material conditions have for the people engaging in these practices. We do not presume actors' intentions or have direct access to the conditions in which they find themselves. Our task is to sort out what they find meaningful on the ground, so to speak, and render it meaningful at a distance. Such a stance assumes that meaning always matters – socially and materially – in making our world what it is.

The Weberian state and its meanings

In this world of ours, states matter a great deal. In the circumstances, we should not be surprised that the term *state* is loaded with meaning, fraught with ambiguity (there is, of course, a huge literature, but see, just for example, Bartelson 2001 and Hay *et al.* 2006). Nevertheless, many scholars today seem to think that, conceptually speaking, the state can only mean one thing. In this context, the Weberian approach to statehood has arguably attained the status of orthodoxy in the mainstream literature (Lemay-Hébert 2009: 23–24), and while being implicitly portrayed as consensual and apolitical, this approach carries specific consequences for scholarly and policy debates. We routinely give Max Weber credit for pinning down the state's core meaning, although Weber was merely articulating what many of his late nineteenth-century contemporaries also believed.

We quote Weber here at some length in order to make clear what his legacy entails.

> Since the concept of the state has only in modern times reached its full development, it is best to define it in terms appropriate to the modern type of state, but at the same time, in terms which abstract from the values of the present day, since they are particularly subject to change. The primary formal characteristics of the modern state are as follows: It possesses an administrative and legal order subject to change by legislation, to which the organized activities of the administrative staff, which are also controlled by regulations, are oriented. The system of order claims binding authority, not only over the members of the state, the citizens, most of whom have obtained membership by birth, but also to a very large extent over all action taking place in the area of its jurisdiction. It is thus a compulsory organization with a territorial basis. Furthermore, today the use of force is regarded as legitimate only so far as it is either permitted by the state or prescribed by it.
>
> (Weber 1978: 56)

There are five issues that Weber pointed up in this passage (taken from the early pages of *Wirtschaft und Gesellschaft*, published posthumously in 1922) that we should like to comment on. In doing so, we will try to tie these five issues to the development of the statebuilding literature and its underlying assumptions.

Stateness as an ideal type

First, nothing in our world fits Weber's description perfectly, or ever will. The concept of the state is just that – a concept or, to use his own words, an 'ideal type'. It is a constructed ideal used to approximate reality by selecting and accentuating certain elements. According to Weber, 'an ideal type is formed by the one-sided accentuation of one or more points of view' following which concrete individual phenomena are arranged into a 'unified analytical construct'; in its conceptual purity, 'this mental construct cannot be found empirically anywhere in reality' (Shils and Finch 1949: 90). Hence, states approximate to a greater or lesser degree Weber's criteria for 'stateness'. Scholars in the field of Comparative Politics have taken to distinguishing between 'strong states' and 'weak states', judged by one or other of Weber's criteria. As Joel Migdal has pointed out, the Weberian idealisation generates 'high expectation for states' (1988: 10), and not just new states, as it takes for granted that fully developed and ideal states are Western liberal democratic ones (Sharma and Gupta 2006: 10–11). One net result is that concern over the possibility of state collapse, failure or weakness often has as much to do with dashed expectations about modern statehood, or the functions that modern states should fulfil following the West's universalist pretensions, as it does with empirically observed collapse of state institutions (Latouche 1996: 103; Milliken and Krause 2003: 1–2). In the process, the Western state is employed as the norm against which all other states are judged, effectively stripping the state from its cultural moorings. Mirroring Edward Said's classical study of *Orientalism*, the failed state concept may be illuminating insofar as our understandings of those who use the concept are concerned (Wilde 2002: 428). An ideal type has become a sociocultural ideal, at least in a post-colonial world where statebuilding is an urgent, endless undertaking. Similarly, peacebuilding and statebuilding have become a new *mission civilisatrice*, an 'act to bring war-shattered states into conformity with the international system's prevailing standards of domestic governance' (Paris 2002: 638).

If the contemporary notion of state is to be at all meaningful, and not merely a 'ragbag synonym of [Western liberal] government', in the words of J.T. Nettl, it must be understood not only as an actor or an autonomous collectivity, but also as a 'summating concept of high societal generality' (1968: 564). For him, the state is 'essentially a sociocultural phenomenon. This follows from the liberation of the concept from exclusive association with particular structures' (1968: 565). In that regard, Weber's conceptualisation (ideal typification, idealisation) of the state has to be understood in conjunction with his conceptualisation of nation. Weber defines the latter as 'a community of sentiment which would adequately manifest itself in a state of its own; hence a nation is a community which normally tends to produce a state of its own' (Gerth and Mills 1948: 176). This development is interesting, yet it begs a conceptualisation as succinct as Weber's treatment of the state. His work seems not to have offered one up. His forthright German nationalism (Mommsen 1984) would have warranted the effort. More importantly, Weber might have addressed the pairing of state and nation as complementary opposites – an exceptionally influential coupling in his own time and since. For this we can thank revolutions in British North America and France as the momentous expressions of popular sovereignty (on sovereignty as the other issue not raised in the quoted passage, see below). Among their many consequences are the nineteenth-century movement for national self-determination, the decolonisation movement of the twentieth century and the resurgence of ethnic politics since 1989.

The pairing of state and nation brings us to the frequently employed division between, on the one hand, 'primordialists' or 'perennialists', who hold that nations are natural units of human association and that they have existed for eternity (van den Berghe 1981), and on the other hand 'modernists' or 'constructivists', who insist on the essentially modern character of national construction (Anderson 1983; Breuilly 1993; Gellner 1983). This division has been nuanced by a number of authors. Some have developed the 'perennialist' position in the direction of the view that nations are modern, but that their 'ethnic roots' are pre-modern (Smith 1986). Others have developed the 'constructivist' position in the direction of the conception that national identity is socially constructed but not necessarily a modern phenomenon (for a discussion, see Rakić 1998). In this whole debate it is the semantics of nation that is essential. As Dominique Schnapper indicates, if one designates by 'nation' any form of historical collectivity, then it is clear that humans have always belonged in collectives, even if their form has varied considerably throughout history (1998: 19). Hence, nations

– that is to say 'ethnies' or pre-national ethnocultural groups in 'perennialist' terms – have always existed. On the other hand, if one calls 'nation' the political form of the contemporary democratic age, it is a relatively recent construction. Thus, for Schnapper, 'sentiments of belonging in a historical collectivity might very well have existed for centuries, but it is only in contemporary times that they founded and justified a particular form of political organization' (1998: 19). In this regard, the *nation state* has to be distinguished from its predecessors, both the traditional and absolutist states (Giddens 1985: 83–121). Its particularity resides in the acceptance of the social control exercised by the state, with the feeling of belonging to a community of fate, of which the state would constitute the political expression. Nation is a social entity 'only insofar as it relates to a certain kind of modern territorial state, the nation-state, and it is pointless to discuss nation and nationality except insofar as both relate to it' (Hobsbawm 1990: 9–10).

Not considering state and nation together effectively privileges interest over passion, detachment over identity and rationalisation over *ressentiment*. In this respect, we can guess that the large number of people today who have made statebuilding a profession are inclined – as we surmise Weber was – to favour technically skilled practices over meanings and their manipulation. We can also guess that the many politicians who are so centrally involved in statebuilding will put the semantics of nation and nationalism to use, summon popular sentiments to the cause and exploit ethnic divisions and prejudice. If the goal is to build an ideal nation state, we can expect to see all sorts of contradictory tendencies to manifest themselves materially and, often enough, violently.

State and violence

Second, Weber enumerated characteristics of the *modern* state while claiming his conceptualisation was abstracted from 'the values of the present day' – presumably including the range of values and meanings associated with the national idea. Drawing on the same nineteenth-century reference points that Weber did, anthropologists have always talked about states in terms sufficiently abstract to include pre-modern polities. From this perspective, states are systems of order whose binding authority implies a potential monopoly on the use of force. Positivist legal theory draws on the same sources and comes to the same conclusions, but it is Weber whom most scholars credit with this general perspective. When they do so, they typically cite Weber's famous essay on 'Politics as a vocation'. There, with no further ado, he defined the state as 'a human community that (successfully) claims the *monopoly of the legitimate use of physical force* within a given territory' (Gerth and Mills 1948: 78, emphasis in text).

There is, however, an implicit contradiction between Weber's general requirement that the state is the only legitimate vehicle for the use of force and his description of a modern state, in which legislation and administration are carefully delimited activities. A strong state must have a strong executive, where authority resides. Yet the modern state must also have constitutionally separated powers. Furthermore, a modern state consists of citizens, on whose behalf it presumably acts, and not just subjects – people subject to the state's authority. Whether these republican principles are conceptually necessary features of the modern state or an Enlightenment bias is open to question – a question further complicated by Weber's failure to consider federal arrangements, which, by fragmenting authority, invariably weaken states.

These conceptual issues have been reflected to a certain extent in the statebuilding literature. Whereas statebuilding was once forged through 'blood and iron' (Tilly 1985), where war and preparation of war played a large part in the formation of European states up to the nineteenth century, the growing influence of norms – notably the rise of the norms of territorial integrity and democratic governance – is altering its very nature. From a process driven by capital and coercion, statebuilding acquired new international dimensions. Many states in the post-1945 world have been externally bolstered from threats to their international status, even as they were threatened by internal collapse. While historically states simply disappeared, divided up into smaller units or conquered by powerful neighbours, 'collapsing' or 'failing' states are now expected to be rebuilt within the same international borders, even if certain scholars either lobbied for a different strategy, 'letting them fail' for instance (Herbst 2004; Luttwak 1999), or underscored that this policy resulted in recognising certain states as sovereign entities notwithstanding the de facto reality on the ground (Jackson 1990). Central to the process is the emergence of the norm of territorial integrity, and the high point of the constitution of this international regime has been seen in the response of the international community to the decolonisation process (Zacher 2001). The colonial territory became the frame of reference for adjudicating competing claims for self-determination and political independence, and the pre-eminence of the territorial integrity principle was consolidated normatively through the UN Declaration on the Granting of Independence to Colonial Countries and Peoples (1960), the adoption of the Organisation of African Unity Charter (1963), the Declaration on Principles of International Law Concerning Friendly Relations and Co-operation among States (1970), and early peace operations, most notably the pioneering UN peacebuilding mission in the Congo in the 1960s.

In this regard, peacebuilding and statebuilding have been considered complementary or even mutually dependent in the literature. Yet, the 'securization of peacebuilding' (Newman 2010), based firmly on the Weberian assumption that the monopoly of the legitimate use of physical force is central to and a unique criterion for the constitution of every state, have had profound and lasting consequences. For Robert Rotberg, for instance, it is according to their performance – according to the levels of their effective delivery of the most crucial political goods, most notably the supply of security – that strong states may be distinguished from weak, failing or collapsing ones (Rotberg 2004: 2). Another example is Martin Doornbos, Susan Woodward and Silvia Roque, defining failing states as 'states incapable to fulfil the basic tasks of providing security for their populace' (2006: 2). Demonstrating how this approach has had far-reaching impacts, even Boutros Boutros-Ghali defines state collapse as 'the collapse of state institutions, especially the police and judiciary, with resulting paralysis of governance, a breakdown of law and order, and general banditry and chaos' (1995: 9). If the provision of security is clearly an important aspect of statehood, there are other dimensions that are left unexplored in this analysis. For Kalevi Holsti, for instance, the strength of the state is defined in terms of 'the capacity of the state to command loyalty – the right to rule' (1996: 82). The overemphasis on security has led authors to consider legitimacy as a mere by-product of successful delivery of public goods. In this context, the contributors to this volume go beyond the strict logics of state capacity to engage with logics of social integration and solidarity.

State and modernity

Third, Weber's conception of the modern state, with its rational administration, separation of powers and law based on uniform rights and duties, implies an evolutionary process. More specifically, for Weber and his contemporaries, this process eventuates in the familiar developmental trajectory of the West, where modernity was invented and then dispersed (or perhaps we should say 'dispensed') to the rest of the world. For anthropologists, the evolutionary process began many thousands of years ago. The 'pristine state' was a response to increased control over material conditions and the concentration of resources, and came into existence when centralised coercion reinforced social stratification as a system of order (see Fried 1967 for a classic exposition). This very fusion is central to 'traditional' political societies found everywhere until modernity took hold.

From this perspective, traditional societies only became modern when stratification ceased to be an ordering principle. This stage in the long-term evolutionary process began half a millennium ago and gained popular support in the Age of Revolutions. Only then could rational administration displace status-ordering, in the process definitively separating state and society. Where there is a modern state, traditional stratification is deprived of its necessary relation to the distribution of resources and will eventually disappear.

Modernisation theory boils this view down to the claim that achievement trumps ascription in the assignment of offices. In the balder versions of this story, status is rendered superfluous, emotions are sublimated and ceremony is reduced to spectacle. In short, modernisation dispatches a vast clutter of once meaningful practices. Even if status, sentiments and ceremony always seem to creep back into the equation (and not only because of nationalism), the modern Weberian state makes rational, regulated authority a regulative ideal. As we have already observed, it is this ideal, with its narrowed range of meanings, to which the professional statebuilders of our own day are so ardently committed.

State and sovereignty

Fourth, Weber insisted that the state has a territorial basis. If by territory we mean land and appurtenances, delimited by fixed boundaries, over which the organisational apparatus of the state has jurisdiction, then this is clearly *not* a distinguishing feature of traditional political societies. Just as clearly, modern states are territorially defined. When territory actually did become a defining feature of the modern state is a matter of controversy. In recent work, Andrew Latham (2012) has made the case for medieval origins and Jeremy Larkins (2010) for the Renaissance. Without examining the matter too closely, most scholars in the field of International Relations simply assume that the Westphalian settlement of 1648 marks the moment at which states systematically began to distinguish themselves from each other by reference to territorial boundaries. It should be noticed, however, that international law was not based on territorial jurisdiction until much later, and that the 'the cartographic revolution of the Renaissance' did not actually translate into sharply drawn state boundaries until the nineteenth century (Branch 2011, quoting p. 11).

In defining the state, Weber conspicuously avoided saying anything about sovereignty. If sovereignty is conceived as an ordering principle within the state – one that locates authority in a single high office, thereby rationalising and regulating the state's organisational apparatus – then this principle dates back to Jean Bodin and Thomas Hobbes, writing in the last decades of the Renaissance. In the passage quoted above, Weber unquestionably accepted sovereignty conceptualised in this way. He may have kept silent on the subject to avoid having to deal, then and there, with the vexing issue of federally divided sovereignty. If, however, sovereignty is conceived of territorially, then this is a later development, for reasons we have just advanced, notwithstanding the fact that many actual sovereigns had long been obliged to deal with each other in accordance with what they understood to be law – the law of nations, later called international law.

Weber's silence on sovereignty is offset, at least in some measure, by his insistence on territory as a basis for binding authority in what we can only regard as a fully modern state. Among social and political theorists, Weber has hardly been alone in neglecting to spell out clearly the link between territory and sovereignty. Scholars in International Law and International Relations have taken this omission as their remit and proceeded to build their fields on the premise that states are, in the first instance, defined by territorial sovereignty – a condition duly recognised among themselves. Most of the contributors to this volume have backgrounds in International Law and/or International Relations, and their perspective on statebuilding reflects just this framework.

More precisely, this volume takes territorial sovereignty as a backdrop and, in effect, examines the changing semantics of sovereignty and the impact of this striking change on statebuilding. For twenty years we have been hearing that sovereignty is eroding, under siege, never what we thought it was, pooling, democratic and so on (see, for example, Keohane 2002; Krasner 1999; Lyons and Mastanduno 1995; Weinert 2007). We are told that globalisation is responsible for whatever is happening to the state's territorial sovereignty. Some scholars acknowledge the impact of globalisation with such terms as post-international, post-colonial and, most of all, postmodern. Some of us consider the possibility that modernity is coming to an end not just because the world is changing so dramatically but also because we no longer think in the received categories of modern discourse – as we speak, whole constellations of meanings are shifting about.

If we are indeed in the midst of a semantic revolution, Weber's conceptualisation of the state goes only so far. Yet Weber was himself engaged in a struggle – the so-called *Methodenstreit* – over whether objective knowledge about subjective states is ever possible. As editors, we interpret Weber as having been ambivalent about the relative merits of interpretative and scientific methods of inquiry. That same ambivalence is reflected in this volume. Our contributors tack between practices and meanings as they come to grips with the imperatives of Weberian statebuilding in a world where modernity itself no longer has a stable meaning. We cannot assume that the administrative personnel tasked with statebuilding share this ambivalence. As we remarked above, they are far more likely to be unambiguously committed to the so-called Enlightenment project of making the world modern.

Weberian state and Hobbesian contract

The fifth and last point we should like to make about Weber's conception of the state returns to the matter of the modern state's relation to the use of force. It should be noticed that Weber did not speak of violence in either version of his definition of the state (although the second one we quoted does add *physical* to *force*). The anodyne phrase 'use of force' takes the violence out of violence – presumably the state's monopoly on the use of force obviates the need to use it very often and, even then, mostly for its demonstration effects. Quite a few postmodern scholars have sought to give violence its due in the modern conception of law and order (see, for example, Derrida 2002). Many other scholars see the state's relationship to violence in Hobbesian terms.

Insofar as the human condition is steeped in violence, the Hobbesian social contract giving the sovereign a monopoly on the use of force is the only plausible alternative. Violence is, at least in principle, excluded from the state except as it is legitimately deployed by the sovereign's administrative staff, acting on behalf of all of us who can no longer act violently in our own defence. As a thought experiment or exercise in rational choice theory, the Hobbesian solution to the problem of endemic violence has considerable appeal. It is far less plausible as a short story about the emergence of the modern state.

There is a longer story, in which violence figures prominently. As told by economic historians and historical sociologists in the last few decades (its proximate source is Frederic Lane's work; see essays collected in Lane 1979), the story starts with the endemic predatory violence of the near-lawless, late medieval West. Warrior kings and princes took advantage of feudal ties to organise proto-states as 'protection rackets'. At the same time, these kings and princes engaged in incessant violence against each other to expand or retain their 'turf'. In effect, as Charles Tilly famously held, state-making and war-making go together; in its origins, the state is a criminal enterprise (Tilly 1985). In this story, the state and its monopoly on the use of force emerged as an unsavoury, utterly unintended consequence of self-interested, highly exploitive behaviour in propitious material circumstances.

The rationalist–materialist emphasis on violence turns the Hobbesian solution to the problem of violence upside down. Yet both ways of thinking about the state's monopoly on the use of force appropriately emphasise the chronic violence surrounding the birth of early modern states. They also warn of the perils that ensue when states fail to work as the Weberian model requires. However, as we mentioned before, as much as the world has changed in half a millennium, statebuilders today are justly concerned about the complex and perhaps symbiotic relation of the state to social and material conditions that foster violence. We hazard to suggest that the subject of this volume offers a paradox and a challenge: the worse things are, the more people are willing to countenance a Hobbesian solution to their woes; the worse things are, the harder it is for people to build the Weberian state that the Hobbesian solution calls for.

Chapter breakdown

Each chapter in this volume addresses the semantics of statebuilding from its own empirical or theoretical perspective. Yet, four overarching and cross-cutting themes emerge in this book, with each distinct theme being linked to a different facet of the semantics of the state and statebuilding.

Rethinking international order

A first group of scholars directly question the commonly accepted meanings and concepts underlying the international (or world) order. Bringing together insights from philosophy, political science, history and international law, together they move towards a post-Westphalian order (Falk 2002), in the process deconstructing the simplistic assumptions associated with the Westphalian moment – whether it is the process of constitution of the modern state (Onuf) or the secularisation politics created via the Westphalian peace (Kratochwil). For Kratochwil, there is also a need to reinterpret the links between the human rights discourse – one of the central normative features of the current world order – and its foundations on human dignity with considerations about the sacred. Similarly, Rakić develops an interpretation of Kant where state-making is intertwined with the idea of a religiously and morally constructed society. In the process, Rakić complexifies substantially our common understanding of democratic peace, and questions the usual ramifications of this 'theory' for philosophy as well as international relations theory.

Nicholas Onuf claims in 'World-making statebuilding' (Chapter 2) that in the last five centuries the state has emerged and then transformed itself in important ways, as has the vast complex of social relations that we call the modern world. Anyone who is involved in statebuilding nowadays must rely on incomplete, confusing, yet normatively controlling layers of blueprints setting standards and limits on the properties states must have to function in the modern world – as societies and in international society. Using a periodisation inspired by Foucault's archaeology of knowledge (the Renaissance, the Classical Age, the Modern Age, Modernism, Late Modernity and the Post-modern Age), Onuf's contribution offers an overview of successive blueprints, each building on the one before. From the beginning the state, as a novel idea, gained its cogency from metaphorical association with bodies and persons, and not, at least initially, from any connection to territory. As a self-conscious activity, statebuilding gains its cogency from Modernist preoccupations with form and function.

Friedrich Kratochwil in his 'Politics, law and the sacred: a conceptual analysis' (Chapter 3) also interprets social change on the basis of reconfigurations of a repertoire. The author questions the myth of secular politics associated with the Westphalian peace, analysing the conceptual issues engendered by the interrelation of religion, state and politics. Thus, Kratochwil investigates how law, religion and politics interact, not as if they were separate 'objects', but as a semantic field. Under conditions of modernity, law can effectively dispense with the 'sacred' and perhaps even with politics by substituting 'human rights'. Since the social world is one of artifice, our concepts are constitutive of our world. Historical analysis can show how the semantics of statebuilding are constitutive in just this sense, and not just a description or icon of a pre-existing reality. The role human rights have under conditions of modernity also ought to be interpreted along the lines of this approach. A semantic field linking statebuilding and the advancement of human rights so closely complicates both as practical, institutionally differentiated activities.

Vojin Rakić's contribution (Chapter 4) focuses on 'Kant's semantics of world (state) making', with the main aim being to clarify Kant's cosmopolitanism. The position Kant developed on international relations cannot be comprehended on the basis of an interpretation of *Toward Perpetual Peace* in isolation from his systematic writings. Rakić argues that the semantics in *Toward Perpetual Peace* relates to what Kant appears to have considered as an intermediate stage of history, while in *Religion within the Boundaries of Mere Reason* his semantics is one that addresses the final purpose of history. In interpreting Kant's understanding of this final purpose of history, Rakić concludes that the concept of the 'Ethical Commonwealth' from *Religion* (defined by Kant as 'a universal republic based on the laws of virtue') implies that in this work Kant's semantics is one of world (state) making. Kant did not believe we could achieve our final historical purpose on our own; we needed Providence to give us a helping hand to achieve it. In the nearer future, on the other hand, Kant was inclined to accept the practices of statebuilding that lead 'merely' to the establishment of a federation of states.

State, society and state formation

A second group of scholars assesses the complex process of state formation and social consolidation beyond the (neo-)Weberian focus on modern institutions. This is a theme also developed to a certain extent by Kratochwil and Onuf in their contributions. Indeed for Kratochwil, the 'sacralisation of the people' was transfigured into the 'nation' as the source of legitimacy for politics and law, where nation lends legitimacy to the state; whereas similarly for Onuf, state and nation have become co-constitutive entities, the nation supplying the state with resources required for rational administration. Iver Neumann contributes to the debate by analysing the complex early state formation of the Eurasian steppe from an anthropological perspective, looking at the nomadic influences on economic and political consolidation. Neumann demonstrates the limits of the Weberian framework when scholars fail to understand it as a relational process between institutions and social structures, drawing instead from a variety of sociological influences, including the Durkheimian sociology of state formation. Similarly, Nicolas Lemay-Hébert develops the limits of the (neo-)Weberian approaches to contemporary statebuilding when understood as institutional reconstruction, bringing to the fore the debates on the sociological understanding of the modern nation state while contrasting Weberian influences with Durkheimian ones. Both chapters contribute, in their own specific way, to a complex dialectic of state and society, where each entity needs to be understood, and finds all its meanings, in the relational process.

In 'The semantics of early state-building: why the Eurasian steppe has been overlooked' (Chapter 5), **Iver Neumann** sheds light on the debates on early complex states as well as the debates on early political organisation in the Eurasian steppe, bringing into perspective one sequence of early state formation, namely that of the Rus'. Neumann explains that his sequence has three parts: the emergence of the Rus' khaganate (about which we know little), the transition to Kievan Rus' (about which we have no knowledge) and the emergence of Kievan Rus'. Once stranger-kings arrive, Neumann argues, they may not settle down immediately, but continue their raiding concurrently with their engagement in state practices at home. The study of early state formation teaches us that no polity was ever an island. Consequently, Neumann concludes that social scientists ought to stop treating polities as closed systems, and approach them instead as relational.

Nicolas Lemay-Hébert analyses the contemporary statebuilding debates from a sociological point of view in his first contribution, 'The semantics of statebuilding and nationbuilding: looking beyond neo-Weberian approaches' (Chapter 6). Lemay-Hébert argues that a narrow form of institutionalism, focusing on institutional reconstruction and the capabilities of the state to secure its grip on society, has prevailed in the literature since Helman and Ratner's seminal article in *Foreign Policy* (1992–93). If it is possible to identify a distinctive Weberian influence in the contemporary statebuilding literature, notably through an overwhelming focus on security and securitisation as the basis of state consolidation, and an implicit definition of legitimacy as *belief* in legitimacy, privileging top-down processes of justification of support for the central authority, it is also true that Weber's influence in social sciences has been somewhat distorted in the process of knowledge production. Many social scientists have reduced Weber's explanation of beliefs to the process of internalisation of these beliefs, oversimplifying state–society relationships and state formation processes. While demonstrating the limits of neo-Weberian approaches to state and statebuilding, Lemay-Hébert also echoes the need to break the tacit neo-Weberian monopoly on state and statebuilding by suggesting a 'legitimacy approach', loosely based on Durkheimian sociology.

Re-assessing liberal statebuilding

The third section includes three contributions which look at the semantics of contemporary statebuilding practices, drawing directly from the liberal peacebuilding debates discussed above. As mentioned previously, the liberal peace refers here to the idea that certain kinds of society will tend to be more peaceful, both in their domestic affairs and in their international relations, than 'illiberal' states. The liberal peace encompasses sociocultural norms associated with peacemaking, as well as the international and national structures instrumental to promoting the liberal peace. Mixing insights from political science, international law and philosophy, the three chapters critically assess liberal statebuilding in three of the main locales of contemporary interventions: the Balkans (Bosnia and Herzegovina, and Kosovo), Timor-Leste and Iraq. Taken together, these chapters contribute to wider debates on sovereignty and legitimacy in a liberal peacebuilding context, and more precisely on the semantics of justification of interventions by international actors.

In Chapter 7, entitled 'Transformative statebuilding, occupation, and international law: friends and foes?', **Jan Wouters and Kenneth Chan** discuss the attitude towards 'transformative' statebuilding during periods of belligerent occupation, using the watershed case of the US-led invasion of Iraq in 2003. International law provides a normative framework for transitional occupation, during which the occupying forces are responsible for securing public order while preserving the defeated state's existing legal and institutional infrastructure. In effect, the international law of occupation does not allow statebuilding as currently practised under international auspices. Wouters and Chan findings suggest that these practices instead draw from a sense of political and moral legitimacy, which in some cases are deemed to supersede the narrower limitations of the law occupation. Judging from post-war Iraq, the demands and difficulties of statebuilding illustrate, and perhaps aggravate, the many tensions, uncertainties and ambiguities in this emerging practice.

David Chandler addresses the semantics of 'political crisis' and 'crisis management' in EU policies of democracy promotion and statebuilding in the Balkans in Chapter 8, 'The semantics of "crisis management": simulation and EU statebuilding in the Balkans'. He uses Baudrillard's concepts of simulation and hyperreality to provide useful insights into these semantics. The outcome of the process of simulation is less the export of democracy than the export of power. This export takes place in an ad hoc and arbitrary manner through the creation of 'simulated states'. These states are what Chandler calls 'ciphers for external power', rather than entities related to their own societies. Moreover, the EU's domination of the Balkans takes the form of a denial of its power and an overemphasis and overpoliticisation of the relations between the EU and its potential Balkan member states. Chandler concludes that this state of affairs is based in the hyperreal construction of the problems of EU enlargement.

Nicolas Lemay-Hébert links the 'empty shell approach' in statebuilding practices with the delegitimisation process that was being experienced by the UN in the cases of Timor-Leste and Kosovo in Chapter 9, 'The semantics of contemporary statebuilding: Kosovo, Timor-Leste and the "empty-shell" approach'. He argues that cultural sensitivity and understanding of local society must be the guiding principles for policy planning and implementation in many statebuilding practices. Political structures created for foreign control, however, tend to be unsuited to local rule. This implies at least a substantive normative shift in the conduct of statebuilding. Consequently, local actors have to be recognised as true partners in the statebuilding process rather than mere recipients of foreign aid. Hence, the empty shell perspective vitiates local ownership. Furthermore, if one wishes to make room for local actors in a participatory framework, authority can hardly be monopolised by the international actors.

Neoliberalism and the state

Finally, a last group of scholars looks at the evolution of the state in a neoliberal context. These two contributions offer a unique framework to understand legitimacy and statebuilding, analysing neoliberal governmentalisation of the state and post-neoliberal capitalism respectively. For Azmanova, the state becomes less responsible but more powerful in terms of its instruments for economic management and reduced social responsibilities, while, for Reid, neoliberalism has found in the ecological discourse of sustainable development a new reasoning to exert its economic logic.

In 'The crisis of capitalism and the state – more powerful, less responsible, invariably legitimate' (Chapter 10), **Albena Azmanova** discusses the reconfiguration of the state-citizens-legitimacy relationship that has taken place over the past twenty years in mature European democracies. Specifically, she examines the transformative dynamics that concern the formation of a new matrix of state–society relations as they affect the semantics of statebuilding. The overly protective 'nanny state' of post-war welfare capitalism, and the 'step-mother state' of the neoliberal late twentieth century (a state which distances itself from society), has been replaced by the 'rich uncle' state – one that readily intervenes to help select actors for the sake of competitiveness in the global economy. What is needed is a readjustment of the relationship between public authority and citizens, something that requires the state to reassume responsibility for the social effects of its economic policy.

In Chapter 11, 'The neoliberal politics of resilience and the spectre of the eco-fascist state', **Julian Reid** depicts how the discourse of sustainable development actively promotes the neoliberal paradigm of society and subjectivity, a paradigm requiring us to prove ourselves by bettering individual and collective resilience. This discourse shifts the locus of concern from the issue of security of merely human life to that of the biosphere. The spectre of the ecofascist state is currently troubling liberal international relations. By advocating the idea that sustainable development will become reality only when we renounce specifically human development, as well as attendant political ideals of progress and security, learning in this process to practise the virtue of resilience, the ecofascist state portrays life for human beings as a finite game of mere survival, while statebuilding adjusts its practices to the rules of this game.

Acknowledgements

In May 2011, the University of Belgrade's Institute for Philosophy and Social Theory graciously hosted a conference on *The State and Statebuilding: Theory and Practice in Retrospect*, on which this book is based. Petar Bojanić and Vojin Rakić organised the conference, with indispensable assistance from Nikolas Rajković, who also suggested the volume's title.

The event triggered the invitation of the Routledge Series on Intervention and Statebuilding for editors to compile a volume devoted to this theme. Several papers from the Belgrade conference are included in this book in their revised form. Chapter 3 and a revised form of Chapter 9 have been published elsewhere, as detailed in the Acknowledgements.

We would like to thank all the chapter authors for their contributions and patience. We also wish to thank Srdjan Prodanović, Deana Jovanović, Jelena Vasiljević, Gazela Pudar and Ana Birešev for their help in organising the Belgrade conference, as well as Nataša Nastić at the Institute for Philosophy and Social Theory. Additionally, acknowledgement goes to Louis Monroy Santander and Mattias Hjort at the University of Birmingham for assistance in the final editing and preparation of the manuscript for publication. Two anonymous reviewers read the initial manuscript and provided insightful comments, for which we are grateful.

It is fitting that this volume is one important result of a conference held in Belgrade, a city where the ravages of state-inflicted violence are still in evidence. It matters to have met in a place where international intervention is no mere abstraction. As a second important result of meeting and talking together, all of us were reminded of the subtle ways in which meanings suffuse practice – in our case the practice of our scholarly craft. By extension, professional statebuilders, politicians and activists, and ordinary citizens fence off Kratochwil's 'semantic fields' whenever they speak about the state as a social reality and statebuilding as a practical activity. As a metaphor, *field* is too limited in semantic thrust. We might better say that 'semantic communities' shape whatever people say through familiar processes of imitation, normalisation and, yes, Weberian rationalisation. Yet another metaphor comes to mind. Pools of meaning overlap and ripple through each other, often in unexpected ways. We expect our discussions in Belgrade to continue rippling outwards in their own way, just as we expect this volume to do so in its own perhaps more predictable way.

References

Anderson, B. (1983) *Imagined Communities: Reflections on the Origin and Spread of Nationalism*, London: Verso.

Aoi, C., de Coning, C. and Thakur, R. (eds) (2007) *Unintended Consequences of Peace-Keeping Operations*, Tokyo: United Nations University Press.

Bartelson, J. (2001) *The Critique of the State*, Cambridge: Cambridge University Press.

Bellamy, A. (2005) 'The "next stage" in peace operations theory?', in A. Bellamy and P. Williams (eds) *Peace Operations and Global Order*, Abingdon: Routledge.

Boutros-Ghali, B. (1995) 'Concluding statement', presented to the UN Congress on Public International Law, New York, March 1995.

Branch, J. (2011) 'Mapping the sovereign state: technology, authority, and systemic change', *International Organization*, 65(1): 1–31.

Breuilly, J. (1993) *Nationalism and the State*, Manchester: Manchester University Press.

Campbell, S., Chandler, D. and Sabaratnam, M. (eds) (2011) *A Liberal Peace? The Problems and Practices of Peacebuilding*, London: Zed Books.

Chandler, D. (2006) *Empire in Denial: The Politics of Statebuilding*, London: Pluto Press.

Chandler, D. (2010) *International Statebuilding: The Rise of Post-liberal Governance*, Abingdon: Routledge.

Cox, R. (1981) 'Social forces, states and world orders: beyond international relations theory', *Millennium: Journal of International Studies*, 10(2): 126–155.

Derrida, J. (2002) 'Force of law: the "mystical foundation of authority"', trans. M. Quaintance, in G. Anidjar (ed.) *Acts of Religion*, New York: Routledge.

Doornbos, M., Woodward, S. and Roque, S. (2006) *Failing States or Failed States? The Role of Development Models: Collected Works*, Madrid: FRIDE.

Falk, R. (2002) 'The post-westphalia enigma', in B. Hettne and B. Odén (eds) *Global Governance in the 21st Century: Alternative Perspectives on World Order*, Sweden: Ministry of Foreign Affairs.

Fried, M.H. (1967) *The Evolution of Political Society: An Essay in Political Anthropology*, New York: Random House.

Gellner, E. (1983) *Nations and Nationalism*, Ithaca: Cornell University Press.

Gerth, H.H. and Mills, C.W. (eds) (1948) *From Max Weber: Essays in Sociology*, London: Routledge.

Giddens, A. (1985) *The Nation-State and Violence*, Cambridge: Polity Press.

Hay, C., Lister, M. and Marsh, D. (eds) (2006) *The State: Theories and Issues*, Basingstoke: Palgrave Macmillan.

Helman, G. and Ratner, S. (1992–93) 'Saving failed states', *Foreign Policy*, 89: 3–20.

Herbst, J. (2004) 'Let them fail: state failure in theory and practice', in R. Rotberg (ed.) *When States Fail: Causes and Consequences*, Princeton: Princeton University Press.

Hobsbawm, E. (1990) *Nations and Nationalism since 1780: Programme, Myth, Reality*, Cambridge: Cambridge University Press.

Holsti, K. (1996) *The State, War, and the State of War*, Cambridge: Cambridge University Press.

Horkheimer, M. (1976) 'Traditional and critical theory', in P. Connerton (ed.) *Critical Sociology: Selected Readings*, London: Penguin.

Jackson, R. (1990) *Quasi-States: Sovereignty, International Relations and the Third World*, Cambridge: Cambridge University Press.

Keohane, R.O. (2002) *Power and Governance in a Partially Globalized World*, London: Routledge.

Krasner, S.D. (1999) *Sovereignty: Organized Hypocrisy*, Princeton: Princeton University Press.

Lane, F.C. (1979) *Profits from Power: Readings in Protection, Rent and Violence-Controlling Enterprises*, Albany: State University of New York Press.

Larkins, J. (2010) *From Hierarchy to Anarchy: Territory and Politics before Westphalia*, Basingstoke: Palgrave Macmillan.

Latham, A.A. (2012) *Theorizing Medieval Geopolitics: War and World Order in the Age of the Crusades*, Abingdon: Routledge.

Latouche, S. (1996) *The Westernization of the World*, Cambridge: Polity Press.

Lemay-Hébert, N. (2009) 'Statebuilding without nation-building? legitimacy, state failure and the limits of the institutionalist approach', *Journal of Intervention and Statebuilding*, 3(1): 21–45.

Luttwak, E. (1999) 'Give war a chance', *Foreign Affairs*, 78(4): 36–44.

Lyons, G.M. and Mastanduno, M. (eds) (1995) *State Sovereignty and International Intervention*, Baltimore: Johns Hopkins University Press.

Mac Ginty, R. (2011) *International Peacebuilding and Local Resistance: Hybrid Forms of Peace*, Basingstoke: Palgrave Macmillan.

Migdal, J.S. (1988) *Strong Societies and Weak States: State-Society Relations and State Capabilities in the Third World*, Princeton: Princeton University Press.

Milliken, J. and Krause, K. (2003) 'State failure, state collapse, and state reconstruction: concepts, lessons and strategies', in J. Milliken (ed.) *State Failure, Collapse and Reconstruction*, Oxford: Blackwell.

Mommsen, W.J. (1984) *Max Weber and German Politics, 1890–1920*, trans. M. Steinberg, Chicago: University of Chicago Press.

Nettl, J.T. (1968) 'The state as a conceptual variable', *World Politics*, 20(4): 559–592.

Newman, E. (2010) 'Peacebuilding as security in "failing" and conflict-prone states', *Journal of Intervention and Statebuilding*, 4(3): 305–322.

Newman, E., Paris, R. and Richmond, O. (eds) (2009) *New Perspectives on Liberal Peacebuilding*, Tokyo: United Nations University Press.

Paris, R. (2002) 'International peacebuilding and the "mission civilisatrice"', *Review of International Studies*, 28(4): 637–656.

Paris, R. and Sisk, T. (eds) (2009) *The Dilemmas of Statebuilding: Confronting the Contradictions of Postwar Peace Operations*, Abingdon: Routledge.

Pugh, M., Cooper, N. and Turner, M. (eds) (2008) *Whose Peace? Critical Perspectives on the Political Economy of Peacebuilding*, Basingstoke: Palgrave Macmillan.

Rakić, V. (1998) 'Theories of nation formation and case selection: the meaning of an alternative model', *Nationalities Papers*, 26(4): 599–614.

Richmond, O. (2005) *The Transformation of Peace*, Basingstoke: Palgrave MacMillan.

Richmond, O. (2011) *A Post-Liberal Peace*, Abingdon: Routledge.

Rotberg, R. (2004) 'The failure and collapse of nation-states', in R. Rotberg (ed.) *When States Fail: Causes and Consequences*, Princeton: Princeton University Press.

Schnapper, D. (1998) *Community of Citizens: On the Modern Idea of Nationality*, New Brunswick: Transaction.

Sharma, A. and Gupta, A. (2006) 'Introduction: rethinking theories of the state in an age of globalization', in A. Sharma and A. Gupta (eds) *The Anthropology of the State: A Reader*, Oxford: Blackwell.

Shils, E. and Finch, H.A. (eds) (1949) *Max Weber on the Methodology of the Social Sciences*, trans. E. Shils and H.A. Finch, Glencoe: Free Press.

Smith, A. (1986) *The Ethnic Origins of Nations*, Oxford: Blackwell.

Tadjbakhsh, S. (ed.) (2011) *Rethinking the Liberal Peace: External Models and Local Alternatives*, Abingdon: Routledge.

Tilly, C. (1985) 'War making and state making as organized crime', in P. Evans, D. Rueschemeyer and T. Skocpol (eds) *Bringing the State Back In*, Cambridge: Cambridge University Press.

van den Berghe, P.L. (1981) *The Ethnic Phenomenon*, New York: Elsevier.

Weber, M. (1978) *Economy and Society: An Outline of Interpretive Sociology*, 2 vols, Berkeley and Los Angeles: University of California Press.

Weinert, M.S. (2007) *Democratic Sovereignty: Authority, Legitimacy, and State in a Globalized Age*, London: UCL Press.

Wilde, R. (2002) 'The skewed responsibility narrative of the "failed states" concept', *ILSA Journal of International and Comparative Law*, 9: 425–429.

Zacher, M. (2001) 'The territorial integrity norm: international boundaries and the use of force', *International Organization*, 55(2): 215–250.

2 World-making, state-building

Nicholas Onuf[1]

> The state is a historical artifact whose existence can be reconstructed by observing semantic distinctions.
>
> (Kessler 2009: 105)

Blueprints

In the last 500 years, the state has emerged and then changed in significant ways, and so has the vast complex of social relations we call the modern world. Familiar periodizations of modernity assume that these parallel developments coincide but that their doing so is no coincidence. To simplify a superabundance of causal connections, we might say that states and the system of states, here called international society, have continuously re-constituted each other over the centuries, and that this process of co-constitution is an integral feature of modernity as a constitutive whole. State-building and world-making occur simultaneously on the basis of blueprints that are periodically but not systematically updated. Anyone building a state today must rely on incomplete, confusing, yet normatively controlling layers of blueprints setting standards and limits on the properties that states must have to function in the modern world – as societies and in international society.

Any effort to characterize social relations relies on metaphors, no matter how conceptually aware the effort is. Speaking metaphorically (and we always do), every concept – every representation of some state of affairs no matter how abstract – was born a metaphor. While I defend this claim later in this paper, it will be noticed that I have already placed great emphasis on a familiar metaphor, *blueprint*. In the first instance, a blueprint is a visual representation of the plan for a building or some other thought-out object of use. By metaphorical extension, a blueprint is any system of linked metaphors, or self-defining semantic field, representing what *we* (some metaphorically identified collectivity: we moderns) think we know about our social arrangements – how they are put together, and how they work, at any given moment. We revise small sections of these blueprints of ours frequently, not always deliberately, in response to practical concerns. Along the way, we even change the way we draw our blueprints – the way that we draw semantic distinctions to represent the particulars of our social arrangements.

This process *looks* continuous and its effects *look like* incremental social change. Nevertheless, when we stand back, we can *see* (a revealing metaphor) that social practices and their metaphorical representation are subject to abrupt changes, and that we can make sense of these changes only retrospectively. To indicate this, I have already used another familiar metaphor. Successive blueprints sit one upon the other in *layers*. All of these metaphors suggest a visual representation of the past and a spatial framing of our relation to it.

Switching to a temporal metaphor (again, one that I have already introduced), each layer constitutes a period in the history of the modern world. With this metaphor in mind, I have adopted and extended the periodization of modernity informing Michel Foucault's archeology of knowledge (1970, 1972). The term *archeology* refers to a familiar practice in the modern world – metaphorically speaking, the practice of digging up the past. Instead of digging up, sorting and reconstructing material objects, an 'archeology of knowledge' exposes the assumptions underpinning what we think we know about the world.

Foucault's idealist construction of epochal change is barely related to changes in material culture (mode of production, technological advances), if at all, and he was notably unwilling to generalize about causes. My own position is also idealist, but with qualifications: epochal changes are observers' constructions, dependent on selective interpretation of the historical record of innumerable changes, many of them material. With this qualification in mind, I have built on Foucault's scheme in order to examine the co-constitution of states and international society, always within the expanding limits, epoch by epoch, of what we can know (also see Onuf 2011).

In my scheme, there are six periods (epochs, ages: all interchangeable metaphors). Modernity begins with the Renaissance (roughly 1500–1650). The Classical age (1650–1800), the Modern age (1800–1900), Modernism (1900–1970) and Late Modernity (1970–) follow. Whether Late modernity is a provisional name for a transition to a Post-modern age is an open question, to which I turn very briefly in my conclusion. I have added two periods – Modernism and Late Modernity – to Foucault's scheme. In my view, they are implied in Foucault's later, genealogical work, when he turned his attention to the state in its modern incarnation. Time and space prevent me from attending to each period as fully as I would like, all the more because the transitions between periods (which I take to be roughly 50 year intervals: 1625–1675, 1775–1825, 1880–1930, 1950–2000, 1970–2020), will detain me more than they did Foucault, for whom discontinuities were sharper breaks, and layers more self-contained, than I see them to have been.

The point of this essay is to provide an overview of successive blueprints, each schematically representing a single epoch, each inscribed on a copy of the one before, each rendering the contents of earlier blueprints less legible. The layers thus documented have permeable boundaries. Nevertheless they demarcate great changes in world-making and state-building. These changes are registered in the characteristic metaphors we put to use during each period. Inscribed as they are on successive blueprints, they continue to dominate our ever-more complex understanding of the state as on-going construction project.

Metaphors

For methodological purposes, Foucault conceptualized periods as *discursive fields*, imagined in layers, each embedding texts to be excavated. Texts are linguistic artifacts; they present the archeologist with evidence of what the people who produced them thought about and, by extension, how their societies worked. Foucault did not call this evidence metaphorical, perhaps because he associated a reliance on metaphors and other figures of speech quite specifically with Renaissance texts. That I do requires me to develop the claim (here, briefly) that concepts are always, ultimately metaphorical (see further Onuf 2010). If they are, then so is knowledge as Foucault understood the term.

As a concept, *metaphor* traces back to Aristotle, who held that metaphors are names of things applied or extended to other things. Even if all metaphors are names (named concepts), he did not claim that all names are metaphors, perhaps because he believed metaphors serve a different, meta-representational function: as figures of speech, they are used for expressive effect. There is, however, nothing in Aristotle's work that would have prevented him, or prevents us, from saying that metaphors are indistinguishable from concepts by reference to what we, as speakers, want them to *do* for us – we seek to make our assertions, as representations of states of affairs, persuasive to others whenever we speak. In this respect metaphors are indistinguishable from similes, which open up and thus expedite the process of metaphorical extension. Even when, as rarely happens, a brand new concept gets a brand new name, the effect is the same: the name circulates, loses any sense of freshness or novelty (by which time, it is 'merely' a concept), and lends itself to metaphorical extension. Any distinction between metaphors and so-called literal concepts ignores or forgets how concepts get to be as we think of them.

Recent decades have seen a renewed interest in metaphors (Ortony 1979, 1993; Lakoff and Johnson 1980, 1999; Gibbs 2005, 2008) and, in particular, in the metaphors reflecting our bodily experience in the world. I suggest that we can sort this inexhaustible supply of metaphors into four kinds. One kind reflects the experience of having to orient ourselves in space and time. A second kind reflects an awareness of our bodies. A third kind reflects our awareness of other bodies metaphorically identifiable as human being like ourselves. A fourth kind of metaphors places our embodied selves in relation to other embodied beings. (In earlier work I treated the last two kinds as one by virtue of their obviously social character.)

All four kinds of metaphors appear in modern texts devoted to the state, but never randomly. From epoch to epoch, writers emphasize one kind or another and link them in distinctive ways. Humanism's triumph over Scholasticism is a familiar trope and an easy way to for us to make sense of the Renaissance as the epoch. For Medieval Christianity, the Resurrection, and thus Christ's *body*, was a controlling metaphor, rendered palpably true by sacrament. Shifting focus from heaven to earth, and from the afterlife to life itself, Renaissance humanists gave the body a new frame of reference. Conceptions of political society as a *person*, *body* or *family* are most clearly inscribed on modernity's early blueprints during the transition from the Renaissance to the Classical age.[2] The metaphorical association of the state with bodies and persons still affects the way we think, most obviously by making states into agents – active members of a society – and not just places.

Students of international relations generally believe that territorial sovereignty is the master principle defining the state as such and directing the development of international society. This point of view relies on a potent metaphor of the orientational kind, namely, that the state is a *container*. The importance of container metaphors for the way we order what we take to be the given or natural contents of the world – make categories, classify things – is inestimable; the metaphor suits most people's conception of concept (Lakoff and Johnson 1980: 19–20). While I do not deny the importance of territory in state-building and world-making, I will try to show that it is a late product of Foucault's Classical age and only becomes dominant in the Modern age.

At the same time, container metaphors combine with body metaphors to form a metaphor of the fourth kind – an ensemble of bodies. International society and the states making it up have the metaphorical properties of a club of clubs, all of which have severely restricted membership criteria. The term *member* is itself revealing: *membrum* means limb or body part in Latin. Even if *club* is less familiar in this context than the other metaphors I have drawn attention to, it is so familiar in other contexts as to be latent in the way we think about states as separate members of a durable ensemble.

A different metaphorical complex marks the Modernist period. Thinking of the state as a *building*, or functionally linked suite of containers, is a modernist innovation that continues to make sense to us. Late modern talk about the state has superimposed the metaphor of *network* on a blueprint where earlier metaphorical associations are still potent. This metaphor would seem to move bodies from rigid containers, such as the state, to more supple social arrangements with more flexible membership criteria.

Post-modern writers seek to strip the state of its multiple, imbricated metaphorical associations. To discredit these metaphors is to dispatch the state itself. Whether this is a plausible program is another question. It can be conclusively answered only when, or if, the metaphorical conjunction of *post* and *modern* clearly identifies an epochal transformation in constitutive premises and processes.

Bodies and persons

Foucault's archeology leaves open the possibility that what we know is constituted by the metaphors we use. I presume just this: all knowledge is an arrangement of metaphors. With Foucault, I hold that what we can know is subject to limits at any given moment, and that it is subject to abrupt shifts discernible in a succession of ages. According to Foucault, a culture's epistemic spaces are stable for long intervals; sudden shifts in the conditions of possibility for systematic thought have wrenching consequences for concepts, values and materially manifest practices, all of which are inscribed on what I am calling that culture's blueprint.

The Renaissance *episteme* starts with what the senses say about the world. Treating things that seem to be alike as indeed alike is the epistemic key, and one that favors an express reliance on metaphors to represent things and their relations. Knowledge is the accumulation of similarities, and the dissemination of knowledge depends on extension by analogy and affirmation by repetition. The *episteme* is its blueprint, and vice versa. With this blueprint, Renaissance humanists could see themselves in relation to the ancients, find an alternative to cyclical or apocalyptic interpretations of the past, and undermine the temporal unity and moral authority of medieval universalism (Fasolt 2004: 16–22).

The Classical age shifts attention from similarities to differences on the assumption that each thing possesses a fundamental nature uniquely its own. Because things are fundamentally different does not mean that they differ in every ascertainable property. For this reason, they can be sorted by the kinds of properties they have in common with some other things. Nature has an order that we cannot perceive directly but nevertheless can make sense of by ordering things. Order is itself to be understood in spatial terms, manifest, however schematically, in grids, tables and, needless to say, blueprints.

In a stern lecture, early in *Leviathan* (1651), Thomas Hobbes railed against 'the use of Metaphors, Tropes, and other rhetoricall figures, in stead of words proper.' Such absurdities stem from not beginning with definitions – 'the Explications of names' – 'which is a method that hath been used onely in Geometry, whose Conclusions have thereby been made indisputable' (Hobbes 1991: 34). Adopting the geometric method, if only metaphorically, Hobbes firmly declared himself a Classical thinker, not subject to the rhetorical excesses of his Renaissance predecessors (but see Skinner 1996, on Hobbes's eventual return to his humanist roots).

Nevertheless, Hobbes metaphorically applied the term *body* to immaterial aggregates of living bodies, as if such a body had material properties of its own. First defining 'SYSTEMES' in expressly metaphorical terms (they 'resemble the similar parts, or Muscles of a body naturall'), Hobbes held that those bodies that people create by contract are either private or political – the latter 'otherwise Called *Bodies Politique*, and *Persons in Law*' (1991: 155, his emphasis). That bodies have heads (recall the *Leviathan*'s famous Frontispiece) undoubtedly gives rise to the enduring metaphorical association of bodies with specifically political properties, such as sovereignty and representation. 'In Bodies Politique,' Hobbes wrote, 'the power of the Representative is alwaies Limited: and that which prescribeth the Limits thereof, is the Power Soveraign' (1991: 155).

It may seem surprising that a text as rigorously Classical as *Leviathan* should so emphatically endorse primary metaphors centered on bodies. Hobbes's rhetorical strategy makes sense, however, in the context of his notoriously grim characterization of the state of nature, in which our bodies make us equally vulnerable to each other's best efforts to protect ourselves from each other. Hobbes's claim of equality applies to 'Naturall Persons,' who proceed to constitute themselves, by contract, into an 'artificiall Person' (Hobbes, 1991: 111–15. Thus constituted, artificial persons are, at least for Hobbes, *sui generis* – hardly equal in size, there is no reason to think them equal in kind.

Hobbes wrote at a time when natural law provided a template for nature's order. The great transitional figure to this time was Hugo Grotius. Never an advocate of natural equality of human beings, Grotius' enduring contribution was to make moral persons the proper subjects of natural law (*De jure belli ac pacis*, 1625; Grotius 2005: 1, 138). Following upon Hobbes, Pufendorf adopted the Grotian conception of moral persons in his great, systematizing treatise, *De jure naturæ et gentium* (1672): 'it follows as command of the law of nature, that every man should esteem and treat another as one who is naturally his equal' (Pufendorf 2005: 224). Natural persons will come together as 'compound moral persons' (Pufendorf 2005: 7), but when they do so, they remain equal, as in nature, and obliged to esteem others.

By implication, equality confers rights on all persons, natural and moral, as needed for them to play their part in nature's order. At the same time, equality imposes corresponding duties on all persons allowing them to exercise their rights. It would seem that Pufendorf was the first to draw this implication, which, of course, we take granted today (Onuf and Onuf 2006: 69–74). Pufendorf did not expressly argue that *all* persons are equal – natural persons would seem to be different in kind from compound persons, since the latter are, as Hobbes emphasized, artificial. Yet Pufendorf's great treatise systematically discriminates between natural persons and nations, as its title, *De jure naturæ et gentium*, indicates. *Gentes*, or nations, are those compound persons that Hobbes called political bodies. As such, they constitute a distinctive *kind* of person for the reason that no one elsewhere has authority over them. Today we unhesitatingly say they are sovereign equals.

Sovereignty

Most discussions of sovereignty begin with Jean Bodin, Grotius and Hobbes, all of them important figures in the transition from the Renaissance to the Classical age. Typically these discussions assume that sovereignty can only be understood as territorial. Were this not so, the familiar claim that sovereignty is indivisible (see, for example, Bartelson 2011) would be difficult to sustain. In my view, these writers never made any such assumption.

Consider this passage from Grotius's *Jus belli ac pacis*:

> Jurisdiction is commonly exercised on two Subjects, the one primary, *viz.* Persons, and that alone is sometimes sufficient, as in an Army of Men, Women, and Children, that are going in quest of some new Plantations; the other secundary, *viz.* the Place, which is called *Territory*.
>
> (Grotius 2005: 2, 457, emphasis in translation)

Sovereignty confers jurisdiction over natural persons in the first instance and then on places, which rather incidentally Grotius referred to as territory. Not only does this textual snippet reverse the now standard practice of giving priority to territorial jurisdiction. It suggests nothing at all about the sovereign, who is, as Grotius made abundantly clear, a moral person with the authority to exercise jurisdiction on behalf of 'a compleat Body of free Persons' – a *civitas*, and not a state, as most translations would have it (including Grotius 2005: 1, 162), a *body*, not a place.

Reading Grotius as an exponent of territorial sovereignty is anachronistic. There is, however, a different kind of text – the conjoined treaties of Münster and Onasbrück, adopted in 1648 – which, we hear today, decisively linked sovereignty and territory and launched the so-called Westphalian system of international relations.[3] Detailed provisions itemize specific places. For example, §73 of the Treaty of Münster names cities and villages that the Austrian Emperor was obliged to surrender to the French King. Most scholars today hold that any such treaty text transfers sovereignty over the places named therein, because the principle of sovereignty entails a clear notion of territorial integrity – places, for most part adjacent, taken together as a whole. By referring to 'Vassals, Subjects, People, Towns, Boroughs, Castles, Houses, Fortresses, Woods, Coppices, Gold or Silver Mines, Minerals, Rivers, Brooks, Pastures,' §74 makes it clear that the places in question are not abstractly conceived territories, but features of a populated landscape.

The treaties were written in Latin, a language in which there is no direct equivalent to the French term s*ouveraineté* or its English translation. Scattered in the Latin text of the two treaties are various forms of the terms *summa*, *superus*, *supremus*, all of which are orientational metaphors indicating status relations among kings and emperors, lords, vassals and subjects. On one occasion, the standard translation of the text offers a list of people and places similar to the one we saw in §74, ending with the words 'and all other things belonging to the Sovereign Right of Territory' (§85, Treaty of Münster). The Latin text reads 'caeterisque omnibus et singulis ad sublime territorii ius,' again suggesting that categories of people and places occupy vertically oriented status relations.

As quoted, the Latin text does not support the conclusion that territory is by itself a rightful or lawful whole. More generally, there is no persuasive evidence that the parties to the Westphalian settlement intended to reconceptualize authority as exclusive control over territory, much less launch a new European order based on any such idea. Nor is there persuasive evidence that anyone writing about sovereignty at the dawn of the Classical age fully grasped the relation between state and territory that we now take for granted. As we would say today, they had worked out a conception of internal sovereignty, one that drew its power from the twinned metaphors of political society as a body of people, and its ruler as a moral person with jurisdictional powers over people and places.

Retrospectively, we can easily see that internal sovereignty in a world of sovereigns implies that all such sovereigns are equal. Writers in the Classical age came to this conclusion only gradually, and only as status distinctions among rulers receded in importance. In 1758, Emmerich de Vattel (2008: 68) could say that

> Nations being composed of men naturally free and independent, and who, before the establishment of civil societies, lived together in the state of nature, – nations or sovereign states are to be considered as so many free persons living together in the state of nature

with no direct reference to territory. Vattel's conception of external sovereignty does not presuppose a boundary between inside and outside or make the state into a container.

Vattel honored the discursive heritage of Grotius, Hobbes and Pufendorf by calling states 'free persons.' States individually have legal personality, and collectively they are bound together by their rights and duties. Decades later, in the transition to the Modern age, Hegel clearly distinguished between the internal and external aspects of sovereignty (*Elements of the Philosophy of Right*, 1821; Hegel 1991: 315, 359). Yet he too did so with no direct reference to territory. Indicatively, the state is 'an embodiment of spirit' (Hegel 1991: 359) – the body as primary metaphor now disembodied.

Containers

We are left with a puzzle. In the Classical age, writers were preoccupied with spatial order, classificatory systems and geometric representations of complex relations. We saw the 'construction of the globe itself as a geometrical object,' but *not*, as Jens Bartelson has claimed, 'its division into distinct territorial portions' (2010: 220). An archeologist of the period cannot fail to notice the dominance of orientational metaphors. Prodigiously comprehensive texts contain an arrangement of containers, defended not as an author's contrivance but as nature's writ. Yet two centuries of writing about what we now call the state show a remarkable consistency in the deployment of the body as a metaphor, and a corresponding reticence about territory as a metaphorical container.

Classical discussions of sovereignty do make use of orientational metaphors. Vertical metaphors inform representations of internal sovereignty. While external sovereignty has no name, the principle of natural equality implies a horizontal orientation that we never see metaphorically developed. The state is a container only insofar as any body must be contained in order to maintain its internal coherence. States have people, land and laws, which together could have been homogenized or abstracted (different metaphors to the same effect) as territorial sovereignty. They were not – not consistently, and certainly not with the affective and normative resonance that we take for granted today.

The Classical age created epistemic conditions under which people could think of sovereignty as territorial and therefore indivisible, or the state as a container.[4] Indeed, the Classical *episteme* made modern cartography possible; its 'geometric foundation ... implicitly encourages the use of lines and homogenous areas to differentiate space' (Branch 2011: 20). Yet sovereigns – 'crowned heads' – did not make maps showing their realms as bounded, homogeneous territories until the Vienna settlement in 1815 compelled them to do so (Branch 2011: 18). Of course, eighteenth-century sovereigns understood that status depended on the 'size' of their realms, acted strategically to absorb neighbors and prevent other sovereigns from doing so, and took advantage of the movement of resources from colonial possessions and across frontiers to increase their wealth. Retrospectively we take the preoccupation with size, power, conquest, marriage, taxes and tariffs as evidence that sovereigns could visualize their realms as clearly demarcated, bounded territories over which they exercised control. They did not – size meant many things (people, land, dynastic connections, fungible resources, perhaps even competence in the conduct of public affairs) – and not just because they had no need to. Without maps, they could not.

The Modern age opened up new possibilities. Systematic map-making and related activities, such as taking censuses, require professionally staffed governments to mobilize and distribute resources for the express purpose of exercising continuous, effective control over resources. We associate this feature of the Modern *episteme* with Weber, for whom rationalization was the key to the state's rapid rise to dominance. This development belatedly substantiates the Classical emphasis on space and recourse to orientational metaphors: rationalized relations of super- and subordination depend on and fill up horizontally contained spaces. Territory displaces the realm, contains political society and grants moral personality a fixed jurisdictional field in which to operate.

How this development fits with Foucault's scheme is not obvious. In part this is because Foucault's account of the Modern *episteme* is difficult to understand, partly because Foucault told only half the story. On his account, history replaces order as 'the fundamental mode of being of empiricities.' History is not simply 'the compilation of factual successions or sequences'; it '*gives place* to analogical organic structures, just as Order opened the way to *successive* identities and differences' (Foucault 1970: 219, 216, emphases in translation). The Modern *episteme* took metaphor out of the Renaissance world of appearances and deployed it in time. By invoking development, evolution and dialectical reasoning, modern thinkers could bring together 'totalities of elements without the slightest visible identity' (Foucault 1970: 265).

Weberian rationalization does not replace order so much as it takes 'the fundamental mode of being of empiricities' to precede order. The same may be said of history. Modern empiricities are stand-alone *things*, positivities – facts subject to isolation, verification, measurement, manipulation – in order to see how those things might be related. This is, of course, positivism, which mandates procedures (the scientific method) for disallowing consideration of most things on any given occasion.

Rationalization and utilitarian thinking inevitably follow from this way of thinking. Like positivist scientists, modern historians start with empiricities and concern themselves with questions of veracity, magnitude and relatedness. They differ from positivists because they organize those empiricities into 'analogical organic structures' (Foucault generalized from what he saw in modern biology to history). When historians do this, they are historicists, and this practice allows them to tell stories selectively based on a superabundance of ascertainable facts.

The one organic structure that modern historians have devoted themselves to most completely is the *nation*. As we hear so often, nations are imagined; they are a Foucauldian 'totality of elements' upon which identity has been imposed. Beginning with the term itself, the importance of body metaphors in the way we talk about the nation is well documented (see, for example, Onuf and Onuf 2006: Ch. 5). Insofar as the nation is a body in the first instance – a body of people loosely held together by common origin or shared traits – then the nation requires a container, which the state supplies. In turn, the nation supplies the state with the resources required for its rational administration. State and nation are co-constitutive, but only insofar as a demarcated, homogenized territory coincides with a specifically homogenized people. Matching state and nation is one of the great projects of the modern age. Notwithstanding the resources devoted to it, this project has succeeded only some of the time, and only then at great cost.

Clubs

The spatial orientation of the Classical age made it conceivable to talk about political societies as if they were containers. The practical realization of this epistemic possibility only took place during the transition to the Modern age, which in turn gave the state-as-container indispensable epistemic support. The spatial ordering of the Classical age also brought forth the grand idea that people are equals, imagined as such on the same level. Pufendorf's picture of human society implies two levels: the level in which people constitute themselves in political societies and the level in which these societies, as sovereign states, constitute themselves as a system or society.

Contemporary students of international relations routinely invoke the same two levels, second (international society) analogous to the first (domestic society), itself conceptualized as the liberal alternative to Hobbes's Leviathan. In my view, the causal dynamics run the other way (Onuf and Onuf 2006: 40–2; Onuf 2013a). First came a 'natural society' of rights-bearing nations (not to be confused with those modern nations I introduced in the previous section). Nations came to acknowledge their 'natural equality' and clarify their rights and duties only gradually. Over the better part of two centuries, natural law treatises documented, validated and expedited this process. If nations are naturally equal as sovereigns and routinely relate to each other by reference to their rights and duties, then by analogy natural persons are equal in their moral autonomy and should be able to relate to each other by reference to established rights and duties. In Britain's North American provinces and in France, violent assertions of popular sovereignty punctuated this more localized process, while in Britain, reformers eventually achieved similar results, often by reasserting historic rights.

As a few political societies variously reconciled republican and liberal premises in the process of modernizing, the small, 'natural' society of nations – assured of their sovereign equality, now more often referred to as states – added members to the club.

In the English language, the metaphor of a social club, as a tightly bound group of people who are therefore like a physical club or weapon, goes back to the Classical age. Clubs are defined as such by exclusionary membership rules. All members are equal; new members must be invited to join. Of course, clubs typically have many additional rules assigning status and offices to members, not to mention rules applicable both to relations of club members and to relations of the club and its members to the 'outside world.' Clubs routinely overlap in membership.

Clubs always have rules or procedures to select, screen and admit new members. When no officers have this duty, admission may result from a decentralized process in which some member (or members) treats some other person as a member of the club, thus making that person a member, but only in relation to the member so acting. In effect the member offering this invitation and the would-be member accepting it become a club whose membership of two persons overlaps the membership of the other club. If no one else in the first club joins the new club, it is likely to atrophy and disappear. If instead other members of the first club follow suit, then the two clubs will gradually merge into one. Indeed, we could say that the second club will swallow the first, but we are more likely to say that the first club has expanded its membership through successive acts of mutual recognition. In the instance of international society, formal rules for what we have come to call the recognition of states emerged in the transition to the Modern epoch.

International society is a small club. Some members were club founders, though hardly in any formal way. Others underwent the process of progressive mutual recognition that I just described. Most recently, admission to membership in international organizations has augmented and gradually replaced pairwise recognition. Only by virtue of being admitted to the club are states sovereign and therefore exclusive membership clubs in their own right. As such, states have developed ever more precise and restrictive membership rules of their own. Only because states constitute themselves as a club does international society exist in the enduring, familiar form that we now see it as having on our blueprints for state-building and world-making as co-constitutive processes. As I have said elsewhere (Onuf 2013a), membership rules stitch states as societies and states in their own society tightly together as a constitutive whole.

Buildings

The Modern *episteme* developed a discontinuity in the last decades of the nineteenth century, one that deepened even after the century's turn. Not only did Foucault overlook this transformation (however much it is implied in his later work on governmentality), so did Weber, whose account of modernity's development centers on our changing relation to the world or, more precisely, on our conscious awareness of our capacity to change the world by rationalizing its contents. And so did members of the Frankfurt School, itself a Modernist development, in developing a critical stance toward modernity and its rationalizing tendencies. Postmodernists are a conspicuous if ambiguous exception to the general tendency. In the very effort to replace Modernism with something equally transformative, postmodernists have paid attention to what makes Modernism an epistemic departure. Regrettably, even they too often use the terms *modern* and *modernist*, *modernity* and *modernism*, interchangeably. There is no great surprise in this: we all speak of modern art when we obviously are referring to work that exemplifies the Modernist discontinuity in the way we represent the world.

To simplify, perhaps unduly (but see Onuf 2009 for a fuller discussion), modernism is a revolution in representation, a reaction against realism (here a synonym for accuracy) as the self-evident object of representation. Modern rationalization and positivism take realistic representation of the things of the world, by whatever medium, as a necessary ancillary to the discovery and manipulation of those things. Logical consistency, precise measurement and instrumental values follow in train. The modernist response to the requirements of realism arose first, or was at least first noticed, in literature and the arts, where representation was an end in itself and not just an instrument for storing and retrieving what we think we know about the world. In literature as in art and music, new ways of using words, actors on stage, pen, paint and chisel in hand, cameras, tonal registers and cultural artifacts took representation beneath the familiar surfaces of things, disrupted the conventional arrangement of those things, and reversed the relation between subject and object. To appropriate a slogan from modernist architecture, if form follows function, then the architect should turn things inside out; esthetics is a matter of exposure.

Modernism also spawned a new generation of human sciences: political science, sociology, psychology and anthropology. Sociologists came to call this process functional differentiation, which they observed everywhere in modern societies as a response to the scale and complexity of social activity.[5] Modernism is not simply about function. Nor is it simply about representation (a feature of modernity that Foucault assigned to the Classical *episteme*). Following Durkheim, the 'high modernist' of social theory, it asks us to represent function first (including the function of representation), and then relate functions to techniques on the one hand, and social arrangements on the other.

In my opinion, functional differentiation is boldly inscribed on the Modernist blueprint for the state. Yet modernist texts in political and social theory leave a different impression. The simple explanation for this odd omission is not an indifference to functional differentiation, but a declared wish to stop talking about the state. Instead modernist political scientists and sociologists talked about political systems, always by reference to their structures, functions and processes – obviously, a highly abstracted set of metaphors. I see in this move a wholesale rejection of the body, person, container and club metaphors so integral to the centuries-long process of turning diverse political societies into those formally equal, functionally similar units that we now call states. This move was bound to fail.

Indeed it had already failed when systems were granted boundaries and subsystems were stipulated; systems are containers, and containers occupy levels. Soon enough we were exhorted to 'bring the state back in.' Rising to the occasion, institutionalists – some positivist and some historicist – tacitly granted functional differentiation its importance by conceptualizing the state as an institution composed of functionally related institutions. Inevitably, some states were identified as strong, others weak, and talk turned to building and strengthening the state.

More or less at the same time systems metaphors prevailed among political scientists, international theorists espoused their own distinctive version of functionalism. Its origins reveal an affiliation with modernism in turn-of-the-century arts and letters (see, for example, Woolf 1916). The internationalist version of functionalism predicted that state agents would gladly surrender technical tasks to experts in international organizations. In the process, they would unknowingly divide sovereignty bit by bit until it would eventually be wholly gone. This theory developed only after governments created functionally delimited international institutions at the very beginning of the Modernist age. This they did to accommodate the technical needs of advanced industrial societies (for example, by standardizing weights and measures).

Even if functionalist theory duly contributed to the emergence of so-called supranational institutions in Europe after World War II, it failed utterly as theory. States did not dismantle themselves in the process of assigning technical tasks to international institutions. They were engaged in a much larger process of functionally differentiating themselves from within (as containers) and then institutionalizing functional differentiated tasks in massive bureaucracies. State-building prompted institution-building among states as club members, and these institutions strengthened states, not weakened them.

Modernist architecture has left a lasting visual imprint on the modern world. Modernist office buildings house the functionally differentiated bureaucracies that no large organization – states, international institutions, corporations, even universities – can do without. City planners are modernists. Modernist architecture has even inspired governments to build brand new capital cities, such as Brasilia, to expedite the 'modernization' of the state. Rationalization and functional differentiation are necessary complements in this process, which can reinforce authoritarian tendencies in the effort to catch up with modernity (Scott 1998: 87–146).

In practice, modernist architecture and city planning have spawned a metaphorical vocabulary we now take for granted. *Blueprint* is an indicative modernist metaphor. Once Marxists talked about superstructure; now we all talk about infrastructure. We visualize states as buildings, and we conceptualize state-building as an activity that depends on a large number of people with diverse technical skills collaborating on carefully laid-out plans that are nevertheless subject to adjustment as new problems and challenges arise. International institutions provide states with technical assistance, mostly by obtaining the services of technicians from other places. Consultants flourish, offering technical advice not just to governments, but to any institution willing to pay for it. There is much discussion of institutional design. Lawyers are everywhere, drafting metaphorical blueprints for metaphorical buildings.

Networks

The epistemic discontinuity that I have identified with Modernism has been with us for at least a century, the Modern age for two centuries. Each *episteme* opened new possibilities in the way we can talk about the world without foreclosing the space that earlier *epistemes* had opened our minds to. Much of what I have said would suggest that the continuing effects of the Modern age and Modernism on the way we talk about the state (and everything else) means that these two ages have not ended. Yet when I introduced my scheme for periodizing modernity, I dated the end of these two ages at 1900 and 1970 respectively. If this seems like a contradiction, then appearances are deceiving.

Epistemes do not successively displace their predecessors (as Foucault seems to have thought) but overlay each other (or so I have claimed). Each layer becomes progressively less legible as new layers are added. Each age has an extended afterglow, as we saw with the state as a container. The Modern age is still easy to read but no longer strictly on its own terms. Everything we say about rationalization, for example, takes modernist differentiation for granted. The continuing, often complementary effects of rationalization and differentiation are so extensive in today's world that they may cast doubt on my claim that we are witnessing another epistemic break, the transition to which began around 1970, with another age ensuing, which I am not alone in calling Late modernity.

The epistemic possibilities of a new age are difficult to recognize close at hand. Transitions are murky affairs. It should be no surprise that I am less confident that we are in the process of entering a new age than I am about the properties of the age preceding. Most observers who think they see an epistemic discontinuity in the making offer globalization as evidence. Often enough, these observers tell us that deterritorialization accompanies globalization – as consumerist culture, productive processes and financial markets globalize, sovereignty *erodes* (a frequent and evocative metaphor) and the modern state ceases to matter as a territorial configuration. I see in globalization something altogether different: striking evidence of functional differentiation wherever people are exposed to the complexities of modernity. This is evidence that Modernism still defines the way we moderns talk about our world. It is a place, now global in scale, where functional differentiation within states has, on balance, increased the state's capacity to respond effectively to the *forces* (another evocative metaphor) that globalization has unleashed.

If, however, we look at the technical correlates of globalization, all of which I take to be integral to the modernist constitution of modernity, it is possible (a Late modern possibility) to glean some evidence that we have indeed entered a transitional moment. The technology in question is overwhelmingly directed to the manipulation and distribution of information; this is 'the information age' (here I rely on Manuel Castells' (2000) *The Information Age*, and especially Volume 1, *The Rise of the Network Society*; also see Onuf 2013b: Ch. 12). Thanks to Late modern technology, we code, store and distribute information, which, by being limitless, weightless and infinitely divisible, does not resemble at all those things that positivists seek to manipulate – take apart and rearrange – with such difficulty and at such great cost. To describe the social implications of our ever easier access to information, Castells has used a metaphor – *network* – that is everywhere in use because we *see* networks everywhere. Marking late modernity is 'the rise of the network society' – one expansive society, and as many societies as there are networks.

Networks depend on flows of information. So-called traditional societies depend on dense networks loaded with locally available information, much of it created and distributed in face-to-face interactions. Yet even these societies have many networks, which, by definition occupy parallel planes in a fixed space: 'A network is a set of interconnected nodes. A node is the point at which a curve intersects itself' (Castells 2000: 501). Because an intersecting set of curves must be located on the same plane, a curve that does not can only be located on a parallel plane (if the planes were not parallel, then they would themselves intersect).

Mapping any one network requires the identification of nodes on that plane and then the connecting lines of information flow. Each map resembles an elementary blueprint. Network maps lay one upon the other; layered networks stratify social space. More concretely (as Castells would have it), the nodes in a social network are agents, whether individual human beings or institutions formed by individual human beings. Each agent in a social network has a status by virtue of participating in that network. Participating in multiple networks, agents acquire a multiplicity of statuses.

Where do states fit in late modern network society? As clubs, states are contained network societies. Yet information is, as we learn daily, harder and harder to contain. Modern states exercise control over land, people, laws and a great variety of resources. Information was once one of those resources a state could hope to control, always at great cost. With the rise of the network society, information leaks, like any gas, from every container that is not perfectly tight. Wherever leaking information ends up defines the always provisional limits of the network society.

The stratification of networks also has implications for the state and its future. States will also experience a proliferation of status-defined networks that inexpensive machinery make readily available to almost everyone almost anywhere. In many of these networks, participants will adopt exclusionary criteria as a means of defining and protecting the status participation affords them, and they will secure resources to institutionalize their activities. In short, these networks will become clubs, in the process stratifying social space within states and beyond them.

With information come networks, with networks come clubs, with clubs comes stratification. Over the last two centuries, most modernizers thought that the whole point of modernity was to eradicate the suffocating old regime of privilege accorded by status, and replace the old regime with a regime of responsible office-holders and rights-bearing individuals. Only the state, as legal person and container, could insure that such a new regime could be instituted; modernizing the state itself was therefore always the first task. Late modernity now casts doubt on the state's capacity to protect the metaphorically rich legacy of epochal social change.

After modernity

Information floods the Late modern world, perhaps to the point that we can no longer find and use the information we need to carry on in the world. If indeed a self-organized world of information effectively takes over our cognitive capacities and leaves us with no more than the trappings of agency, then we may have entered a time of epochal transition. Given the conditions of possibility granted us by successive *epistemes*, we cannot know until we have reached the other side of the transition. Insofar as modernist thought and the social sciences reaffirm 'the strange figure of knowledge called man' (Foucault 1970: xxiv), they remained within the confines of the Modern *episteme*. In my reconstruction, modernist thought and the social sciences add new blueprints to the growing pile of blueprints that tell us how modernity came to be the layered epistemic whole that it is. Inscribed on those blueprints is an ever stranger 'figure of knowledge' whom we call ourselves.

Clearly, then, the 'disappearance of man' would mark the appearance of an entirely new Post-modern *episteme* (Foucault 1970: 386). That strange figure cannot be dissociated from five centuries of institutional support, of which none has been more central than the state. If the figure of man were to disappear, so would all of those many superimposed blueprints on which we constantly rely, in the first instance to tell ourselves who we are. And so would the state in all of its metaphorical richness. Successive *epistemes* have made it possible for states to be what they have become, or are capable of becoming, just as they make us what we are. Without a new set of Post-modern blueprints, we cannot even begin to imagine what our figurative successors will have created for themselves.

Notes

1 Presented at the Conference on *The State and State-Building: Theory and Practice in Retrospect*, Institute for Philosophy and Social Theory, University of Belgrade, May 5–7, 2011. Revised and presented at a colloquium, Instituto de Relações Internationais, Pontifícia Universidade Católica do Rio de Janeiro, September 14, 2011. I am grateful to Jon Strandquist for advice and assistance and to Paulo Estevez, Raphael Gonçalves Marreto, Harry Gould, Stefano Guzzini and Anna Leander for helpful comments.

2 In this essay, I give no further consideration to the family as a metaphor for political society in general and the state in particular, or to paternal authority as a metaphor for

internal sovereignty. The emblematic figure for this way of thinking in the Classical age is Robert Filmer, whose *Patriarcha* served John Locke as a foil in the first of his *Two Treatises of Government* (1689). Nor do I consider the relation of families to their homes and thus their 'homelands.'

3 The two treaties are available in their original Latin and various translations from Acta Pacis Westphalicae: www.pax-westphalica.de/ipmipo/index.html.

4 Readers may notice that I have ignored federation as a state-form in this essay. Suffice it to say here that the 'spatial logic' of federalism is eminently Classical – containers are ordered in ascending levels (Onuf 1998: 55–7) – and that federalism in practice, as an eighteenth-century development, has not fared well in the Modern age.

5 Some sociologists hold that functional differentiation is a mark of the Modern age, while I see this process to have accelerated markedly with Modernism. See for example Luhmann (2002: 111, his emphasis):

> The breakdown of what we may call (following Otto Brunner) *old-European semantics* became inevitable when society changed its primary form of differentiation, when it shifted from the very elaborate order of hierarchical stratification, conceived of as 'the order,' to the primacy of functional differentiation.

References

Bartelson, J. (2010) 'The social construction of globality,' *International Political Sociology*, 4(3): 219–25.

Bartelson, J. (2011) 'On the indivisibility of sovereignty,' *Republics of Letters: A Journal for the Study of Knowledge, Politics, and the Arts*, 2(2), available at: http://rofl.stanford.edu/node/91 (accessed 6 February 2012).

Branch, J. (2011) 'Mapping the sovereign state: technology, authority, and systemic change', *International Organization*, 65(1): 1–36.

Castells, M. (2000) *The Rise of the Network Society*, 2nd edn, Oxford: Blackwell.

Fasolt, C. (2004) *The Limits of History*, Chicago: University of Chicago Press.

Foucault, M. (1970) *The Order of Things: An Archeology of the Human Sciences*, trans. A.M. Sheridan Smith, New York: Random House.

Foucault, M. (1972) *The Archeology of Knowledge*, trans. A.M. Sheridan Smith, New York: Pantheon Books.

Gibbs, Jr., R.W. (2005) *Embodiment and Cognitive Science*, Cambridge: Cambridge University Press.

Gibbs, Jr., R.W. (ed.) (2008) *The Cambridge Handbook of Metaphor and Thought*, Cambridge: Cambridge University Press.

Grotius, H. (2005) *The Rights of War and Peace*, 3 vols, ed. by R. Tuck from J. Barbeyrac's edition of 1738, trans. J. Morrice, Indianapolis: Liberty Fund.

Hegel, G.W.F. (1991) *Elements of the Philosophy of Right*, trans. H.B. Nisbet, Cambridge: Cambridge University Press.

Hobbes, T. (1991) *Leviathan*, Cambridge: Cambridge University Press.

Kessler, O. (2009) 'Toward a sociology of the international? International relations between anarchy and world society,' *International Political Sociology*, 3(1): 87–108.

Lakoff, G. and Johnson, M. (1980) *Metaphors We Live By*, Chicago: University of Chicago Press.

Lakoff, G. and Johnson, M. (1999) *Philosophy in the Flesh: The Embodied Mind and Its Challenge to Western Thought*, New York: Basic Books.

Luhmann, N. (2002) *Theories of Distinction: Redescribing the Descriptions of Modernity*, Stanford: Stanford University Press.

Onuf, N.G. (1998) *The Republican Legacy in International Thought*, Cambridge: Cambridge University Press.

Onuf, N.G. (2009) 'The ambiguous modernism of Seyla Benhabib,' *Journal of International Political Theory*, 5(2): 125–37.

Onuf, N.G. (2010) 'Escavando a "comunidade internacional": por uma arqueologia do conhecimento metafórico,' *Contexto Internacional*, 32(2): 253–96.

Onuf, N.G. (2011) '"Modern order/disorder": notes for a future archeologist,' in R. Marlin-Bennett (ed.) *Alker and IR: Global Studies in an Interconnected World*, Abingdon: Routledge.

Onuf, N.G. (2013a) 'Recognition and the constitution of epochal change,' *International Relations*, 27(2): 121–140.

Onuf, N.G. (2013b) *Making Sense, Making Worlds: Constructivism in Social Theory and International Relations*, Abingdon: Routledge.

Onuf, N.G. and Onuf, P. (2006) *Nations, Markets and War: Modern History and the American Civil War*, Charlottesville: University of Virginia Press.

Ortony, A. (ed.) (1979) *Metaphor and Thought*, Cambridge: Cambridge University Press.

Ortony, A. (ed.) (1993) *Metaphor and Thought*, 2nd edn, Cambridge: Cambridge University Press.

Pufendorf, S. (2005) *Of the Law of Nature and Nations*, 4th edn, trans. B. Kennett, Clark, NJ: Law Book Exchange.

Scott, J. C. (1998) *Seeing Like a State: How Certain Schemes to Improve the Human Condition Have Failed*, New Haven: Yale University Press.

Skinner, Q. (1996) *Reason and Rhetoric in the Philosophy of Hobbes*, Cambridge: Cambridge University Press.

Vattel, E. (2008) *The Law of Nations, Or, Principles of the Law of Nature, Applied to the Conduct and Affairs of Nations and Sovereigns, with Three Early Essays on the Origin and Nature of Natural Law and on Luxury*, trans. T. Nugent, Indianapolis: Liberty Fund.

Woolf, L.S. (1916) *International Government: Two Reports*, New York: Brentano's.

3 Politics, law, and the sacred

A conceptual analysis

Friedrich Kratochwil

Introduction

The ‘return’ of religion has not only engendered new conflicts in world politics, it has also fundamentally challenged the Western political project, which allegedly rests on a strict separation of the public and private sphere. Religion is supposed to play a role only within the confines of the latter, as it is considered a ‘privately held belief’. Of course, this project is neither shared by all Westerners, nor is it necessarily persuasive to other cultures. Thus within the emerging global sphere it is by no means clear whether such a strict separation can muster assent (Barbato and Kratochwil 2009: 1–24). For this reason some thinkers, such as Habermas (2003) and Connolly (1999), among many, have attempted to formulate a new approach in which ways of overcoming the displacement of religions to the ‘private/personal’ realm are explored, in order to harness the semantic potential of religion for the establishment of a discourse on global order, while avoiding at the same time the establishment of a particular orthodoxy or of a millenarian political project based on the notion of absolute ‘truth’.

Irrespective of what we think of the realisability of those proposals, one thing seems clear: that the strict dichotomy of religion and politics cannot be consistently maintained, precisely because the freedom of religion is one of the fundamental rights protected by law, and thus religion, the state, and politics are intertwined. In this article I want to probe the *conceptual problems* that are engendered by these links. In doing so I want to correct that part of the Westphalian myth which maintains that the ‘secular politics’ of modernity had its origin in this ‘contractual’ settlement. Certainly the pre-eminence of the pope was substantially diminished thereby, since state churches supplanted the encompassing notion of a church of all believers, but it took some time before the semantics of ‘religion’ and ‘rule’ mutated from a public and official concern to a largely ‘private’ affair.

While these arguments are certainly not new, it is useful to mention some of these points in passing, since much of the traditional international relations literature does not fully appreciate the ‘historicity’ or the complexity of the conceptual problems, and therefore cuts itself off from understanding certain problems of contemporary world politics. Four points seem relevant in this context. There is first the methodological issue that derives from the widely shared assumption (propagated, for example, by positivism) that the social world can be studied in the same way as 'natural facts' (the world 'out there'), and that the problem of meaning, so important for social theory, is one of reference (this is a chair, not a dog!). But if meaning is not simple reference – what does, for example, 'sovereignty' correspond to since we cannot point to a 'thing' in the outer world – then meaning is conveyed by how we *use* our concepts, as Wittgenstein suggested. In other words – and this is my second point – meanings are embedded in the links a concept has to other concepts within a semantic field, as Quine also showed (Quine 1980: 20–46, quote at 42f).[1] In the case of sovereignty we get at its meaning not through 'definitions' or simple abstraction from observations, but through an analysis of the related concepts, such as domestic jurisdiction, autonomy, self-defence, citizenship, diplomacy, etc. The issue is no longer one of 'matching' a concept with an object in the 'world', but of investigating the semantic field and the practices that are thereby allowed, enjoined, or demanded. Such an investigation has by its very nature to become 'historical', as we are examining how conceptual change works itself out in the self-understanding of the actors in actual practice, and in the critical reflections on this process of social reproduction. Such an analysis obviously cannot be reduced to some 'history of ideas' (who said what), or to some grand narrative, such as that of 'progress', where meaning derives from where something is placed (is it 'progressive' or 'reactionary', is the West (East) in 'ascendancy' or in 'decline'?).

This leads me to my third point. In order not to fall victim to such errors, I want to show that, despite the decline of organised religion, the 'secularisation' thesis (see Norris and Ingelhart 2004; for an opposing view, see Berger 1999; also Hurd 2008; Taylor 2007) of public life is problematic. It not only misses important elements in the increasingly global discourse that disconnects 'religion' from the state and concrete societies, but it fails to show why and how this process exhibits quite different patterns in different regions of the world. This calls into question the unidirectional secularisation narrative and the different, but related, 'end of history' argument. Since I have dealt with some of these issues in another place I do not want to rehearse those arguments further (Barbato and Kratochwil 2009).

Fourth, both debates submerge the conceptual issues in a narrative of progress by treating them as problems that are either largely passé or ought to be handled by insisting on a purely secular conception of the 'primacy of the right over the good'. By focusing here on the semantic interplay of politics, law, and the 'sacred' – since it is the latter that bestows legitimacy on the other two by linking them *(religare)* to some source that is 'set apart' – I want to show that the narrative of progress is hardly 'progressive' (in the sense of increasing our understanding), since the problems are not passé but still with us. In addition, the heuristic fruitfulness of the approach outlined here lies in examining the semantic field of religion and politics through the prism of 'law', thereby also challenging some of the fundamental tenets of traditional (international) law and of 'cosmopolitan' politics. It suggests that 'religions' do not have the monopoly for millenarian derailments, since even 'secular' projects, such as human rights, have that crusading potential. The reason for this at first surprising fact is that clashes between incompatible values that characterise the realm of *praxis* must be mediated by historically contingent *political* means, not by logical fiats (assumptions, definitions)[2] or allegedly foundational arguments, be they based on God, reason, nature, or subjective rights.

As in the case of modern deontological ethics from Kant onwards, which focused mainly on the problem of the justifiability of norms, the real problems of *praxis* lie in the dilemmas created by colliding duties or in bringing a concrete problem under different descriptions which require (justify) different norms. Concrete problems are only marginally helped by establishing the validity of these norms due to their rootedness in universal values. Thus to depict the legal system as a system of norms – without due account that closure can be reached only in the act of interpretation of the law – seems misleading. Rather, such a perspective stresses the need for an agreement on certain shared practices instead of assenting to certain norms dependent upon their derivation from universal principles.

Similarly, while important value questions have re-entered the political discourse in the name of 'human rights', relatively scant attention is paid in mainstream international relations theory to the constitutive *political* implications of these conceptual innovations (Shapcott 2001; Reus-Smit 2004), although their system-transforming capacity is recognised in political theory (Linklater 1997) and humanitarian law. But even here the critical reader is frequently surprised by the optimism, even naiveté of the analysis, as if no fundamental rethinking were required, and the state project could now be projected onto the global sphere with the only question remaining of how 'thick' or 'thin' the institutional structures and new political identities would have to be. To that extent, the new developments such as *jus cogens* and obligations *erga omnes*, or the emerging 'community of courts', or the transnational networks of norm entrepreneurs, are simply taken as harbingers of a 'cosmopolitan' turn in world politics. Here everything seems to fit like a hand in a glove, by which the liberal project with its primacy of the 'right' over the 'good' – best exemplified in Rawl's *Law of the Peoples* (Rawls 1993a, 1993b) – reaches its completion.

Admittedly, I am quite sceptical of such 'designs' and their teleologies, and suggest instead that a more fine-grained analysis of the semantic field of law, the sacred, and politics is required. Such an analysis has to transcend the conceptual fetters of a history of progress, of the communitarian/cosmopolitan divide, of the secularisation debate, or even of the Schmittian/Kelsenian dichotomies of law and politics. In this respect I argue that with the emergence of the human rights discourse – which can be taken as a 'religion for agnostics' – some of the very same problems arise at the intersection of politics, law, and religion that we encountered before with more traditional faiths. To that extent, my analysis is not primarily interested in mapping what 'faith-based' organisations do and how they have become part of global civil society, but is concerned rather with the viability of the political project claiming that through the emergence of law based on 'human dignity' the difficulties of the historical mediations between politics and the 'sacred' can be avoided. In short, this chapter is a critical gloss of some parts of international relations theory, of certain strands of international political theory, and of some approaches to human rights law.

It is the inevitable tension between the universal claims embodied in many religions and the actual limitations engendered by the plurality of different societies and political systems that interests me both historically and analytically. I maintain that today we witness again the clash between a universalist creed centred on 'human dignity'[3] and the contingencies of history and politics. To that extent, the problem of 'religion' is not just limited to some traditional faiths, or some historical experiences that have been overtaken by events, as the secularisation debate suggests. Rather, 'religion' stands for a system of meaning that provides guidance by taking certain things 'out' of the ordinary and keeping them separate and beyond reach by 'sacralising' them. This 'separation' between the sacred and the profane was used by Durkheim (Durkheim 1912/1965) and other sociologists of religion in order to assess religion's role in social life. Since under present conditions the link between the law and its legitimising source, i.e. God, the state, or the 'people', has been eclipsed, the question arises whether 'human dignity' can provide such a 'sacred' foundation as is sometimes intimated by the 'cosmopolitan' or 'world order' discourses,[4] or whether such attempts are likely to derail into millenarian and/or imperial projects (for a critical assessment, see Marks 1997; Koskenniemi 2004).

One could – with reason – object to such a project, as it seems to be nearly entirely based on the 'Western' tradition and its conceptual puzzles. They are not necessarily the same ones that would emerge from an examination of other traditions or from a comparative analysis. My justification for limiting my analysis to the Western traditions is threefold. For one, given the limitations of a chapter in a book, one could hardly do justice to the complexities arising out of an engagement with another tradition or out of a comparison of several of them. While this may sound like a cop-out, there is a second, more substantial, reason for staying the proposed course. For better or for worse, international law and the discourse of subjective human rights – admittedly Western creations and perhaps conceptual creations of debatable merits – have become the mainstay of the international discourse on 'world order' which attempts to link domestic, sub-national and supranational institutions and practices. While it certainly would be quite heroic to assume that we have reached a 'consensus' or that this discourse is able to satisfy the criteria of an 'ideal speech situation' *à la* Habermas or of Rawl's 'Laws of the People' (Rawls 1993b) – even though the latter might well turn out to be 'imperial project', as suggested below – they do represent a discursive formation that not only philosophers and lawyers, but also practitioners (from those in foreign ministries to those working in NGOs) use. To that extent, an examination of the semantics of this discourse is hardly an idle undertaking.

Again, irrespective of the conclusions we might draw from the above analysis, the interdependencies between law, religion, and politics in this 'Western' discourse do not seem accidental, but point to their necessary intertwining in different political projects over time. As Carl Schmitt (1922/2005) and Eric Voegelin (1986; see also Voegelin 1952) observed – though from quite contrary perspectives – most modern political concepts have their roots in religion. But there is even more to it, and this represents actually my strongest reason for engaging the problem of politics, religion, and law through a 'case study' rather than large-scale multivariate analysis, as I claim that a heuristically fruitful framework for comparative analysis could emerge from it that leads us far beyond the particular case.

As the historical record shows, new forms of political rule appeared in a variety of places and periods together with the advent of 'higher' religions, and the question of whether this shows that a 'universal' structure is at work or that it is perhaps only a historical coincidence can be left for further research. The fact remains that in lieu of the acephalic orders of segmented societies, *hierarchies* formed and the incorporation of various 'tribes' into one 'people' or 'realm' became possible (for an extended discussion, see Luhmann 1999). Here 'the people' of the Covenant uniting under God's law provides the historical example and also the template for later re-enactments, as in the case of the Puritans. The Pharaonic Empire and the Aristotelian *synoikismos* of various Greek clans under a new 'political' law represent another historic instance of the same phenomenon (Maier 1990). As the etymology of this new principle of social differentiation (hierarchy) suggests, the connection between 'rule' *(archein)* and the 'sacred' (*hieros*) is deeply embedded in our political imagination and language, even if historical ruptures and different trajectories have reconfigured these links significantly. In short, I want to examine this intersection of law, religion, and politics by focusing on the 'sacralised' source that bestows legitimacy for political rule, but which remains a 'source' always beyond politics and law.

Bearing these considerations in mind I develop my argument in the following steps. In section two I address the myth of a purely secular, contractarian international order created by Westphalia, since this seemed the only rational way of managing the unbridgeable religious differences that had led to an exhausting war. That this interpretation needs some modification is evidenced by the fact that well into the nineteenth century international treaties were often concluded by the invocation of the 'most holy and undivided trinity',[5] which showed the continued relevance of religious symbolism. Similarly, the main source of legitimisation in politics remained the *Dei gratia* principle (by the grace of God), domestically as well as internationally, until the time when 'the people' become the ultimate source of legitimation.

In section three I investigate what happens if, together with sovereignty and the state, 'the people' have also largely disappeared and the abstract ideal of 'human dignity' serves now this legitimising function. I use ideal types for tracing the changes in the semantic field, rather than attempting to provide a full-fledged explanation in a causal, or 'evolutionary' form (Luhmann 1980, 2002). Since this piece is a conceptual analysis and not a predictive/explanatory account, it resembles more a 'constitutive' explanation (Wendt 1999: Ch. 2).

I also do not want to suggest that a 'world law' or 'cosmopolitan law', i.e. a law free from, and superior to, politics, is in the offing. As a matter of fact, the conclusion (section four) casts a critical look at the human rights discourse and at the potential of imperial projects, or of a 'rule of lawyers' instead of a 'rule of law'.

Westphalia and the 'people' as a 'source' of law

According to the classical lore popular among lawyers (Gross 1948) and international relations specialists, it was Westphalia that brought about the decisive break with medieval 'universalism'. It not only removed the pope from politics but laid the foundation for the modern secular order both domestically and internationally. As such, these assertions are, if not downright wrong, at least essentially misleading, as the discussion below suggests. Without entering into an extensive debate about the accuracy of these characterisations, which has engendered a huge literature, some brief remarks are in order.

For one, historical research has shown that Westphalia was not a radical new beginning, but rather a midpoint in the slow transformation of feudal society into territorial orders (Ossiander 2001). Similarly, although interventions for religious purposes were no longer self-justifying after the Westphalian settlement, something far from a 'secular' order developed. Four political 'mediations' were of particular importance in finding a way to deal with the problems that had led to one of the longest and bloodiest conflicts. The first concerned the illegitimacy of religious 'pretexts' for justifying interventions, while at the same time rooting membership in the club of 'sovereigns' in a common tradition of the *res publica Christiana*. A second mediation concerned the acceptance of 'exile' for religious dissenters and their 'toleration' elsewhere. A third implied the modification of the *cuius regio eius religio* rule since changes in the profession of faith by the sovereign was after Westphalia no longer binding upon the subjects. The fourth mediation consisted in a carefully designed 'corporate' compromise between Protestants and Catholics in the institutional make-up of the Holy Roman Empire (for a discussion on the constitution of the Empire see Aretin 1993–97, particularly the first volume) (or also several city governments) which attempted to ensure domestic tranquillity rather than simply 'debunking' religion as a fact of socio-political relevance.

Thus religion continued to play a constitutive role (Philipott 2001) in supplying the legitimacy for the ruling houses – the *Dei gratia* invocation as ultimate source of authority did not cease – but also buttressed the emerging bureaucratic order of the state and justified the 'disciplining' of their respective populations. For the first time political authorities possessed the means of reaching their subjects where before only an indirect relationship had existed, via their overlords and lesser nobles. Thus aside from the impetus of war-making and of furthering commerce (in order to finance war-making) – rightly emphasised by Hintze (1975: Ch. 5) and Tilly (1992) – the role of 'established churches' for the state project can hardly be underestimated, as Schilling (1992) has shown.

Similarly, although indubitably the power of the pope significantly declined, this was perhaps less the effect of secularism than of the de-feudalisation of societies, which deprived the pontiff of a significant source of power. Under the old practices of medieval politics the pope was not only accorded the right to dispose of the titles of all 'islands' (Sicily!), or of land wrested from the 'infidels' (East Prussia), but also to mediate disputes between vassals and their lord, and exceptionally also transfer titles in case the overlord's conduct was considered not in keeping with his obligations (Grewe 2000: Ch. 1–3). Although this power never went so far as to deny the right to rule of a wayward lord – even though some canon lawyers made such a claim – it led to the significant practice of 'infoedeisation'. This practice was the basis of the threats and bargains between the pope and the feudal nobility, of which the 'ban' (connected with absolving the subordinates from any obedience to their overlord) and emperor Henry IV's desperate journey to Canossa (1077) are good examples. The last flickerings of this controversy, cast in the more general terms of the 'supremacy' of either spiritual or secular power, can be seen in the exchange between Cardinal Belarmine and Hobbes in the seventeenth century.

True, the pope's protest of some of the terms of the Westphalian peace no longer carried a veto power even among catholic princes; nevertheless, he continued to wield considerable influence. After all, he did manage to get the coalition together to repel the last attack of the Ottoman Empire on Hapsburg (1683) and thus saved not only Vienna and the Empire but the existence of the *res publica Christiana*. This latter term was used by the new 'sovereigns' to signal their membership in a larger system. It demarcated the insiders from the outsiders, although some 'system-transcending' relations, such as the alliance between Louis XIV and the Sublime Porte, existed. However, such alliances were considered illegitimate, except *in extremis* (Grotius 1625/1925: 190). In a similar fashion, the religious legitimisation of Ottoman power as rulers over all 'true believers' prevented a secular, merely contractual, understanding of the emerging 'system', and it took until the treaty of Paris (1856) ending the Crimean War to incorporate the Sublime Porte into the sanitised version of the club of now 'civilised' nations.

How much the 'symbolic power' of religion still mattered even at the beginning of the nineteenth century can be seen from the fact that long after the victory of 'reason' and of the 'nation' as the ultimate legitimating sources, Napoleon, as an opportunistic *parvenu* of this revolution, still found it necessary to receive a crown from the pope. In short, in contrast to the narrative of epochs, or of progress in which 'ideas' or social forces appear and disappear like the figures in a pageant, we see that even transformative changes seldom result in the total elimination of the previous elements (Tocqueville 1835/1840/1952). As in the case of evolution, new species usually do not simply displace existing species, but rather give rise to new configurations with new equilibria and niches, in which the new and old coexist.

Furthermore, even in cases where concepts emerge with radically new meanings the question remains whether or not they can be interpreted as total displacements instead of only taking over (some of) the functions of the replaced concepts. The cult of 'reason' during the French revolution soon took on religious overtones and Robespierre's crusade for 'virtue' had all the trappings of messianic enthusiasm. This is not to deny the strongly anti-clerical character of the revolution and the stridency of the *laicité* argument that still reverberates in French politics today. But it does call into question the traditional notion of 'secularisation' through progressive enlightenment[6] – quite aside from the fact that the enlightenment project also comprised a good number of Deists and Pietists, who were anti-establishment and perhaps even anti-clerical, but certainly not 'secularists' in the modern sense.

To that extent, the similarities between religious concepts and our 'modern' political vocabulary (Schmitt 1922/2005; Voegelin 1986) is not so surprising after all. It is surprising only if we have bought into the problematic belief that existential issues – and both religion and politics deal with existential issues – are cognitive only, and that 'progress' consists not only in leading man out of his ignorance but in suppressing the 'irrationality' of his emotions. Here Hobbes – certainly not an opponent of the rational pursuit satisfying one's desires – saw perhaps more clearly that a political association cannot be based only on the 'rational pursuit' of individual interests and on dispute settlement. Precisely because various 'sources of quarrel' such as envy and honour are endemic to social life, the indifference of the 'rational actor' – who is neither envious nor benevolent – can only be the result of the new 'discipline' to which the 'subject' has to submit. But such a project is possible only when the sovereign is able to keep all members in 'awe'. It is therefore no accident that it is not 'interests' but 'awe' which the 'mortal God' – the new Leviathan – inspires, that makes the 'pursuit of happiness' by the subjects possible. Significantly, 'awe' refers to the ambivalence of emotions, comprising both attraction and repulsion (the awful), that is deeply implicated with the 'sacred', as students of religion, Otto (1971) and most recently Agamben (1998), have pointed out.

Here I do not want to follow up on these thoughts, frequently adduced as an explanation for why religions can become sources of destructive violence even though they provide – at least in their 'higher' forms – powerful symbolisations of the unity of mankind (Appelby 2000). Rather I want to focus on the mediating role of 'law' for modern politics. Order is now created largely through 'legislation' as law is *made* and no longer simply discovered in either God's will, in nature, or in customs. Order is also no longer the result of periodic rites and sacrifices, as the rite of *hieros gamos*, or the reading of entrails, or the sacrifices performed by the *pontifex maximus*, show. Different from those traditional and primordial means of 'setting things right', which have their origin in magic and which prescribe certain detailed *activities*, law tackles the problem of creating order *cognitively*. The advantage of such a strategy lies partly in its 'impersonal' character, which addresses all (i.e. a potentially unlimited audience) and is not dependent on actual presence at those 'restorative events' or even on actual existential experiences (which, for example, cults or rites try to re-enact). Thus the original 'awe' can now increasingly be transformed into a question of ascertaining the 'validity' of a law, which in turn can be done by tracing the specific law back to a 'source'. Here of course the 'legislator' in the continental tradition and the 'judge' making the law in the common law tradition become the most salient sources.

In short, such a 'cognitive turn' allows for the proliferation of norms answering to greater social differentiation and to the 'practical' problems arising from it. It frees law from the archaic notions that social order can only be maintained by answering violations through identical retributions. By internalising validity and thus reducing legitimacy to 'legality' – so that the question why some prescription is binding can be answered by looking to the 'authorising' (secondary) rule – law attains (near) closure (Hart 1961). Nevertheless, there remains the issue of the 'extra' legal legitimising source – be it the authorising *Grundnorm* or the several 'sources' – that transcends law and resists a reduction of the problem of validity to one of legality. Occasionally this leads to some rather strange formulations, such as in the case of the international committee of lawyers assessing the Kosovo intervention. In their report they came to the conclusion that the intervention was 'illegal' but 'legitimate' (Independent International Commission on Kosovo 2000). In short, behind the internal justification ('legality') there always looms the issue of an 'ultimate' authorisation, be it 'the people' or some other 'source' that is put beyond reach and beyond the ordinary.

Thus even Kant, with all his emphasis on 'reason', invokes the 'sacred', although it has here more the semblance of a (useful?) fiction than the appearance of some encounter with the transcendent. But if intrinsic to the notion of the 'sacred' is its being 'set aside' ¾ as something that has to be treated differently than the common or profane ¾ as Durkheim (1912/1965) argues, then we find even here some 'religious' roots for the concept of law. In one rather strange section of his *Metaphysics of Morals* Kant writes in regard to the obligatory character of law and its legitimising source:

> If a subject having pondered over the ultimate origin of the authority now ruling wanted to resist this authority, he would be punished, got rid of or expelled (as an outlaw *(exlex)* in accordance with the laws of this authority, that is with every right. – A law that is so holy (inviolable) that it is already a crime even to call it in doubt in a practical way, and so to suspend its effect for a moment, is thought as if it must have arisen not from human beings but from some highest, flawless lawgiver; and that is what the saying 'All authority is from God' means. This saying is not an assertion about the historical basis of the civil constitution; it instead sets forth an idea as a practical principle of reason: the principle that the presently existing authority ought to be obeyed, whatever its origin.
>
> (Kant 1797/1996: 462)

Similar arguments are made by Rousseau, not only about the 'lawgiver' (Rousseau 1762/1976: 22f) who is endowed with near-divine capacities, but also when he 'socialises' the people by 'removing' them from the daily encounters and particular deals they make with each other, by distinguishing the *volonté generale* from the *volonté de tous*. The individual as part of 'the people' has to keep personal preferences in abeyance, having to choose in accordance with criteria that would be best for all. 'The people' are also distinguished from the existing multitude, since they emerge out of the *alienation totale* and the moral change induced by the social contract, which substitutes in man's conduct 'justice for injustice' and transforms him 'from a stupid and ignorant animal into an intelligent being and a man' (Rousseau 1762/1972: 42ff).

But precisely because the concept of the 'people' requires such a distancing from the ongoing interactions, it widens the perspective of the agents, since the choices of today will affect future generations. Only in this way can the community be constituted as an ongoing and trans-generational concern. In the same vein, being one 'people' also presupposes a common recognition of who belongs to 'us' and who is a 'stranger'. But the reflection of who 'we' are also raises the question of where we came from (for a more general discussion, see Kratochwil 2006). It is therefore no accident that soon the 'nation' – with its allusions to the presumed 'naturalness' of a common ancestry – replaces the 'state' as the centre of attention.[7] As a matter of fact, it is not 'consent' or participation in common matters – a crucial element underlying the ancient concept of the *res publica* – but the *nation* that lends legitimacy to the state.

All these important 'historical' problems do not come into focus by the master metaphor of modern politics, i.e. the 'contract', which 'assumes' that these questions have been settled. After all, people must know who the others are with whom they contract, and they must develop a non-myopic conception of a self and of their interests in order to keep this resulting association an ongoing concern. As all contractarians realise, the social contract *is* special. It is not simply a contract that one can easily undo by a contrary action or by opting out (with or without compensation). But if this is the case, then the specific nature of *political obligation* has to be addressed (for a more extensive discussion, see Kratochwil 1994).

Liberal contractarians do this badly, either by assuming the permanence of the contract or by arguing that otherwise a return to the state of nature is inevitable (Hobbes). Another alternative is to construe the state as a mutual 'benefit association' and to 'imply' consent by such innocent acts like 'travelling on a highway', as does Locke. But his solution of 'implied consent' is problematic, as any presumption that an action implies consent requires a prior rule to that effect. Of course, such rules can be passed even for future generations, but it is not clear what 'consent' is then doing here. It is the *rule* that has been passed by others (my forebears) and not my voluntary uptake which is then decisive. Without some presupposed notion that the laws of a community are binding on its 'members', to which they *qua members* owe loyalty, the argument becomes incoherent. Rawls's construction of a 'just' community suffers from the same problem. He simply *assumes* that the problem of membership has been solved. Here Carl Schmitt saw the problem more clearly. Issues of membership *are* 'political' in the foundational sense (Schmitt 1927/1996), and they cannot be resolved by the application of universal principles (such as common humanity, universal reason, or whatever).

It is in this way that 'the people' come to see themselves as the authors of their laws, and in this way a 'constitution' can claim 'loyalty' and respect for the limiting and enabling conditions of political order. Obviously, the duties flowing from loyalty are quite different from those resulting from contracts or universal norms. To that extent, the specific obligations do not sit well with the attempts of an ethics that tries to 'ground' all obligations in universal principles. The only duties that are particular and accepted in this foundational discourse are the ones that derive from contractual undertakings. But even here the foundation is provided by the universal principle that promises have to be kept.

What the rhetoric of universalism simply leaves out, however, are those duties which are more contingent and cannot be directly derived from 'ultimate' principles. This is the case with 'loyalty': it is owed to those people and institutions who define us as *historical* particular subjects, i.e. establish who we 'are'. One might be obliged to strangers, due to promises made or to the general principles underlying their status as persons which require recognition. But one can only be 'loyal' to friends and others who are or have become part of 'us'. Loyalty connects us to particular groups and invokes specific historical experiences. It cannot be tailor-made as a freestanding 'de-contextualised' structure that is imposed upon a group. The 'law' must be the repository of peoples' particular experiences and of meaning, even if the produced 'text' satisfies the criteria of justice and makes reference to universal human values. Consequently, Hirschman considers 'loyalty' as one of the fundamental social mechanisms that cannot be reduced to either 'exit' or 'voice' (Hirschman 1970).

The usual tendency to explain, for instance, our political obligations in terms of the 'justice' of the regime whose subject we are misses precisely the point that we, as e.g. Frenchmen, have special obligations to abide by French law and not by those of Australia or Switzerland, even if the latter are also 'just regimes'. These 'special obligations' are therefore not the result of the benefits we receive in the pursuit of our goals, ¾ as we could be tolerated outsiders ¾ or from the general maxim that laws are necessary to avoid conflict and regulate interferences. Even universal values that are part of our political projects will not do. Rather, the obligations derive from the realisation of who we are as historical beings.

The issue here is not to rehash the mistaken idea of a 'primordial' existence of a people that 'gives' itself a constitution, or to argue that since this 'theory' is clearly problematic, any other 'multitude' can be integrated through contract. The point is rather to understand that law is not only a coordination device, regulating the interactions among 'rational' self-interested actors, but also a vehicle of sense-making whose constitutive function is deeply embedded in our historical experiences and our political imagination. To that extent it is true that 'the people' is not a pre-political 'fact' but rather a strategy of sense-making, in which 'fictions' are established and put beyond question, as the Kantian quote above indicated. In short, the notion of politics is narrower than that of justice and wider at the same time. It is narrower since it introduces *particularity* as an important dimension of meaning and sense-making in human life; and it is at the same time wider by showing that, aside from common universal concerns arising out of our status as persons and agents, there are those obligations which are the result of particular positions and roles in which we find ourselves as members of families, corporations, states, or nations. To that extent, we have to realise that such 'special' duties and rights are apparently an unavoidable part of our social life.

The universality of 'human dignity'

This rather philosophical argument is of decisive importance for international law and its role in present international politics. Given that the existing state boundaries are less and less able to serve their steering purposes in a globalised world, and given that migration flows have dramatically altered the composition of historical 'peoples' or 'nations', the question is of how 'law' is able to respond to these changes. But equally important is the delegitimisation of 'the people' and their 'will' as ultimate source of law, perhaps due to the atrocities of the Nazi regimes and the persistence of genocidal tendencies in the present. Here the invocation of universal human rights, the growth of transnational legal networks, or even of a tutelary notion of sovereignty, making its exercise dependent on the 'responsibility to protect' (International Commission on Intervention and State Sovereignty 2001), have been interpreted as harbingers of the growth of a new 'cosmopolitan law'. They promise to revolutionise international law and make out of the 'practical association' (Nardin 1983) a 'constitutional' order for mankind (Fassbender 1998).

These are of course important developments, which have all spurred their own debates on constitutionalisation, or the inherent fragmentation of the international legal order, or the judicialisation of world politics (Abbott *et al.* 2000), or on transnational 'principled' networks and their impact, or on the growth of transnational administrative (for a further discussion see Krisch 2006) law, to name just a few. Here I shall limit myself to the question of how these changes have had an impact on bestowing legitimacy through sacralisation. Thus my focus is – in keeping with the argument made above – not so much on the causal account of the spread of ideas, or on the issue of origin. My interest is rather the internal dynamics of the semantic field and the change in legal and political practice thereby engendered.

As we have seen, within historical time, custom (*mos maiorum*), the law of God, of nature, and later, the 'will' of the sovereign, and – when sovereignty became an attribute of the *populus* – of the 'people', all have served this function. This of course spawned debates whether international law was really law since it does not possess a clear hierarchy of norms, and even if we accepted that its 'sources' provided viable 'secondary rules', their heterogeneity and the lack of a clear reference point such as the *salus publica*, or the will of the people, made it often even difficult to decide what the law is.

Both the introduction of human rights and, later, of the more abstract notion of 'human dignity' seemed to provide a way out of the well-known conundrum of a positivist conception of international law (McDougal 1966). But the question remains if such a conceptual move is able to deliver what it seems to promise: the emergence of a cosmopolitan law based on universal principles. Kant's caveat concerning the critical inquiry into the 'ultimate origins of the authority now ruling' and his limitation of cosmopolitan right to a right 'to visit' (Kant 1795/1996: 328), rather than opting for a fully fledged panoply of subjective rights, should give us pause.

Somehow it seems, however, that these principles such as human dignity are so compelling because of their universality and because they can dispense with any political and historical mediation. But despite near-universal rhetorical support for human rights, democracy, and the rule of law, and the considerable material resources committed to their implementation, the record of these programmes shows that they can be successful only if the 'subjects' are persuaded to 'cooperate' (Carother 2006). Obviously, 'local knowledge', shared interpretations, and 'politics' still matter. But this recognition considerably undermines claims to universality, 'innateness', or a supreme value that can bestow legitimacy on a trans-historical canon of rights.

At this point some clarification concerning the language game of 'universality' seems in order. In keeping with the intentions of the chapter I want to examine what kind of 'work' the invocation of universal values does in political and legal arguments. This raises several conceptual problems. On the most basic level 'universality' is opposed to 'particularity' and thus seems to suggest that the universal is to be preferred to the particular. This is in keeping with the Kantian idea that, for example, laws should be equally applied to 'all' cases similarly situated, and universality as 'universalisability' provides a defence against capricious exceptions and idiosyncratic justifications.

When law differentiated itself from custom, and when the encounter with other societies showed the great variability of existing norms, the sophists' challenge was that law was not derived from the value of justice but was a function of strengths, i.e. the right of the stronger, or at best, a convention (the *physei/thesei* debate). It was countered by an appeal to 'nature' or to a cosmic order, so that only a law in agreement with these universal standards could claim validity. Here Antigone's plea justifying her resistance to Creon's law is often adduced, as was the stoic conception of law based on the existence of cosmic order.

There are three problems with those arguments. For one, there is the equivocation of 'law' that does not distinguish between a nomic generality, exemplified, for example, by the law of gravity, and normative claims to universality. Without a belief that normative ordering can be deduced from ontology, this deprivation of a legal (or moral) obligation from the 'order of things' is problematic. Similar difficulties arise in the context of the 'greater inclusiveness' argument, often mentioned by advocates of 'cosmopolitan' law. Anyone familiar with the actual Sophoclean *text* of the drama (as opposed to some of the current interpretations linking it to some stoic notions of 'cosmic' law) will notice that

Antigone's plea for burying her bother is based on the old custom predating the polis. It imposed particular duties on family members and the clan. It is against this 'particularity' that Creon's edict was directed, forbiding burials of anyone killed in civil unrest. It tried to establish a more 'inclusive' order, i.e. a law applicable to all citizens, in order to end the feuding among the powerful families. When Antigone appeals to a standard 'behind' all law – which supposedly lends validity to the particular law – she actually wants to have her actions respected in terms of the particularistic custom and not of the more inclusive law now 'universally' binding all citizens, or perhaps even all mankind. Thus the 'universal' she appeals to is not the abstract and more inclusive 'universal' but the concrete particular, based on a way of life of a traditional society. This might seem a controversial interpretation, but as Segal (1983) has shown, Antigone's arguments address (in the guise of events in a mythical past) important political arguments that were occasioned by the Cleisthenic reforms in Athens and the conflict between matrilineal and patrilineal descent for organising politics. The vocabulary used is here of particular importance (and usually gets lost in translation).[8] Thus something more is going on here than just dealing with a problem in terms of the formal categories of extension, whereby the more general contains the particular, as for example Kristeva argues with cosmopolitan intent – *pace* Montesquieu.[9]

The example raises two further issues: one, that the concept of universality is equivocal, and two, that it is not freestanding, so that without further specifications, arguments of universality do very little work. Prominent here are issues of exclusion vs. that extension that interact in the use of the term 'universal'. On the one hand, 'universality', when used in the sense of universalisability, serves as a criterion of exclusion, separating a core of norms which we distil from existing normative catalogues or idiosyncratic prescriptions and which we consider as binding on 'rational' beings. Thus when considered in this sense, the term cannot be 'wider' in the way that the more general is wider in an extensional sense. The other use is precisely based on extension: the more frequent *is* then the more universal, as its observed commonality is taken as an indication of 'what people want'. But again it is easy to see that the argument about a common practice hides an additional normative premise, and is not simply a statement of scope. This problem is well known from the discussion of 'custom' in (international) law. Since not all common regularities, such as getting a stylish haircut or drinking tea at certain time, have normative standing, this 'pull' is often supplied by arguing that the regularity is an indication of an underlying 'value'. Among global 'constitutionalists' and even in the International Law Commission one finds prominent advocates who maintain not only that the legal system contains a hierarchy of norms, but that this hierarchy corresponds to a set of global values that should inform the law-making process. Here the convergence on a particular prescription is taken – perhaps in a Right-Hegelian fashion – as an indication of an underlying universal value at work.

But such a nearly causal inference seems rather heroic. For one, values like principles or norms in general provide 'reasons' for action but are not their efficient cause. To that extent, the conclusion from an effect back to the value as its cause is logically doubly problematic.[10] Even such a fundamental norm as the one against torture might get adopted not necessarily because of the realisation of a common global value. Alternatives could be that, for example, we know that torture 'does not work' (since frequently it does not deliver the crucial information, even though victims will admit to anything), or that – based on historical experience – the non-prohibition creates significant negative externalities, or that it is counterproductive by creating 'martyrs', etc. Of course, many, perhaps most of us, might be deeply shocked by the affront to human dignity. But this does not entitle us to jump to the conclusion that a universal value explains such an agreement. Given the widespread use of torture, the many 'reservations' attached to the legal instruments and the nature of the lenient remedies for violations – especially when read in conjunction with the abandonment of the notion of criminal responsibility by states – makes one wonder whether the universal value argument can be sustained.

But even if we accept it *arguendo*, our problems are not over. Values, like principles, are compatible with diametrically opposed rules implementing them, so that the hierachisation of norms, principles, and values quickly loses its ordering function. For example, the realisation of peace through disarmament was the dominant lore after the First World War. But during the Cold War, 'peace' was based on deterrence and arms control, necessitating rearmament. Both regimes can preserve peace, but point in different directions. Similarly, the recent emphasis on 'robust peace-keeping' seems quite at odds with the original idea of preserving peace through policing a border by means of neutral 'observers' serving at the pleasure of the parties to a conflict. In any case, practical choices call for judgement and political mediations. These choices are contingent, since usually a multiplicity of values is at stake that defy a fixed ordering once and for all, and since the situations are normally describable in a variety of ways, requiring a choice among different rules and different value trade-offs. Here de-contextualised values are of little help despite their 'universality'.

The best indication that appeals to the supreme value of human dignity do little work is provided by the ever-expanding catalogue of human rights, bridging the gap between the lofty values and actual practice. Furthermore, the move to subjective rights implies that everything desirable has now to be recast in the language of individual rights. Democracy suddenly becomes an individual 'right to democracy', the environment is protected by the subjective 'right to a clean environment', and 'development' is somehow wished into existence by the postulation of a 'right to development' (Barsh 1991). It needs not much reflection to conclude that the construal of these 'rights' is the result of considerable conceptual befuddlement. The last 'right' at least can arguably be understood as a 'manifesto claim', i.e. as a grievance. In the absence of a clearly defined class of correlative duty-bearers, a flaw in the existing order is identified, awaiting further specific initiatives to address the problem.

The other two 'rights' are simply based on faulty reasoning. To put it bluntly, the 'right' to democracy is not a human right accruing to human agents as part of their status as agents. Since democracy is a way of organising a society for collective purposes, not a subjective right inherent in, or explicating the notion of, personhood or agency, it involves a category mistake of the first order not to see this difference (Cohen 2004). Similar difficulties arise if the protection of the commons is 'derived' from an individual 'human right'. A more appropriate conceptualisation would be one of common ownership that explicitly prohibits individual appropriation and individual taking. But this requires something like a notion of 'corporate' rights which are irreducible to individual rights.

Since the 'protection' of individual rights is now the *spiritus rector* of the legal enterprise, the notion of 'crime' and of prosecution become important. This is, of course, a *novum* for international law, whose classical 'countermeasures' – including acts of force – were only designed to bring the wayward state back into the fold. But given the enormity of the task, i.e. providing equal and universal justice, it is hardly surprising that such aspirations have to be sacrificed on the altar of contingent reality. The result is an ever-widening gap between aspiration and practice. Most grave breaches of law in the international arena are still dealt with by 'neglect', as Rwanda, Darfour, and Srebrenica demonstrate, and one need not be a 'realist' to see that particular interest and saliency, rather than universal values, do most of the explaining.

But even in cases of humanitarian intervention or criminal prosecution – admittedly few and far between – there are some conceptual issues worth pondering. Justice is not to be gained through the even-handed and general application of existing rules by independent judges, who are subject to the constraints of a constitution or particular political system. Instead, law is supposed to work quasi-freestanding in the newly opened up space of international 'universality' and through some form of 'exemplary justice', which is occasionally visited upon individuals, be they state agents or 'private' persons. My suspicion is that the persuasive force of individual 'criminalisation' in international law has less to do with its expected effectiveness or its prospective ordering function – as a matter of fact, the record of highly selective enforcement makes a mockery of that hope – and more to do with the ideology of 'progress' (Haltern 2006). It is the near-messianic hope for a transformative change resulting from the contestation of the state's monopoly of legitimate force. True, the right to punish was always a jealously guarded right of states. But whether sporadic verdicts of tribunals 'above' the state can instil new loyalties by speaking in the name of 'human dignity', 'collective humanity', or the 'international community' seems rather doubtful.

The imprecision of naming the authority for holding individuals 'responsible' is telling. Is the relevant group the community of states, the 'domestic' order which has incorporated certain universal principles, the 'peoples' of the world, or 'humanity' at large? These are no idle verbal games. It seems that having purged law of all historical peculiarities and contingencies, the identifiable thrust of the argument requires a narrative of the end of the state, or even of 'history'. In this sense, 'humanity' itself and not only 'mankind' in its contingent diversity becomes the all-encompassing point of reference. Both the 'peoples' and the (concrete) people of a given order have vanished. What remains is 'human dignity' as the ultimate source from which all law emanates and to which it refers back (Slaughter 2004: 267; Slaughter and Burke 1990).

But since 'humanity' cannot act, the Schmittian question of *quis judicabit* is the real problem. In short, such a state of affairs is an open invitation for imperial projects, pursued perhaps somewhat quixotically by enthusiasts who see norms 'cascading' (but strangely enough never degenerating, or giving rise to disregard and circumventions), pushed by an 'activist' judiciary – hardly rooted in a constitutional structure and a functioning political process – or by great powers, perhaps even by a coalition of the willing, who feel empowered by the universalist nature of their goals. Politics, eliminated because of its contingent and particular character, is likely to return with a vengeance. It will do so not as the 'art of the possible', but more likely as a fundamentalist creed which is cynically manipulated or, still worse, is actually believed, engendering what Durkheim called 'religious effervescence'.

Conclusion

In a way the discussion has brought us back to the beginning, although with a more sceptical take on the secularist notion that law under conditions of modernity can effectively dispense with the 'sacred', and perhaps even with politics, by substituting 'human rights' for it. Instead of beginning, as is usual, with some 'operational' definitions of religion, law, and politics that treat the social world as if it consisted of 'natural kinds', I argued for an analysis of how law, politics, and religion interact in a semantic field. Since the social world is one of artifice, our concepts are not mere descriptions or icons of a pre-existing reality, but constitutive of our world. But such an analysis necessarily becomes also 'historical' since it is through the configurations and their changes that the meaning of the terms is disclosed.

As a first step I examined therefore the 'secular myth' of Westphalia. The historical record is clear: far from a purely secular order based on contract, what emerged from Westphalia were the 'establishment' churches and the legitimisation of rulers by means of the *Dei gratia* principle. Several *political* solutions were found for the intractable problems that had pitted Protestant dissent against Catholic orthodoxy.

In keeping with my argument about the need to look at law, religion, and politics not as separate 'objects' but as a semantic field, I inquired into the 'sacralisation' of 'the people' in modernity. This notion emerged from the contractarian metaphor but was soon transfigured into the 'nation' bestowing legitimacy onto the state and its laws. In a second attempt I examined the difficulties of a legal order which has 'sources' of, but lacks a central point of reference for, legitimisation, as is the case in international law. This leads then either to the conceptualisation of a secondary order based on the 'self-limitation' of sovereigns, or on their 'consent' as the main source of legitimation. With the dissolution of the nation-state, the alleged convergence on 'human dignity' has to serve as the ultimate foundation.

My critical questions and doubts were less based on the 'foundational' elements in the human rights discourse but rather on the 'abstract' universality that this strategy implies. Having eliminated crucial terms from the discourse, or denuded the remaining ones of any historical and political context – even the 'person' seems to have disappeared – the pride of place is now given to an abstract 'human dignity'. As the 'universal' value it needs, of course, to be concretised again. This is done by a motley array of subjective rights declared to be 'human rights'. The result is a strange mixture of an abstract, sacralised humanity and a quite specific way of life that supposedly best instantiates it. This, I argued, is not an innocent conceptual move. Despite the 'political neutrality' bestowed upon these rights by 'universality', they are likely to invite imperial or millenarian political projects. Those derailments of politics are familiar from fundamentalist religious conflicts, when the goals pursued are no longer treated as fallible political experiments, but become self-justifying ordinances.

But if we are not to engage in imperial projects, the *political mediations* rather than abstract universal norms and values should be our concern. This might be less inspiring than the goal of liberating mankind. But whatever is lacking in the more modest goals of actual political projects in limited, imperfect orders, we have to realise that this 'lack' is simply a reflection of the human condition, all dreams of omnipotence notwithstanding. Thus, despite the various dilemmas we encounter, despite the lack of secure answers to existential questions, and despite the pervasiveness of conflict, the world is not simply a war of all against all, or a Manichean struggle between the children of light and the children of darkness. As certainly as there is no one answer to the existential problems, there are certainly *some* answers to *some* of our problems in practical life. Finding them without the comfort of totalising ideologies or messianic promises by keeping the 'sacred' sacred, i.e. separate, is the predicament we all share as finite, historical beings.

Notes

1 The totality of our so-called knowledge or beliefs, from the most casual matters of geography and history to the profound laws of atomic physics or even pure mathematics and logic, is a man-made fabric which impinges on experience only along the edges. Or, to change the figure, total science is like a field of force whose boundary conditions are experience. A conflict with experience at the periphery occasions readjustments in the interior of the field. Truth values have to be redistributed over some of our statements. Re-evaluation of some statements entails re-evaluation of others, because of their logical interconnections.... Having re-evaluated one statement we must re-evaluate some others, which may be statements logically connected with the first or may be the statements of logical connections themselves. But the total field is so underdetermined by its boundary conditions, experience, that there is much latitude of choice as to what statements to re-evaluate in the light of any single contrary experiences. No particular experiences are linked with any particular statements in the interior of the field, except indirectly through considerations of equilibrium affecting the field as a whole. If this view is right, it is misleading to speak of the empirical content of an individual statement – especially if it is a statement at all remote from the experiential periphery of the field.

2 In this context it is no accident that in Hobbes' Leviathan the sovereign is the 'fixer of signs' and that this 'performance' allows for no contestation. Here the problem of praxis is reduced to one of 'truth' which is authoritatively established by 'command'. One of the implications of this semantics is all 'knowledge', even that of governance has to satisfy the criteria of logic and 'theory' (unequivocality, universality, necessity, etc.). Against the Aristotelian tradition that conceptualises the realm of praxis quite differently, he tries to establish an *episteme* that proceeds 'more geometrico', i.e. in the way in which the theorems in geometry are derived from – as Descartes would later say – 'indubitable' assumptions.

3 See for instance the preamble of the International Covenant on Civil and Political Rights: 'Recognizing that these rights derive from the inherent dignity of the human person', entered into force 23 March 1996, 999 UN Treaty Series, 171.

4 For the latter, see the late Myres McDougal's prolific writings in international law. For a programmatic statement, see McDougal (1966).

5 See the Treaty of Paris in 1783, and aside from common European practice, even the US signed treaties with such a preamble, as in the case of treaties with Russia (1832) and with Paraguay (1859). I owe this thought to an email from Michael Myerson, Prof. of Law at University of Baltimore.

6 In sociology the secularisation argument was attacked first by Thomas Luckmann (1967) and its criticism engendered the later work by Thomas Berger (1990).

7 Of course the physical reality of 'birth' establishes nothing since it is only by connecting the institutional fact of 'citizenship' with this physical (brute) fact – in Searle's parlance – that establishes my status as a member. Consequently, not nature but 'the law' is determinative and other bases for ascription might be provided (naturalisation).

8 See, for example, Antigone's plea with Creon (verses 522–523) and with her 'common self-wombed sister' Ismene. As Segal suggests:

> The tie through blood alone through the womb, Antigone makes the basis of her philia, *Philia* which includes notions of love, loyalty, friendship and kinship, is another fundamental point of division between Creon and Antigone…
>
> CREON: The enemy (*echthros*) is not a loved one (*philos*), not even when he is dead.
>
> ANTIGONE: It is my nature to share not in enmity, but in loving (*symphilein*).
>
> Creon here repeats his political definition of *philos* from his first speech (182–183) but now it is opposed by Antiogone's fierce personal loyalties. Once more the sameness of the womb cuts through the principle of differentiation that separates *philos* from *echthros*. Creon's politisation of burial distinguishes between the two brothers as hostile political forces. 'The one he promotes in honor, the other he dishonors (22). To Antigone, however, those 'of the same womb' are worthy of the same degree of honor (time) and love (philia).
>
> (Segal 1983: 173f.)

9 Julia Kristeva (1993: 28) quotes Montesquieu in her plea for a 'more inclusive cosmopolitanism':

> If I knew something useful to myself and detrimental to my family, I would reject it from my mind. If I knew something useful to my family, but not to my homeland, I would try to forget it. If I knew something useful to my homeland, but detrimental … to mankind I would consider it a crime.

10 It is doubly faulty since values like norms values are contra-factually valid, they do not cause a result in a causally efficient manner. Two, in logic the reversal of the inference from 'if p then q' is invalid (i.e. if we observe q and infer p). This conclusion could only be justified if the proposition is: 'if and only if p then q': if it rains the street is wet, but the street being wet does not establish rain as the antecedent cause, since it might be due to a break of the water main or to street cleaning.

References

Abbott, K., Keohane, R.O., Moravcsik, A., Slaughter, A-M., and Snidal, D. (2000) 'The concept of legalization', *International Organization*, 54(3): 401–19.

Agamben, G. (1998) *Homo Sacer*, Stanford: Stanford University Press.

Appelby, R.S. (2000) *The Ambivalence of the Sacred*, Lanham, MD: Rowman & Littlefield.

Aretin, K.-O. von (1993–97) *Das Alte Reich 1648–1806*, 3 vols, Stuttgart: Klett-Cotta.

Barbato, M. and Kratochwil, F. (2009) 'Towards a post-secular order?', *European Political Science Review*, 1(3): 1–24.

Barsh, R.L. (1991) 'The right to development as a human right: results of the global consultation', *Human Rights Quarterly*, 13(3): 322–38.

Berger, P. (1999) 'The desecularization of the world: a global overview', in P. Berger (ed.) *The Desecularization of the World: Resurgent Religion and World Politics*, Washington, D.C.: Ethics and Public Policy Center.

Berger, T. (1990) *The Rumour of Angels*, New York: Anchor.

Carother, T. (2006) *Promoting the Rule of Law Abroad*, Washington, D.C.: Carnegie Endowment.

Cohen, J. (2004) 'Whose sovereignty: Empire vs. international law', *Ethics and International Affairs*, 18(3): 1–24.

Connolly, W. (1999) *Why I am not a Secularist*, Minneapolis: University of Minnesota Press.

Durkheim, E. ([1912] 1965) *The Elementary Forms of Religious Life*, New York: Free Press.

Fassbender, B. (1998) 'The UN Charter as the Constitution of the international community', *Columbia Journal of Transnational Law*, 36: 529–619.

Grewe, W. (2000) *The Epochs of International Law*, Berlin: de Gruyter.

Gross, L. (1948) 'The Peace of Westphalia 1648–1948', *American Journal of International Law*, 42(1): 20–41.

Grotius, H. ([1625] 1925) *De Jure Belli ac Pacis*, ed. and trans. by F. Kelsey, Indianapolis: Bobbs Merrill.

Habermas, J. (2003) *The Future of Human Nature*, Cambridge: Polity.

Haltern, U. (2006) 'Tomuschats Traum: zur Bedeutung von Souveraenitaet im Völkerrecht', in P.-M. Dupuy, B. Fassbender, M.N. Shaw, and K.-P. Sommermann (eds) *Festschrift für Christian Tomuschat*, Kehl: N.P. Engel Verlag.

Hart, H.L.A. (1961) *The Concept of Law*, Oxford: Clarendon Press.

Hintze, O. (1975) 'Military organization and the theory of the state', in F. Gilbert (ed.) *The Historical Essays of Otto Hintze*, Oxford: Oxford University Press.

Hirschman, A. (1970) *Exit, Voice, Loyalty*, Cambridge, MA: Harvard University Press.

Hurd, E.S. (2008) *The Politics of Secularism in International Politics*, Princeton: Princeton University Press.

Independent International Commission on Kosovo (2000) *The Kosovo Report*, Oxford: Oxford University Press.

International Commission on Intervention and State Sovereignty (2001) *The Responsibility to Protect*, Ottawa: International Development Research Centre.

Kant, I. ([1795] 1996) 'Towards perpetual peace, third definitive article for perpetual peace', in M.J. Gregor (ed.) *Immanuel Kant: Practical Philosophy*, Cambridge: Cambridge University Press.

Kant, I. ([1797] 1996) 'The metaphysics of morals', in M.J. Gregor (ed.) *Immanuel Kant, Practical Philosophy*, Cambridge: Cambridge University Press.

Koskenniemi, M. (2004) 'International law and hegemony', *Cambridge Review of International Affairs*, 17: 197–218.

Kratochwil, F. (1994) 'The limits of contract', *European Journal of International Law*, 5(4): 465–91.

Kratochwil, F. (2006) 'History, action and identity', *European Journal of International Relations*, 12(1): 5–29.

Krisch, N. (2006) 'The pluralism of global administrative law', *European Journal of International Law*, 17(1): 247–78.

Kristeva, J. (1993) *Nations without Nationalism*, New York: Columbia.

Linklater, A. (1997) *The Transformation of Political Community*, Cambridge: Polity Press.

Luckmann, T. (1967) *Invisible Religion*, New York: Macmillan.

Luhmann, N. (1980) *Gesellschaftsstruktur und Semantik*, Frankfurt: Suhrkamp.

Luhmann, N. (1999) *Die Gesellschaft der Gesellschaft*, Frankfurt: Suhrkamp.

Luhmann, N. (2002) *Die Religion der Gesellschaft*, Frankfurt: Suhrkamp.

Maier, C. (1990) *The Greek Discovery of Politics*, Cambridge, MA: Harvard University Press.

Marks, S. (1997) 'The end of history? Reflections on some international legal theses', *European Journal of International Law*, 3: 449–77.

McDougal, M. (1966) 'Some basic concepts about international law: a policy oriented framework', in R.A. Falk and S.H. Mendlovitz (eds) *The Strategy of World Order. Vol. II: International Law*, New York: World Law Fund.

Nardin, T.L. (1983) *Morality and the Relations of States*, Princeton: Princeton University Press.

Norris, P. and Inglehart, R. (2004) *Sacred and Secular: Religion and Politics Worldwide*, Cambridge: Cambridge University Press.

Ossiander, A. (2001) 'Sovereignty, international relations and the Westphalian myth', *International Organization*, 55(2): 251–87.

Otto, R. (1971) *The Idea of the Holy*, Oxford: Oxford University Press.

Philipott, D. (2001) *Revolutions in Sovereignty*, Princeton: Princeton University Press.

Quine, W.V.O. (1980) '*From a Logical Point of View*', Cambridge, Massachusetts: Harvard University Press.

Rawls, J. (1993a) *Political Liberalism*, New York: Columbia University Press.

Rawls, J. (1993b) 'The law of the peoples', in S. Shute and S. Hurley (eds) *On Human Rights: The Oxford Amnesty Lectures*, New York: Basic Books.

Reus-Smit, C. (2004) *The Politics of International Law*, Cambridge: Cambridge University Press.

Rousseau, J.-J. ([1762] 1976) *Social Contract*, ed. by C. Crocker, New York: Washington Square Press.

Schilling, H. (1992) *Religion, Political Culture and the Emergence of Early Modern Society*, Leiden-New York: Brill.

Schmitt, C. ([1922] 2005) *Political Theology*, Chicago: University of Chicago Press.

Schmitt, C. ([1927] 1996) *The Concept of the Political*, Chicago: University of Chicago Press.

Segal, C. (1983) 'Antigone: death and love, Hades and Dionysos', in C. Segal (ed.) *Greek Tragedy: Modern Essays in Criticism*, New York: Harper and Row.

Shapcott, R. (2001) *Justice, Community and Dialogue in International Relations*, Cambridge: Cambridge University Press.

Slaughter, A.-M. (2004) *A New World Order*, Princeton: Princeton University Press.

Slaughter, A.-M. and Burke-White, W. (1990) 'An international constitutional moment', *Harvard International Law Journal*, 43(4): 866–76.

Taylor, C. (2007) *A Secular Age*, Cambridge, MA: Harvard University Press.

Tilly, C. (1992) *Coercion, Capital and the European States, AD 990–1992*, Oxford: Blackwell.

Tocqueville, A. de ([1835/1840] 1952) *L'Ancien Régime et la Révolution*, Paris: Gallimard.

Voegelin, E. (1952) *New Science of Politics*, Chicago: University of Chicago Press.

Voegelin, E. (1986) *Political Religions*, Lewistown, NY: E. Mellen Press.

Wendt, A. (1999) *Social Theory of International Relations*, Cambridge: Cambridge University Press.

4 Kant's semantics of world (state) making

Vojin Rakić

Democratic peace and cosmopolitan democracy

Kant scholars have offered a variety of differing interpretations of his cosmopolitanism. There are two basic positions concerned with this debate, and a third, which can be seen as a refinement of the second.[1] The first position mostly focuses on *Toward Perpetual Peace* (*TPP*), while the second and third follow the semantics of world (state) making. I will argue that the third stance is the most appropriate reflection of Kant's standpoint, linking it to the dismissal of the currently prevailing liberal peace project in statebuilding – a project with Weberian underpinnings. In addition, I will attempt to demonstrate why *Religion Within the Boundaries of Mere Reason* (*RBMR*) is essential for understanding Kant's cosmopolitanism. I will contend that it offers insights into Kant's semantics of world (state) making, whereas his republicanism and federalism from *TPP* remain within the boundaries of the semantics of Weberian statebuilding. All in all, I will reconstruct Kant's position in international relations primarily by observing the semantic distinctions between *TPP* and *RBMR*.

The first position focuses on Kant's dismissal of a world state in sections of *TPP*. Here Kant raised his concerns regarding the potential for uninhibited despotism in a world republic, and voiced his preference for a lawful federation under commonly accepted international law. Some advocates of the first position, such as Ferdinand Teson, contend that the first definitive article of *TPP*, stipulating that the civil constitution of every state should be republican, can offer a transition from Kant's moral philosophy to his political theory – because every state within the federation is required to be representative and to respect human rights without the presence of an overarching global authority (Teson 1998: 105). Moreover, Teson believes that Kant was the first philosopher to establish the link between domestic freedom and the foundations of international law:

> Not only did he [Kant] have the vision to predict modern international organization for the maintenance of peace; he also explained, for the first time, the connection between domestic freedom and the foundations of international law. In essence, he foresaw the human rights revolution of the twentieth century.
>
> (Teson 1992: 56)[2]

A variant of this first position establishes a connection between the features that are intrinsic to liberal states and peaceful relations among them (Doyle 1983; Russett 1993; Owen 1996). All in all, proponents of this 'democratic peace (DP) thesis' are committed to the idea of popular sovereignty and the notion that the citizenries of territorially fixed units are sufficient as mechanisms of international reform.[3] It is possible to assert that this standpoint became the dominant view on the subject in the 1990s, since the realist paradigm had been weakened in the years after the Cold War (see Franceschet 2000: 280).

Those proponents of DP, however, who link features that are intrinsic to liberal states to peaceful relations among them (attributing this stance to Kant) might be accused of misunderstanding Kant's republicanism: it can be argued that an identification of Kant's republicanism with contemporary liberalism is misplaced. In fact, such identification implies unjustified trans-historical interpretations:[4] the liberal notion that someone can do whatever they want as long as they do no wrong to anyone else is different from Kant's 'republican' conception of freedom as 'the warrant to obey no other external laws than those to which I could have given my consent' (Kant 1912a, Ak. 8: 350).

The second position also claims to have a Kantian heritage. It advocates that Kant envisaged a world republic and that he was seeking a community of individuals independent from states, i.e. of politically autonomous moral agents. It is a paradigm that during the 1990s and 2000s presented an alternative to the DP thesis. But this 'cosmopolitan democracy (CD) paradigm' has earlier origins (e.g. Bull 1977; Wight 1987). Hedley Bull notes the following: '[Kantian] imperatives enjoin not coexistence and cooperation among states but rather the overthrow of the system of states and its replacement by a cosmopolitan society' (Bull 1977: 25). According to Bull, however, the sole force that can bring warring states together is the force of one will over all others, which makes the idea of a world union unattractive. Wight even came up with the realist interpretation that Kant's preference for a world state originated from his alleged inclinations towards the idea of world conquest (Wight 1987: 226).[5]

CD theorists disagree with DP exponents that the state is the sole basis of individual autonomy. They replace the DP paradigm of territorially based sovereignty with the idea of multiple, overlapping, state-transcending forms of democratic governance. David Held is possibly the principal proponent of this thesis (see Held 1995), but Archibugi (1995a, 1995b, 1998), Linklater (1996, 1998), Franceschet (2000, 2002), Della Porta (2006) and Marchetti (2008) have added new insights to his ideas.

Critiques of the second position were frequently based on Kant's explicit dismissal of a world republic in sections of *TPP* in which he argued that such a republic contains the danger of unrestrained despotism. The third position is in its key aspects a response to these critiques. In that sense, it can be seen as a refinement of the second position. It accepts the idea of a future world republic, although it emphasises that such a republic was not Kant's *immediate* choice.[6] It lays down that Kant advocated a federation for practical and political reasons, but also believed that something more than a federation was required to achieve the ultimate purpose of history, i.e. the cosmopolitan ideal. Hence, Kant saw a global federation as a stage in history's path towards a world republic (Cavallar 1999). Some Kant scholars have come up with the interpretation that Kantian ideal theory requires individuals to live under the common civil laws of a cosmopolitan republic and that the idea of a federation was merely Kant's second-best choice (Laberge 1998). If 'second-best choice' is interpreted as a stage on history's path towards the ideal of a global state (i.e. as an intermediate 'blueprint', to use the formulation by Nicholas Onuf in Chapter 2 of this volume), this interpretation is also in line with the third position.

Unlike the second, the third position does not suppose that Kant favoured a world republic as an immediate political goal, but rather that he believed in the progress of humankind towards a cosmopolitan order. Such an order would be some kind of long-term destination of history. One of the strengths of this interpretation is that it can accommodate Kant's conviction that any progress towards a future global order would have to be voluntary and that a willingness to accept such an order needs to be preceded by humanity's greater ethical maturity.

It is the third interpretation of Kant, marked by an unwillingness to make trans-historical interpretations linking his republicanism to contemporary liberalism, that can be related to the dismissal of the currently prevailing liberal peace project in statebuilding. The case for dismissal is forcefully argued in this volume, notably by Nicolas Lemay-Hébert in Chapter 6 and David Chandler in Chapter 8. Kant's notion that a future global order has to be accepted voluntarily is relevant here. Only then will such an order be sustainable – due to humanity's appropriate 'ethical maturity'. It cannot impose its values on nations like on an 'empty shell'. A willingness to look at social processes beyond the Weberian state and to strive for 'local ownership' in statebuilding is essential for its success.

But it is not only essential for successful statebuilding. It also helps humanity to abandon its 'second-best choice', i.e. the Weberian state in a global federation or the Weberian state in 'EU member statebuilding' (Chandler), and move in the direction of a cosmopolitan order that Kant envisioned as the ultimate purpose of history. Hence the semantics of Kantian cosmopolitanism (interpreted in line with the third position) and the semantics of post-Weberian statebuilding appear to send us related messages. But let us see now to what extent the third position is justified.

Kant's path to world (state) making

Kant developed the foundations of his philosophy in his major systematic writings. Among them, *RBMR* (published in 1793) was the last large, systematic and, for our purposes relevant, work before an important event that might have determined Kant's writings in later years. As is well known, Kant's practical philosophy cannot be fully understood if the role that Providence plays in his system is ignored. But after the publication of *RBMR*, Kant's diminishing involvement in religious and theological matters is noticeable. A striking silence on these matters characterises two of his works frequently cited in relative isolation from Kant's other writings when his approach to international relations is being studied. They are principally *TPP* (published in 1795), but also a number of relevant sections on 'Public Right' from *The Metaphysics of Morals* (1797). How did this change of attitude in Kant's thinking come about? How is it possible that in these two studies Kant fails to concentrate on a concept that is essential for his system of practical philosophy, and has the potential to answer critical issues pertaining to international relations: the concept of Providence, and the ideas that Kant derives from it?[7] What changed his semantics of international relations?

I propose to seek an explanation in a noteworthy event that occurred in 1794: the decision by the Prussian authorities to undertake repressive actions against Kant due to his writings on religious matters. After the publication of *RBMR* and *The End of All Things* (1794), the Prussian King, Frederick William II, authorised an official letter to Kant (signed by Frederick William's 'Minister of Education and Religious Affairs') in which he was accused of 'misusing' his philosophy to 'distort and disparage many of the cardinal and basic teachings of the Holy Scriptures and Christianity'. The letter also demanded that Kant 'give an account of himself' and be guilty of no similar faults in the future, lest he be the object of 'unpleasant measures' for his 'continuing obstinacy' (Wood 1996: xx). It was dated 1 October 1794.

Eleven days later Kant did indeed give an 'account of himself' and replied that his writings were purely philosophical and hence were not an attempt to evaluate the Holy Scripture and Christianity. Regarding the second point, however, Kant pledged 'as your Majesty's most loyal subject' not to discuss publicly any form of religion, whether natural or revealed, either in lectures or in his writings (Wood 1996: xxi). This was undoubtedly an important event, one that might shed light on why *TPP* and *The Metaphysics of Morals*, written *after* the ban was imposed, are devoid of the necessary theological component, including seriously elaborated concepts of God and Providence and the semantics derived from them (as obvious 'forms of religion, whether natural or revealed').

In November 1797 (four months after the publication of *The Metaphysics of Morals*) Frederick William died and Kant was no longer bound by his personal promise, which had been given to the *specific* monarch. In 1798, *The Conflict of the Faculties* appeared, containing Kant's last major printed reflections on religion.[8] Hence, in the period between Frederick William's letter of October 1794 and 1798, Kant did not publish anything on religious and theological matters. In the light of the relevance of these issues for Kant's practical philosophy in general and his position on international relations in particular, therefore, it is possible to argue that *TPP* (and the relevant sections of *The Metaphysics of Morals*) must be viewed as statements with only a relative value for issues they address or fail to address.

Which writings, then, can give us more complete insights into Kant's views on relations between states as an element of his political philosophy and system of ethics? Apart from *TPP* and the aforementioned sections of *The Metaphysics of Morals*, it is important to understand the ideas Kant develops in *Groundwork of the Metaphysics of Morals* (1785), *Critique of Practical Reason* (1788) and, as already underlined, *RBMR*. These works are systematic writings in which Kant deals with his practical philosophy. The most important of them might well be *RBMR*, because it was the last work of the type in which Kant wrote as a philosopher who could still freely express himself. The implications of this might be quite serious. If *RBMR* contains thoughts that are sufficiently relevant for a proper understanding of Kant's position on international relations, it is an essential piece of reading on the subject. I will now attempt to show that this is indeed the case.

In interpreting *RBMR*, I begin by highlighting something that is significant for an understanding of Kant's conception of relations between states. It is also important for understanding the role 'perpetual peace' plays in his semantics of international relations. This is that, for Kant, the aim of perpetual peace cannot be achieved by political means alone. In his own words:

> Such is therefore the work of the good principle – unnoticed to human eye yet constantly advancing – in erecting a power and a kingdom for itself within the human race, in the form of a community according to the laws of virtue that proclaims the victory over evil and, under its dominion, assures the world of an eternal peace.
>
> (Kant 1907a, Ak. 6: 124)[9]

What can we conclude from this? Evidently that the success of the project sketched in *TPP* must depend on something other than politics. That something is for Kant 'the work of the good principle', i.e. the moral progress of the human being. But moral progress has a point of convergence with political progress. This point of convergence is fully outlined in *RBMR* – another reason *RBMR* should be given serious consideration.[10]

But where do moral and political progress converge? In the previous quotation Kant uses a revealing semantics, talking about 'the good principle' working 'within the human race' in the direction of the creation of 'a community according to the laws of virtue'. This semantics should not be understood independently from Kant's perception of Christianity as a religion that sends us a moral message that calls for the unity of humanity – a unity that will in the final instance result in the formation of a world state. That indicates why issues pertaining to international relations occupy a significant place in *RBMR*: Kant there asserts that the ultimate aim of human progress is that 'the human being ought to leave the ethical state of nature in order to become a member of an *ethical community (commonwealth)*' (Kant 1907a, Ak. 6: 96, my emphasis).[11] Kant envisions this commonwealth as 'an association of human beings merely under the laws of virtue' (Kant 1907a, Ak. 6: 94).

The idea of an ethical commonwealth is anticipated in *Groundwork of the Metaphysics of Morals* and *Critique of Practical Reason*. In both works Kant writes about the *summum bonum*, or the highest good, and defends the position that this can be attained only in a perfect community. In *Critique of Practical*

Reason he refers to the achievement of the 'highest good in the world' as the 'necessary object of a will determinable by the moral law' (Kant 1908, Ak. 5: 122). In *Groundwork*, Kant describes the perfect community by using the term 'Kingdom of ends' (Kant 1903, Ak. 4: 433; and elsewhere). Let us for a moment call to mind something that is essential for Kant and central to the concepts that are addressed here: the idea of the free person. Only a person with a free will is capable of acting morally, because he *wills* to act morally. Hence, the achievement of the highest good and the Kingdom of ends is only possible by free individuals.

In political commonwealths all citizens are in an ethical state of nature (Kant 1907a, Ak 6: 95). That is not the case in an ethical commonwealth, in which they are 'united under laws without being coerced, i.e. under *laws of virtue* alone' (Kant 1907a, Ak. 6: 95). The concept of the ethical commonwealth, moreover, extends to humanity in general (Kant 1907a, Ak. 6: 96). Kant writes:

> Hence, a multitude of human beings united in that purpose [of a political community] cannot yet be called the ethical community as such but only a particular society that strives after the consensus of all human beings (indeed, of all finite rational beings) in order to establish an absolute ethical whole of which each partial society is only a representation or schema.
>
> (Kant 1907a, Ak. 6: 96)

Kant describes an ethical commonwealth as 'a universal republic based on the laws of virtue' (Kant 1907a, Ak. 6: 98). It is something to which humans should aspire, but which can only be achieved with the help of Divine intervention (Kant 1907a, Ak. 6: 99). Kant writes: 'Hence an ethical community is conceivable only as a people under divine commands, i.e. as a *people of God*, and indeed *in accordance with the laws of virtue*' (Kant 1907a, Ak. 6: 99, my emphasis). In other words, no matter how unachievable the ethical commonwealth might appear to us, Providence will give us the help we need – but not if we remain inactive. On the contrary, we should direct our efforts towards our moral improvement and the creation of this ethical commonwealth.[12]

The ultimate purpose of politics is the goal of an ethical community in which individuals are guided by '(the duties of) virtue'. This means that Kant is entirely clear about the need for the subjection of the political sphere to ethical principles. The highest political good and the highest moral good, however, can only be achieved simultaneously. And that can happen exclusively in a world community, a community of human beings, in a world state – not in a federation of states. This appears to contradict Kant's advocacy of a federation of states in *TPP*. Apart from the argument concerning 'uninhibited (global) despotism', we find in *TPP* the following closely related statements:

> The idea of the right of nations presupposes the *separation* of many neighbouring states independent of one another; and though such a condition is of itself a condition of war (unless a federative union of them prevents the

> outbreak of hostilities), this is nevertheless better, in accordance with the idea of reason, than the fusion of them by one power overgrowing the rest and passing into a universal monarchy.
>
> (Kant 1912a, Ak. 8: 367)

and:

> … a federative condition of states having as its only purpose the avoidance of war is the sole *rightful* condition compatible with the *freedom* of states.
>
> (Kant 1912a, Ak. 8: 385)

How can one explain this discrepancy in Kant's thinking, apart from raising the issue of the ban on his freedom of expression at the time *TPP* was published? How to account for Kant's changed semantics of international relations? It might be argued that Kant envisions the ethical commonwealth as the Church:

> An ethical community under divine moral legislation is a *church* which, inasmuch as it is not the object of a possible experience, is called the *church invisible*.
>
> (Kant 1907a, Ak. 6: 101)

But at various other points in *RBMR*, Kant makes clear that the ethical commonwealth is more than one particular church. It is *the* one, true, invisible Church, but also 'a universal *republic* based on the laws of virtue' (Kant 1907a, Ak. 6: 98; my emphasis). The fact that Kant uses the term 'republic' to describe the ethical commonwealth indicates that he did not understand it merely as a sort of spiritual community. The invisible Church, the universal republic or world republic, 'the good principle' working within the human race towards 'a community according to the laws of virtue', the *summum bonum*, the perfect community, the Kingdom of ends, the ethical commonwealth – all these terms refer to Kant's view of the point of convergence of moral and political progress of the human being. This point is thus also one at which the Church and the political community converge. Consequently, the ethical commonwealth is more than the Church.

Elsewhere in *RBMR* Kant writes that

> the will of the world ruler … invisibly binds all together, under a common government, in a state inadequately represented and prepared for in the past through the visible church.
>
> (Kant 1907a, Ak. 6: 122)

The 'Church invisible', on the other hand, is the true representative of the morally progressed human, subject to a *common* government in a *common* state. Accordingly, this 'Church invisible' and the world state are the indispensable embodiments of a future humanity – a community of human beings who are united in an ethical commonwealth.

How does Kant account theoretically for his view of a continuous progress of the human race for the better (formulated in *RBMR* in a variety of ways, e.g. as 'the continuous advance and approximation towards the highest possible good on earth' [Kant 1907a, Ak. 6: 136])? This question cannot be answered without looking at one of the main features of Kant's practical philosophy: duty. Let us recall that for Kant it is our duty to act in accordance with the moral law and to assume that humanity continuously progresses for the better. Acting in accordance with the moral law means, among other things, always treating human beings as ends in themselves, and never only as a means towards other ends. This will finally result in what Kant calls the 'Kingdom of ends'. In *TPP*, Kant writes that it is our duty to realise the 'condition of public right, even if only in approximation by unending progress', and that consequently perpetual peace will be realised at an accelerated pace (Kant 1912a, Ak. 8: 386). Hence, it is duty that is the basis of perpetual peace, the Kingdom of ends, the world state, the Church invisible, the ethical commonwealth. Our obligation to assume that all these concepts will be realised makes them realisable.[13]

It is useful to link these thoughts with Kant's postulations on the immortality of the soul and the existence of God in his *Critique of Practical Philosophy*. Kant derives the postulation on the immortality of the soul from his understanding that the highest good (morality) can only be accomplished by assuming an endless development of the human capacity for good. The highest good can only be achieved in eternity. Because of that, it is our moral duty to assume the immortality of the soul (Kant 1908, Ak. 5: 122 and 5: 123). Concerning the existence of God, Kant provides us with a related argument: the achievement of the highest good is not possible without God, and hence it is duty that makes us postulate God's existence (Kant 1908, Ak. 5: 124). He writes:

> Now, it was a duty for us to promote the highest good; hence, there is in us not merely the warrant but also the necessity, as a need connected with duty, to presuppose the possibility of this highest good, which, since it is possible only under the condition of the existence of God, connects the presupposition of the existence of God inseparably with duty; that is, it is morally necessary to assume the existence of God.
>
> (Kant 1908, Ak. 5: 125)

and:

> the moral law leads through the concept of the highest good, as the object and final end of pure practical reason, *to religion, that is, to the recognition of all duties as divine commands, not as sanctions* ... but as essential laws of every free will in itself.
>
> (Kant 1908, Ak. 5: 129)

It can be seen here in Kant's own statement that the moral law and the concept of the highest good lead to religion, and that hence *RBMR* is the logical extension of *Critique of Practical Reason* and of *Groundwork*, as well as, arguably, the culmination of Kant's thoughts on practical philosophy.[14]

Kant's apparent semantic incoherence in *TPP* as compared to *RBMR* (a federation of states vis-à-vis a world state) might suggest that he had quite different aims in the two works. He apparently described two different historical 'blueprints'. In *RBMR* he endeavoured to give an account of the final condition which humanity should attain (and is gradually attaining). In *TPP* he was concerned with the intermediate phase, the stage to which humanity ought to aspire in the more immediate future. At that stage, a world state is still not achievable – because of the imperfections of humanity. After humans have made sufficient moral progress, a universal state and Church will become possible. Before that, a federation of states will have to suffice.

In interpreting Kant's semantics of international relations, one therefore needs to have a clear picture of the stage of the future (or 'blueprint') Kant is referring to: the distant future (i.e. the approximation of the final stage of human development) or the more immediate future. *RBMR* deals more with the former, *TPP* with the latter. There are at least two crucial reasons why it might be justified to believe that Kant cared more about the former. First, in *RBMR* he made a systematic attempt to position his thoughts from that work in the framework of his entire system of practical philosophy. For instance, the ethical commonwealth in *RBMR* is an extension of the Kingdom of ends from *Groundwork*. It is also an extension of the 'highest good in the world as a necessary object of a will determinable by the moral law' to which Kant refers in *Critique of Practical Philosophy*. Second, Kant must have been less dedicated to the thoughts he expressed while his freedom of speech was restricted than to those he developed in the periods when he could freely express himself. Hence, his semantics of the future world (society), including the role Providence plays in its establishment – notions that are developed in *RBMR* – appear to deserve greater attention than his semantics of this and related subjects addressing the more immediate future. Kant expressed the latter considerations in *TPP* and the aforementioned sections of *The Metaphysics of Morals*.

Furthermore, in contrast to *TPP*, Kant's cosmopolitan project in *RBMR* is not based on states but on moral individuals guided by the *Vernunftreligion*. If the line of reasoning from the previous paragraph is accurate, Kant's notion of universal moral purpose outshines his political handling of international relations.[15] His moral semantics surpasses his political treatment of the subject.

This brings us to another problem Kant has perhaps exposed himself to in *TPP*: the 'status quo bias'. Although it is unusual to associate this bias with Kant, he might have fallen victim to it during the period of the ban on his freedom of expression. Since Kant could not at that time have expressed his thoughts on matters that might have a religious foundation, in *TPP* he could not develop further his key conceptions about the ethical commonwealth, the one true Church and one world state. This left him with the possibility of discussing international relations in an abridged form, and Kant opted for the least painful solution – to discuss his concepts on relations among states from the point of view of the present state of affairs and the relatively near future. That skewed his thoughts in *TPP* towards the status quo in international relations. In other words, Kant's semantics of statebuilding in *TPP* is based on the concept of federalism, republicanism and international law that guarantees universal hospitality. In *RBMR*, on the other hand, Kant's semantics of statebuilding becomes one of world (state) making, with the concept of the 'ethical commonwealth' figuring as essential.

But is the attainment of something that goes far beyond the status quo realistic? Although Kant believed that humans do not have the capacity to achieve the ethical commonwealth and a universal state on their own, he thought that the help of Providence would eventually result in the development of a community of humanity and a world state. Nevertheless, it is possible to dispute that Kant *unambiguously* advocates one global state in *RBMR*. Even though he uses the term 'republic' in describing the ethical commonwealth, Kant's references to it through the expression 'Church invisible' do instil some ambiguity. In order to shed more light on this uncertainty, it is useful to consider, in addition to Kant's own statements, what the logical implications of his fundamental ideas are for international relations.

In that regard, it is worth emphasising that it appears quite incongruous to envision an ethical commonwealth as the *summum bonum*, and at the same time to consider this highest good to be achievable only in a federation of states. Such a federation can only be necessary as an intermediate stage of development of international relations.[16] Its rationale would be based on the need of humans to preserve a connection with their ethnic and political communities, in order not to be robbed of their cultural specificity and their rootedness in Weberian states. But why the need for such ties in a community of humanity, in a commonwealth of the highest good? Can we imagine the highest good and a community of humanity as a condition in which humans are divided along ethnic and political lines? Such a division is conceivable only at some halfway stage on the path to a global state. That is the 'blueprint' Kant talked about in *TPP*. But the only logical consequence of Kant's concepts discussed in *RBMR* is one global state. That state would be an embodiment of the ethical community, as well as the worldly side of the 'Church invisible'.

The concept Kant has developed does not envision organisational solutions at the global level. He remains focused on his semantics of Providence and one true Church, believing that they will ensure that his entire project will succeed in the end. The true Church, not being any one in existence, will be an institutionalisation of the moral progress of the human being. Although the natural path of history may gradually lead humans to a just and civilised order, justice and peace have to be instituted in the final instance as a result of conscious moral choice. In international relations, therefore, as in religious matters, Kant relies on the moral improvement of humanity and on justice as a point towards which history leads us. Accordingly, moral progress of the human being will be institutionalised both in one true Church and in one global state. In other words, morally advanced humans (progressing in morality up to the distant future) will be the essential ingredients in this religious and political order. Furthermore, only moral improvement of humanity (and world justice as its final result) can ultimately ensure peace. Hence, perpetual peace is also one important (though generally less visible) theme of *RBMR*: Kant asserts there unambiguously that 'the good principle' (i.e. moral progress) is the vehicle that 'assures the world of an eternal peace' (Kant 1907a, Ak. 6: 124).

The future global order is thus one in which the state and the Church are in a harmonious relationship, because they aspire to the same aims: justice and peace. In an ethical commonwealth, as envisioned by Kant, reasons cease to exist for competition for power among people and thus also between the global state and the one true Church. The ethical commonwealth is a just, peaceful and harmonious commonwealth in which the state and Church meet each other again, no longer as competitors but as partners in a common project. Hence, the dialectical development throughout history of the relations between the state and the Church will move the Church from an intruder in political affairs, via an institution that is separated from the state (the current situation in liberal societies) to a future in which its competition with the state is superseded (*aufgehoben*). In such a future, the Church and (world) state are partners, forming an ethical commonwealth of morally perfected humans.

It is also at this point that the connection between Kant and Kratochwil's view of politics, law and religion becomes transparent. Kant's interpretation of world (state) making is related to the idea of a religiously and morally constructed society. For Kratochwil, the idea of a Westphalian secular state assumes an immediate separation of religion and politics. But the 'sacred' has been preserved post-Westphalia. Systems of norms (such as human rights law) have religious foundations. They focus on concepts of punishment and the holiness of law that are derived from European Christianity. In fact, modern law cannot effectively dispense with the 'sacred' by substituting abstract entities such as 'human rights'.

Kant's ethical commonwealth, on the other hand, is a 'sacred' (read 'morally superior') entity of the future. The contemporary semantics of human rights endeavour to give these rights a similar status. But Kratochwil is critical of them. It seems that, intentionally or not, he interprets the present as Kant's intermediate stage on the path of humanity towards the ethical commonwealth. On the remaining part of that path the semantics of 'sacredness' of human rights is to develop into a moral semantics of the ethical commonwealth. That is when the Church and the state will re-establish a close relationship – an ethical partnership consisting of morally superior humans.

Conclusion

It can be concluded that the advocates of the third position in the typology presented in the first section appear to have come closest to understanding Kant's changing semantics in international relations, specifically by interpreting his federation as an intermediate stage on the historical path of humanity towards a world state. However, they generally seem oblivious to the fact that key arguments for their position are to be found in *RBMR* – specifically in Kant's conception of the ethical commonwealth. In *RBMR* Kant makes clear that this commonwealth is a future community of morally sophisticated humans that is marked by justice and peace. Such a community is the final destination and purpose of our moral and political development. We have to guide ourselves towards this purpose; we can count on Providence in our endeavours, while we have to direct our short-term strategy to another 'blueprint' – one marked by the establishment of a federation of states as a precursor to a world state.

The foregoing does not imply, however, that Kant's belief in a world state necessarily requires his comprehensive philosophy of religion. Nonetheless, some of its elements are of key significance if Kantian cosmopolitan semantics is to be fully illuminated. As has been demonstrated, they include relevant sections of *RBMR* that deal with the ethical commonwealth as humanity's final destination and with Providence as our invisible guide to it. In this commonwealth the legal-political becomes congruent with the ethical (after it has been divorced from the religious with post-Westphalian secularism – as interpreted in this volume by Friedrich Kratochwil).

In *RBMR*, it is the semantics of the ethical commonwealth, Providence, the *summum bonum* and world state making that transcends the semantics of republicanism and federalism from *TPP*. Most relevant for our purposes is that Kant's federalism from *TPP* appears to have been superseded by world state making in *RBMR*. In other words, if Kant's federalism is understood as a stage on the path of history to the ethical commonwealth – a world republic founded on virtue – it is justifiable to conclude that Kant's semantics of republican and federalist statebuilding from *TPP* was a precursor to his semantics of virtue-based world state making from *RBMR*.

Furthermore, as I have argued in the first section, Kant's semantics of world (state) making can offer substantial foundations for the semantics of post-Weberian statebuilding. The latter might be interpreted as a move from a semantics of the Weberian state, a state that might be in a union of the type promoted in *TPP* or in a European union (perhaps additionally legitimised or 'sacralised' by a human rights discourse) to a semantics of Kantian cosmopolitanism. But post-Weberian statebuilding has still not abandoned Kant's intermediary blueprint. It is not yet the historical stage that Kant interprets as the ultimate purpose of history. This purpose is in the domain of the semantics of the ethical commonwealth. Such a commonwealth requires world (state) making by morally advanced humans.

Notes

1 I am indebted here to Brown (2005). My typology, however, is not identical to Brown's.

2 This did not prevent other scholars from focusing on the perceived contradiction between Kant's respectful attitude towards state sovereignty and his desire for cosmopolitan reform (Franceschet 2002). Where the issue of human rights is concerned, we will see later that the 'human rights revolution of the twentieth century' is not a

Kantian concept. It is rather, as Kratochwil argues in Chapter 3 in this volume, an abstract entity that modern law utilises in order to substitute for the 'sacred'.

3 For a formulation of the 'democratic peace thesis' and a review of corresponding literature, see Franceschet (2000: 280–288).

4 I owe this formulation of the contextual setting to Nicholas Onuf.

5 On CD traditions see Mitrany (1966) and Long (1995a, 1995b).

6 See the argumentation in Matthias Lutz-Bachmann (1997: 59–77).

7 In *TPP* and *The Metaphysics of Morals* Kant does address the concept of Providence (or God), but generally more in passing, avoiding a discussion of its role like the one he provided in *RBMR* and most of his other systematic writings.

8 Because *The Conflict of the Faculties* does not elaborate in depth on Kant's essential ideas on international relations, I do not analyse this work here. It is sufficient to mention that its second part offers some empirical evidence for Kant's belief that the human race is progressing towards the better. This evidence is based on the perceived enthusiasm for the French Revolution among disinterested observers of the event (Ak. 7: 85). But in light of the fact that in *RBMR* Kant offers a broad and organised discussion of his notions related to ethics and political philosophy, including international relations, it is justified to say that this work was Kant's last systematic and openly expressed elaboration on the matter.

9 The English translation of *RBMR* used is the Cambridge edition of the works of Immanuel Kant (Kant 1996).

10 Here I partly follow the argument in Williams (1983). Williams perceives *RBMR*, whether or not exaggerating its role, as 'perhaps the most committed of Kant's works' (Williams 1983: 261).

11 It is possible to translate the German *Gemeines Wesen* as 'community' or as 'commonwealth'. Both terms have been used by different translators, as well as by different Kant students. My belief is that in most contexts the term 'commonwealth' gets closer to the meaning of *Gemeines Wesen.* Moreover, the German term *Gemeinschaft* is commonly translated as 'community'. I therefore use the term 'commonwealth' more frequently here, although not exclusively.

12 For Kant's own formulation, see Ak. 6: 100–101.

13 It is worthy of mention that Kant makes a distinction between duty in an ethical sense and duty in a legal sense. This distinction, however, primarily applies to the current state of affairs. With the passing of time, its relevance fades. As we approach the ethical commonwealth, we act more and more in accordance with the moral law. Our legal and political sense then becomes increasingly congruent with our moral sagacity.

14 There is, however, one important difference between our obligation to assume perpetual peace and related concepts (e.g. the ethical commonwealth and the Kingdom of ends) and our duty to assume the immortality of the soul and the existence of God. In the first case, the fulfilment of our duty (our realisation of the moral law and our assumption that perpetual peace will be realised in the future) will finally result in perpetual peace, whereas our moral duty to assume the immortality of the soul and the existence of God will not result in these assumptions becoming reality.

15 Such a viewpoint is also in line with Kant's *Idea for a Universal History With a Cosmopolitan Aim*. Here Kant asserts, in the ninth proposition, that 'the perfect civil union of the human species' will not be furthered by politics, but by philosophy – specifically by its cosmopolitan endeavours: 'A *philosophical* attempt to work out universal world history according to a plan of nature that aims at the perfect civil union of the human species, must be regarded as possible and even as furthering this aim of nature' (Ak. 8: 29, emphasis added).

16 Here I use the formulation 'intermediate stage of development of international relations' as a logical extension of Kant's teleological conception of history guided by Providence.

References

Archibugi, D. (1995a) 'From the United Nations to cosmopolitan democracy', in D. Archibugi and D. Held (eds) *Cosmopolitan Democracy: An Agenda for a New World Order*, Cambridge, UK: Polity Press.

Archibugi, D. (1995b) 'Immanuel Kant, cosmopolitan law and peace', *European Journal of International Relations*, 1(4): 429–456.

Archibugi, D. (1998) 'Principles of cosmopolitan democracy', in D. Archibugi, D. Held and M. Kohler (eds) *Re-imagining Political Community: Studies in Cosmopolitan Democracy*, Stanford: Stanford University Press.

Brown, G.W. (2005) 'State sovereignty, federation and Kantian cosmopolitanism', *European Journal of International Relations*, 11: 495–522.

Bull, H. (1977) *The Anarchical Society*, New York: Columbia University Press.

Cavallar, G. (1999) *Kant and the Theory and Practice of International Right*, Cardiff: University of Wales Press.

Della Porta, D. (ed.) (2006) *The Global Justice Movement: Cross-national and Transnational Perspectives*, New York: Paradigm.

Doyle, M. (1983) 'Kant, liberal legacies, and foreign affairs (parts I and II)', *Philosophy and Public Affairs*, 12(3): 205–235 (I) and 12(4): 323–353 (II).

Franceschet, A. (2000) 'Popular sovereignty or cosmopolitan democracy liberalism, Kant and international reform', *European Journal of International Relations*, 6(2): 277–302.

Franceschet, A. (2002) *Kant and Liberal Internationalism: Sovereignty, Justice and Global Reform*, New York: Palgrave.

Held, D. (1995) *Democracy and the Global Order: From the Modern State to Global Governance*, Stanford: Stanford University Press.

Kant, I. (1903) *Grundlage zur Metaphysik der Sitten* (*Groundwork of the Metaphysics of Morals*), Ausgabe der Preußischen Akademie der Wissenschaften (Ak. 4).

Kant, I. (1907a) *Religion innerahalb der Grenzen der bloßen Vernunft* (*Religion within the Boundaries of Mere Reason*), Ausgabe der Preußischen Akademie der Wissenschaften (Ak. 6: 3–202).

Kant, I. (1907b) *Metaphysik der Sitten* (*Metaphysics of Morals*), Ausgabe der Preußischen Akademie der Wissenschaften (Ak. 6: 205–493).

Kant, I. (1907c) *Konflikt der Fakultäten* (*Conflict of the Faculties*), Ausgabe der Preußischen Akademie der Wissenschaften (Ak. 7).

Kant, I. (1908) *Kritik der praktischen Vernunft* (*Critique of Practical Reason*). Ausgabe der Preußischen Akademie der Wissenschaften (Ak. 5).

Kant, I. (1912a) *Zum ewigen Frieden* (*Toward Perpetual Peace*), Ausgabe der Preußischen Akademie der Wissenschaften (Ak. 8).

Kant, I. (1912b) *Idee zu einer allgemeinen Geschichte in weltbürgerlicher Absicht* (*Idea for a Universal History with a Cosmopolitan Aim*), Ausgabe der Preußischen Akademie der Wissenschaften (Ak. 8).

Kant, I. (1996) *Religion within the Boundaries of Mere Reason*, ed. and trans. A. Wood and G. Di Giovanni, Cambridge, UK: Cambridge University Press.

Laberge, P. (1998) 'Kant on justice and the law of nations', in D. Maple and T. Nardin (eds) *International Society: Diverse Ethical Perspectives*, Princeton: Princeton University Press.

Linklater, A. (1996) 'Citizenship and sovereignty in the post-westphalian state', *European Journal of International Relations*, 2(1): 77–103.

Linklater, A. (1998) *The Transformation of Community: The Ethical Foundations of the Post Westphalian Era*, Cambridge, UK: Polity Press.

Long, D. (1995a) 'The Harvard School of Liberal International Theory: a case for closure', *Millennium: Journal of International Studies*, 24(3): 489–505.

Long, D. (1995b) 'Conclusion: inter-war idealism, liberal internationalism, and contemporary international theory', in D. Long and P. Wilson (eds) *Thinkers of the Twenty Years' Crisis: Inter-War Idealism Reconsidered*, Oxford: Clarendon Press.

Lutz-Bachmann, M. (1997) 'Kant's ideal of peace and the philosophical conceptions of a world republic', in J. Bohman and M. Lutz-Bachmann (eds) *Perpetual Peace: Essays on Kant's Cosmopolitan Ideal*, Cambridge, MA: MIT Press.

Marchetti, R. (2008) *Global Democracy: For and Against*, London and New York: Routledge.

Mitrany, D. (1966) *A Working Peace System*, Chicago: Quadrangle Books.

Owen, J.M. (1996) 'How liberalism produces democratic peace', in M.E. Brown, S.M. Lynn-Jones and S.E. Miller (eds) *Debating the Democratic Peace*, Cambridge, MA: MIT Press.

Russett, B. (1993) *Grasping the Democratic Peace: Principles of a Post-Cold War World*, Princeton: Princeton University Press.

Teson, F.R. (1992) 'The Kantian theory of international law', *Columbia Law Review*, 92(1): 53–102.

Teson, F.R. (1998) 'Kantian international liberalism', in D. Maple and T. Nardin (eds) *International Society: Diverse Ethical Perspectives*, Princeton: Princeton University Press.

Wight, M. (1987) 'An anatomy of international thought', *Review of International Studies*, 13: 221–227.

Williams, H. (1983) *Kant's Political Philosophy*, Oxford: Basil Blackwell.

Wood, A.W. (1996) 'General introduction', in A.W. Wood (ed.) *The Cambridge Edition of the Works of Immanuel Kant – Religion and Rational Theology*, Cambridge, UK: Cambridge University Press.

5 The semantics of early statebuilding

Why the Eurasian Steppe has been overlooked

Iver B. Neumann

How is it that man is born the same, but everywhere he is different? Humankind has a biological unity, but its social and political organization demonstrates huge differentiation. For nineteenth-century anthropologists, the political differences, which will be my broad theme in this chapter, was a key puzzle. They tried to solve it by placing different modes of organization along a time axis, and then argue that the differences were due to mutations. The observable variations here and now were really sequential, and they were only temporary. This evolutionary answer has fallen into disrepute, but it has, and is still, framing the anthropological debates about early states. It is still the answer to beat today. We have a problem, however. With the hunters and gatherers all but gone from the face of the earth and the pastoral nomadic way of life disappearing fast (Khazanov 2001: 6), soon we will no longer be able to collect data on them by means of observation. So, due to expedience and also since a science needs the fullest possible universe of cases, the anthropologist will have to turn to the study of history.

The aim of this chapter is to survey the debates on early complex states as well as the debates on early political organization in the Eurasian steppe with a view to theorizing one sequence of early state formation, namely that of the Rus'. The Rus' were Vikings who moved south along the riverways and established what, in an evolutionary perspective, is the first stirring of a Russian state, called the Rus' khaganate. The key underlying theme is that external relations should be given their due in the study of early complex polities.

The chapter falls into three sections. In section one, I précis the anthropological account of the early state. Given that the state has been defined as a political form of sedentary populations, steppe polities have not really been given that much attention within this tradition. Section two of the chapter therefore sketches some key themes from the literature of steppe empires that we need in order to proceed to section three, which gives a broad outline of the case. In conclusion, I argue that we must bring nomads into our studies of early polities, and treat the issue of state formation as a relational one.

The field of the early complex state in cultural anthropology

Lewis Henry Morgan – and also his most important early follower, Friedrich Engels – hypothesized how polities change from a nomadic to a sedentary form. By polities I mean a group of humans that has a self-reflected identity or 'we-ness', a capacity to mobilize resources and a degree of institutionalization and hierarchy (cf. Ferguson and Mansbach 1996: 34). Morgan highlighted how

> ... all forms of government are reducible to two general plans, using the word plan in its scientific sense. In their bases the two are fundamentally distinct. The first, in the order of time, is founded upon persons, and upon relations purely personal, and may be distinguished as a society (*societas*). The gens is the unit of this organization; giving as the successive stages of integration, in the archaic period, the gens, the phratry, the tribe, and the confederacy of tribes, which constituted a people or nation (*populus*). At a later period a coalescence of tribes in the same area into a nation took the place of a confederacy of tribes occupying independent areas. [...] The second is founded upon territory and upon property, and may be distinguished as a state (*civitas*).
>
> (Morgan 1963: 6)

In *The Origin of the Family, Private Property and the State* (1884/1985), Engels latched onto Morgan's reflections on property and synthesized them with Marx's analyses of capital accumulation. The thing to note is that the world was once peopled by nomads, organized in person-based political structures. Then they settled down and adopted the state as their principle of political organization. It is easy to spot Darwin's thinking on evolution here, but even more basically, this is in sync with the broad sweep of European nineteenth-century political thinking, whether in an explicitly teleological guise as in Hegel, or in the more implicit version of Kant, himself a sometime geographer and, it could be argued, early anthropologist. A neo-Kantian like Durkheim (1992: 54) may refer to Hegel's historiography as 'mystical', but Durkheim himself nonetheless clearly and explicitly cherished the idea that humankind is evolving towards a goal, which to him is the world state. Durkheim's point of departure is also how the rulers extract from and lay down the law for the rulers but, contrary to Engels, he sees this as inevitable and obvious. Every society is, by necessity, despotic.

For Durkheim (1992: 91), the state first incorporates itself as a small cadre, organized independently of society:

> the State is nothing if it is not an organ distinct from the rest of society. If the State is everywhere, it is nowhere. The State comes into existence by a process of concentration that detaches a certain group of individuals from the collective mass.
>
> (Durkheim 1992: 82)

When the state is young, it has few ties to society, but the more it grows, the more democratic it becomes.

As I will attempt to demonstrate below, Durkheim is on the money when it comes to specifying how state formation begins as a business undertaking by some clan or lineage, only to transmute into something more rooted in everyday interaction. This is not to say that there are no problems with Durkheim. One problem is his insistence on viewing the state as organic. Another is the teleology Durkheim shares with Morgan. There is nothing wrong with teleology as such. If you drive down a motorway in Greece and it leads nowhere, there will be a sign to warn you that you have to make a turn. That sign reads 'Telos'. Telos simply means end. Telos may also mean end goal, but it is a commonplace of the human condition that goals exist. Aristotle even refers to one of his four types of causality as teleological, and gives the example of building a house. If the goal of the builders is to build a house, then the fact that this thought exists is a cause of the building of the house. Fair enough; if what it takes for A to cause B is 1) that A is different from B, 2) that A happens before B in time and 3) that B would not have happened if A had not happened first, then teleological causality exists. The problem for subsequent anthropologists was not necessarily teleology as such, but the level at which it was postulated, namely world history. How could humanity have a common goal that it did not even know about? That would be bad Darwinism. With no sky hook to a god or to History, anthropologists were tempted to let go of the idea of the state as the common evolutionary goal of humanity.

Not everyone stopped doing evolutionary work. At the LSE, Finnish anthropologist and LSE professor in sociology Edvard Westermarck kept using evolutionism in his work, and his students, who did the same, were active into the 1950s. By that time, evolutionary thinking was re-invigorated by a neo-evolutionist turn. The key works were arguably Leslie White's (1949) *The Science of Culture* and Julian Steward's (1955) *Theory of Culture Change.* Evolution is an inner dynamic. Consequently, evolutionists are not big on relations. Morton Fried (1967: 232) stated explicitly that pristine states, by which he meant states that emerge in settings where there was no such thing before, emerge in a vacuum.

Elman Service (1975) worked out a typology of evolutionary stages – bands, tribes, chiefdoms, states – that is still the coinage in evolutionary circles and beyond. Service's debt to Morgan is obvious, and he demonstrates his debt to Durkheim when he underlines how the origins of the state may be traced to how a small band of warriors take tribute from a larger population which thereby enters into a subaltern position, but which at least in principle gains military protection from other marauders (Service 1975: 300). Here Service is aligned with historical sociologists like neo-Durkheimian Charles Tilly, who quips that war makes states, and states make war. Marshall Sahlins, who started his career as Service's collaborator, went on to do groundbreaking historical work on chiefdoms in the Pacific. Sahlins also inspired a key work on the transition from chiefdom to state (Earle 1997). On the basis of wide-ranging comparative work, Claessen and Skálnik (1978: 640) defined the early state as

> a centralized sociopolitical organization for the regulation of social relations in a complex, stratified society divided into at least two basic strata, or emergent social classes – namely, the rulers and the ruled – whose relations are characterized by political dominance of the former and tributary obligations of the latter, legitimized by a common ideology.

In 1977, there emerged an important alternative way of framing studies of the early complex state, when Jane Schneider (1977) brought Immanuel Wallerstein's world-systems model of a core, semi-peripheries and peripheries into the field (Peregrine 2007). The world-systems approach highlights the importance of relations *between* polities. There are problems with the way this is done, however. As Gil Stein (1999: 37) puts it,

> The power of core areas is often overestimated because researchers tend to conflate ideology, politics, and economics, so that if evidence for one form of influence is found in the periphery, by metonymic extension, the other forms are presumed to be present as well.

To take but one example, the Byzantine domination of its geographical peripheries, such as it was, depended on the spread of religious and legal practices more than on trade and military conquest (the Byzantines always tried to leave the use of force to allies from the steppe).

The alternative presented by Stein is to analyse early states by means of relational approaches other than world-systems theory such as the peer polity interaction model of Renfrew and colleagues (Renfrew and Cherry 1986), where the point is to study the emergence of, say, Sumer or Greece as a case of emergent clusters or systems of polities, rather than on an individual basis.

Turning to a study of relations may seem an obvious thing to do for a science that specialises in interaction, but in the field of early state studies, it has not been the thing to do. Let me mention an additional reason for that, namely the general popularity of Max Weber's thesis from 'Politics as a Vocation', that claimed monopoly on the use of force is the key factor in statebuilding. The benefits of drawing on Weber are obvious, but that reception has also come at a certain cost. If Weber's focus on the extension of specific units is read not as a relational process, but as something as it were unfolding from within (noting that that within is what is being created, not something that is already actually there) a consequence may be that 'the histories of interrelated peoples become territorialized into bounded spaces', to quote the Venezuelan anthropologist Fernando Coronil (1996: 77). Generally, and this is now a rather belaboured point, what we are seeing is an ontologizing of territorially bounded units.

A Chicago anthropologist with the unlikely name of Adam Smith lampoons the evolutionary story about early complex states as follows.

> It begins with the Pristine State – an original, authochonous political formation built on radical social inequality and centralized governmental institutions that emerged first on the alluvial plain between the lower Tigris and

> Euphrates Rivers and in the Nile River valley. Sometime later, the Pristine State developed in a handful of other regions, including northern China, the Indus valley, Mesoamerica, and the Andes mountains. The Pristine State generally assumes one of two possible forms: regional state (for example, Old Kingdom Egypt) or city-state (for example, the interlinked urban polities of Early Dynastic southern Mesopotamia). As the Pristine State grew in complexity, it influenced surrounding regions either through imperial expansion or inter-regional political economy, thus sparking subsequent episodes of 'secondary' State formation. At the end of this ever-expanding network of secondary States lies the modern incarnation that, through its articulation of capitalist production and global colonialism, brings the State to its current position as *the* extant political formation.
>
> (Smith 2003: 17–19)

Smith's alternative is to look more at the very practices of state formation, and less at classification. To sum up so far, the field of early states studies has demonstrated that the evolutionary story is unsustainable. Discarding it outright would, however, be to commit an ahistorical error, since it would be impossible to understand how we came to ask the questions that we now ask without taking the lingering importance of the evolutionary approach into account. The last thirty years have seen a change of perspective towards a relational approach, which may counter evolutionism's endogenous perspective on the processes concerned, and a practice approach, which may validate forms of political organization in their own right and specify variation. Note that the field's turn towards a relationist ontology and an epistemology focused on the level of practice are both in sync with wider moves in the social sciences (cf. especially Emirbayer 1997; Schatzky *et al.* 2001).

The Steppe

Morgan and Engels explicitly saw the sedentary experience as a key precondition to the emergence of the state. Since they also discarded the importance of specific inter-polity relations to state emergence, it followed logically that they devoted little attention to nomadic experiences. The field of early state studies has largely followed their example. Even one of the key scholars in this field through the last half century, Jack Goody, does not attend to this area. For example, in his magisterial study of kinship in Eurasia (Goody 1990), the steppe, the womb of all the societies that he actually does study, is simply read out. If we want to set up a relational perspective on early state formation, in the forest zone bordering on the Eurasian steppe particularly, but also, say, for the case of the Franks around the year 800 (Charlemagne pronounced himself emperor after having beaten the Avar steppe empire), the steppe should not – I'd argue cannot – be overlooked. For this, we have to turn to the specialized literature.

Anatoly M. Khazanov (2001: 1), Ernest Gellner Professor of Anthropology at the University of Madison-Wisconsin, kicks off a recent edited volume on

Nomads in the Sedentary World by noting that our knowledge of how nomads have impacted sedentary populations is rather tentative. Khazanov maintains that the following phenomena are key to an investigation of Eurasian steppe nomadic influences on sedentary societies:

> There was the notion of charisma and the divine mandate of rule bestowed upon a chosen clan. There were specific models of rule (including dual kinship), imperial titles, and imperial symbolism. There was the notion of collective or joint sovereignty, according to/which a state and its populace belong not to an individual ruler but to all members of a ruling clan or family as corporate property, and a corresponding appanage system. There were specific succession patterns based on different variations of the collateral or sacred rotating system and seniority within a ruling clan. With these we meet a patrimonial mode of government which implied a redistribution of various kinds of wealth among vassals, followers, and even commoners.
>
> (Khazanov 2001: 4–5)

No small matters, and all of them are in play where the Rus' are concerned. We find continuity in patterns of political organization in the steppe from the very earliest period of which we have archaeologically based knowledge and through the Mongol empire. Since the written sources are so much better for the Mongols than for their predecessors, their empire may serve as a convenient point of departure for generalization.

Chinggis's key tool was his imperial guard, which had at its core his classificatory brothers (*anda*) and people who had chose to leave their tribe to follow him personally (*nöker*). The guard included representatives of all the Mongolian tribes, which was in effect Chinggis's extended household, numbered around 10,000 at the outset of his conquests. Again, this seems to have been the way in which previous steppe empires rose as well. Some charismatic leader would arise, score some spectacular successes, build a following, and enroll conquered tribes in his entourage.

Success in warfare by the head of the steppe empire, the khagan was ascribed to Tenggri, a shamanistic sky entity worshipped by many Mongols and known to have been worshipped by previous empires as well. Note that the title of khagan was linked to the heavenly realm, which is to say that it could not just be usurped by anyone. There had to be some kind of *translatio imperii* involved. Conversely, if luck was running thin, the luck was said to have left the khagan, and he could be killed. If he was not killed in this manner, a system of succession kicked in whereby the empire was divided between his sons, with the youngest son being the one who should in principle inherit the hearth (i.e. the centrally placed part of the empire). He also became the khagan, with the brothers becoming merely khans. In principle – and this was a principle which usually held until a new empire arose – the khagan had to be from the same patrilinear line as his predecessors.

Raiding and preferably subduing sedentary populations into paying tribute was a traditional nomadic pastime which, if successful, resulted in empires. There is a key issue here, however, and that is whether conquest, which was undoubtedly the all-consuming goal for the Mongol empire, was also a steady goal for earlier empires. The traditional view, which received its classic formulation by French academician René Grousset in 1939 (Grousset 1970), was that, given the chance, steppe nomads would escalate attacks from raiding to tribute-taking to conquest. Boston anthropologist Thomas Barfield (1989) has a more nuanced view of the relationship between the steppe empires and sedentary populations, the largest and most enduring of which were the Chinese, Persian and Roman empires. Barfield holds that nomadic and sedentary dynasties rose together, but that the nomadic ones actually fell due to inner dynamics, largely because of succession crises. The concurrency was due to the dependence of steppe shadow empires on sedentary polities. Given an even level of technology and the fact that the resource base available in the steppe was fairly stable, the surplus needed to run an empire could only come from taxing or raiding caravans, and from raiding and tribute-taking from the sedentaries. Barfield notes that, if the nomads' goal was to maximize gain, then conquest would not have been an optimal strategy, as it would tie up nomadic resources and block the creation of new ones by the sedentaries. An 'outer frontier strategy', whereby the nomads could engage in raids that would bring in the resources, which could be distributed amongst the nomads and so in turn sustain a nomadic force which could raid even more, would be better suited. It is a frankly functionalist argument, which, following Durkheim's thesis that functionalist and causal explanations should always complement one another, has to be put to the test for each steppe empire. Naomi Standen (2005), who is amongst the many who are sympathetic to Barfield's thesis, highlights the complementary theme of recognition. Nomadic leaders seeking recognition from sedentary leaders might also be better served by an 'outer frontier strategy' rather than by conquest, which would erase the one whose recognition was sought in the first place. Note that nomadic empires could shop from their entire southern and eastern perimeter; the Huns, for example, tried their hand at raiding the Chinese frontier before they turned to the Roman one. Note also that, since the empires consisted of conquered peoples from all over the steppe, they were all multi-ethnic and multi-lingual. So were the sedentary empires off which they lived.

Khazars, Vikings, Byzantines and the Rus' Khaganate

Armed with these insights, let us now take a look at how early state formation worked in one specific case. The area where Rus' early state formation takes place is the forested zone on either side of the great rivers Dnepr and Volga, from the Baltic Sea in the north to the Black and Caspian Seas in the south. The forest density was such that the rivers were crucial for communication. From around 4000 BC, when the glacier receded, a whole string of peoples – Kelts, Cimmerians, Scythians, Sarmatians, Goths, Huns – came this way. The Huns were probably mainly Turkic-speaking, as were all their successors up until the Mongols (who came and conquered Rus' in 1238).

In the forests and along the steppe zone there were Finno-Ugric and Slav-speaking tribes. These people constituted possible objects for raiding and trading. Note that neither the territory as such, nor the people considered as a whole, were particularly coveted by any of the possible rulers involved. Although raids may be seasonal, serving as a regular additional base of income, they cannot by definition be a template from which to rule. It is only with tribute-taking (whether in the form of humans, goods or money), which depends on the tribute-takers imposing some kind of virtual presence once absent, that we may talk about relations that are stable enough to warrant the use of the concept of rule.

Making an argument from silence, we may assume that the Khazars were the first permanent tribute-taking polity in the area. Kiev, which two centuries later was to become a key centre of a Rus' state formation, was founded by the Khazars as an outpost. When, in the ninth century, Vikings from the North appeared and formed the first polity centred on this area, it was the Khazars against whom they had to compete. Archaeological findings document a Scandinavian presence from the middle of the seventh century. By the beginning of the ninth century, they were residents (Noonan 1986: 339). By 839, we know from the Annals of St. Bertin that they had established a polity known as the Rus' Khaganate. To quote the leading Khazar scholar, Peter Golden,

> As for the Rus' qaghanate, we know nothing concrete about its origins. Both Pritsak and the writer of these lines concluded that there must have been some marital connection between the Khazar qaghanal line and the Rus' rulers. Pritsak suggested that the founder of the line was a Khazar Qaghan who fled the Kabar (Qabar) revolt in the 830's and 'found refuge in the Rus' factory (trading post) dominating the vital Volga-Donets route from the region near Iaroslavl'–Rostov. I also argued for a blood tie because anything less, in steppe Eurasia (the most important audience for such imperial pretentions), would have been meaningless.
>
> (Golden 2001: 32)

Meaningless, because we are talking about a khaganate, and the title of khagan was not, as discussed, to be assumed lightly. Noonan (2001: 90) argues that it was adopted, and remained in use into the eleventh century, because the Rus' were intimately involved with the peoples of the steppe and

> were aware that Khazar pretentions to universal empire were something to be reckoned with. [...] If it had not been for the Khazars, much of southeastern Europe would have been conquered by the Umayyads and 'Abbasids and subsequently incorporated into the Islamic world. The Rus' of Kiev undoubtedly knew this history and understood how the mandate of heaven had helped the Khazars keep the Arabs out of southern Russia and Ukraine.

The Viking pressure on Khazar trade and tribute-taking was a key precondition for the downfall of the Khazar empire. Noonan (2001) makes the case that the title of khagan was not only taken over from the Khazars (of which there is little doubt), but that it was specifically intended to ease the transfer of tribute-paying from one (Khazar) khagan to another (Rus') and generally to stake a claim first to equality and then to succession.

The crucial period in centralizing tribute collection by driving out the Khazars, taking over their role as tribute taker and their base in Kiev, as well as increasing the regularity of their payment, was the tenth century. The Byzantine emperor reported that the Rus' prince made the rounds to collect tribute (*polyudie*). It has been suggested that what we have here is an example of a practice that has been called 'one of the focal points of the embryonic state', namely the royal tour:

> This phenomenon, named *gafol* or *feorm* in Anglo-Saxon, *veizla* in Ancient Scandinavian, *poludie, poludavanie,* or *goszczenie* in the Ancient Slav dialects, *makahiki* in Hawaiian, etc., was spread almost universally. [... It] is an institution whereby the ruler – the political or ritual head of the Early State (chief priest, sacred king) – or some other person acting in his place (his heir, vice-roy, vice-regent, envoy, etc.) makes his rounds of his dominion (the subject communities) following a prescribed traditional route to perform his duties and enjoy his privileges.
>
> (Kobishchanow 1987: 108)

In effect, the king and his people peripatetically dined off their subjects. The royal tour is a more routinized and ritualized form of tribute-taking than the 'popping by' practised by the Khazars, and it points towards the even more differentiated practice of taxation on the other. In the case of the Rus' khaganate, the *gafol* seems to have been a short-lived practice, for in our key source, the Russian *Primary Chronicle*, it is recounted how middlemen were soon sent to live amongst the subjects and collect tax from the local tribes.

If we hark back to Durkheim's view of early statebuilding, the case of the Rus' seems to fit his general outline pretty well. A small cadre, first Khazars, then Vikings, appear and take tribute from the locals, offering protection against other possible tribute-takers in return. The interface between the Vikings and the local Slavs and Finno-Ugrics begins to thicken, first by means of the *gafol*, then by the Viking deployment of tax-collecting middlemen amongst the natives.

Kiev emerged as the leading town in the second half of the tenth century, just as the Khazar empire died away. If Viking inroads were one precondition for its fall, another was its religious organization. Originally shamanistic, Khazaria was also touched by the early missionary activity of Islam as well as by missionaries from Byzantium bringing orthodox Christianity. The Khazar leading stratum, who also knew about Judaism from the Jewish community at Kherson on the Northern coast of the Black Sea, reacted by converting to Judaism. The religious turmoil that followed in the multi-confessional empire was one precondition for its downfall, and the Rus' leaders would probably have seen things in these terms. When Prince Vladimir, who followed the Old Norse religion of his parents, became prince of Kiev in 980, the Khazarian empire's demise seems to have been one of the factors installing in him a newfound interest in religion (Martin 2007: 6). Vladimir sponsored the erection of a pagan temple on a hill at the very heights of the city. Seven gods had their statues here: Perun, Sazhbog and Stribog were Slavic gods, Semargl had started life as an Iranian deity, and so may Mokosh; the last two gods seem to have been Norse. After a few years Vladimir found Christianity to be a better social glue. If we follow Durkheim and think of religion as the community's celebration of itself, it is not particularly surprising that a divided pantheon gave way to a common deity.

In order to Christianize the inhabitants of Kiev and the rest of his subjects, Vladimir had to lean on religious specialists from Byzantium. As seen from sedentary Byzantium, the Rus' nomads to the north had posed a challenge from the start. One of Byzantium's counter-moves had been missionary activity. Vladimir's christening of Kiev established a layer of general symbolism to the state-building project. Note that the Christianizing followed a military alliance. The Byzantine emperor Basil II had suffered defeat against the nomadic Bulgars and needed Vladimir to send him Viking reinforcements that could defend Constantinople. In return, he offered his sister Anna as a marriage partner. Vladimir sent Vikings as agreed and eventually succeeded in marrying Anna. The theme of recognition is clearly in evidence here.

As seen from Byzantium, where thinking about barbarians was historicized, taming them was expected to take its time. A key effect looked for in Christianizing was acceptance of the accompanying empirical ideology, which turned on how the *basileus* or emperor was the earthly head of *all* Christians:

> According to the Eusebian formulation, the emperor is the viceregent of God, the mimesis or 'living icon of Christ' ('zosa eikon Christou'), and he rules the *Basileia*, the Christian commonwealth, which is in turn the terrestrial counterpart of God's kingdom in heaven. Since there was only one God, it followed inevitably that there could be only one empire and therefore only one true religion
>
> (Geanakoplos 1976: 39)

Byzantine historian Chrysos (1992: 35) postulates a three-layered process at work once the cult of Christianity was in place. First, the new ruler was welcomed into the family of kings. A discursive prerequisite for this was Christianization, but expedience often had its way, and the practical record is patchy in this regard. Following 100 years of Christian penetration, Vladimir forcefully had his Kievan subjects baptized in 988 (for the circumstances, see Poppe 1976). Second, there was an assimilation of Byzantine social attitudes. Third, and as a formalization of the second layer of the process, there were laws. In order to drive this process, the Byzantines availed themselves of a number of, mostly diplomatic, practices. Sure enough, the first codification of laws (unknown to us in its original form) was Vladimir son's Iaroslav's *Russkaya Pravda* (Franklin and Shepard 1996: 217).

The major drama of Rus' statebuilding in the eleventh and twelfth centuries revolved around the religious and legal practices taken over from Byzantium. As predicted by recent scholarship on early complex polities, it is clear that Rus' was more under the sway of Byzantium in the religious sphere than in others, and it is far from clear in what degree the Rus' periphery may be said to have been dominated by the Byzantine 'core', even in the religious sphere. Franklin (2002: 518, 521) concludes a close reading of relevant textual material by stating that Kievan writers 'had very little available information on the Byzantine empire' and that there simply was a 'lack of interest' amongst them. Franklin (2002: 518) finds a 'deliberate pattern', where 'at each stage of transmission, translators, scribes, editors and local writers are unanimous in their disregard for the imperial heritage of the country from which they took their religion'.

Franklin (2002: 529), who is a Cambridge historian, points to an alternative legitimizing source for Rus', one that will hardly surprise the anthropologist, namely kinship. 'Kinship' is *rod* in Russian, and it was 'resonant with echoes of deep traditional belief: belief in the fertility-cult of Rod'. He points out how *rod*, 'kinship', is the root of other words in Russian, such as *narod*, which now approximates to German *Volk*, and *priroda*, 'nature'. The founding myth of Rus' turned on how the first stranger-king, Ryurik in Russian, Rörek in Old Norse, was called in. As spelled out in the *Primary Chronicle* (Cross and Sherbowitz-Wetzor 1953: 49–50), local tribes said to the Rus' that 'our land is vast and abundant, but there is no order in it. Come and reign as princes and have authority over us!' Rurik and his two brothers came with all their kin, and settled down in different townships. The theme of brothers acting in partnership is of course well known from other cultural settings as well. It takes on particular significance for Rus' statebuilding, for it became a principle for the next eight centuries that only Rurikids could become Rus' princes. The immediate succession after Rurik is a bit hazy, and that haziness envelops the question of paternity as well, but except for that, the only known case of a princely title being held by a non-Rurikid in the pre-Mongol period was that of the boyar Vladislav, who was proclaimed prince of Galicia and ruled around 1212–1214 (Vernadsky 1948: 227).

Since Rörek was a Viking, probably from today's Denmark, he would have been firmly planted in a patrilineal tradition, with primogeniture being one principle of succession (just one possible principle, for princely and kingly titles were, particularly in pre-Christian times, often contested in direct combat between warriors who had proven themselves in battle). However, from the mid-eleventh century and into the sixteenth centuries, the prescribed system of succession in Rus' lands was the *Lestvitsa* or *Lestvichnaya sistema* (from a root also to be found in steps and staircase) or, in English, collateral seniority. It spelt out that the oldest brother should inherit Kiev, and then the younger brothers other cities, presumably in some ranked order. Once a prince died, his brothers moved up, and his oldest son entered the order from some lowly point, i.e. as the prince of some small town. Brothers became cousins, cousins became second cousins, and the fights surrounding succession became ever more messy. But the point I want to make is where this succession system, a key structuring principle of political organization, came from. We first hear about it in 1054, when Yaroslav the Wise divided the Rus' lands between three of his sons. Since it did not come from the North, it must have risen locally. But how? None of the sedentary neighbouring polities had it, they all stuck to primogeniture. But, as noted above, the nomads of the steppes had it. Indeed, the only other place where this system is known to have existed is amongst the Inner Asian peoples (Halperin 1987: 18). It is, of course, possible that collateral succession was simply an idea of Yaroslav, but ideas come from places. Most probably we have in the Rus' succession system yet another example of how relations with the steppe nomads shaped the early Rus' polity.

Conclusions

If we reflect on the importance of the case of Rus' for the literature on early complex polity formation, the first factor that comes to mind is that the importance of nomadic influences for economic organization, particularly trade, as well as for political organization, has to be taken into consideration. Furthermore, the distinction itself is in need of differentiation. Once stranger-kings arrive, they may not settle down immediately, but continue their raiding concurrently with their engaging in state-building practices at home. An evolutionary reading of the practices of the Rus' stranger kings would be that we have here an intermediary stage between the nomadic and the sedentary. Note, however, that we have touched on another case which demonstrates this evolutionary reading to be superficial. Noonan writes about the early model for the Rus' polity, the Khazar steppe empire, that

> Khazar domination and the resulting Paz Khazarica fostered the emergence of a diversified economy throughout the Qaghanate in which pastoralism, agriculture, apiculture, viticulture, foraging, and craft production could all flourish. Such a highly diversified economy had only existed earlier under the Scythians and later under the Golden Horde. Extensive agriculture and a developed craft production were only possible when a well organized 'nomadic' state provided the necessary peace and security. They could not flourish when the steppe was dominated by 'stateless' nomads.
>
> (Noonan 2001: 91)

In this quote, Noonan puts nomadic and stateless between inverted commas, for the existence of agriculture is the key defining trait of a sedentary polity, and the Khazars had it. If we jump to the other side of the Eurasian steppe, to the Tchukchi, they are famous for having bothered Morgan's evolutionary mind, for although they were nomadic at the time of Morgan, they had clearly been sedentary before. This fact was corrosive rust on the iron evolutionary law that peoples go from being nomadic to being sedentary. Now, the Khazar case demonstrates that entire early complex polities may do the same thing. Under the pressure of the Mongol invasion in the mid-thirteenth century, the Magyar court, which was by then Christian and firmly ensconced in sedentary ways, reverted to certain steppe practices, sartorial practices amongst them. The steppe continued to influence sedentary practices. Barry Hindess (2000) is amongst the many who have recently reminded us that the assumption that, toing and froing aside, people will normally be settled in the society to which they belong, is not historical. On the contrary, periods like the present one, marked by extensive migration, have alternated with periods when sedentariness was the rule. While pastoral nomadism is becoming a thing of the past, other forms of nomadism survive and may even be intensified, with unpredictable political consequences. The students of the state – whether the early state or the contemporary one – ignores nomadism at their peril.

The point may be widened to relations as such. Early state formation may have as one precondition relations between competing wannabe stranger-kings; in this case, between Khazars and Vikings. Furthermore, one precondition for the way in which the winners go about their state-building may be relations with former rivals, as was the case with the Vikings and the Khazars. Again, the form of state-building may also depend on a struggle for recognition, as Russian state-building shaped up partially as a result of a struggle for recognition from the Byzantine emperor. Yet another relational factor which emerges here is the need of state-builders to limit the political presence of others; for the Rus' rulers, it was a key point to keep the Byzantines and the peoples of the steppe, primarily Pechenegs and Khipchaks, at bay. The recent trend in the study of early complex polities towards taking inter-polity relations more seriously should be applauded and extended.

The age of nationalism, where knowledge production focused on sharpening boundaries between polities, is over. One thing we may learn from the study of early state formation is that no polity was ever an island. One scholarly boon of today's globalization may be that anthropologists stop treating polities as close systems, and approach them instead as what they always were, namely relational.

References

Barfield, T.J. (1989) *The Perilous Frontier: Nomadic Empires and China, 221 BC to AD 1757*, Cambridge, MA: Blackwell.

Chrysos, E. (1992) 'Byzantine diplomacy, A.D. 300–800: means and end', in J. Shepard and S. Franklin (eds) *Byzantine Diplomacy. Papers from the Twenty-fourth Spring Symposium of Byzantine Studies, Cambridge, March 1990*, Aldershot: Variorum.

Claessen, H.J.M. and Skálnik, P. (eds) (1978) *The Early State*, Den Haag: Mouton.

Coronil, F. (1996) 'Beyond occidentalism: toward nonimperial geohistorical categories', *Cultural Anthropology*, 11(1): 51–86.

Cross, S.H. and Sherbowitz-Wetzor, O.P. (eds) (1953) *The Russian Primary Chronicle, Laurentian Text*, Cambridge, MA: Medieval Academy of America.

Durkheim, E. (1992) *Professional Ethics and Civic Morals*, London: Routledge.

Earle, T.K. (1997) *How Chiefs Come to Power: The Political Economy in Pre-History*, Stanford: Stanford University Press.

Emirbayer, M. (1997) 'Manifesto for a relational sociology', *American Journal of Sociology* 103(2): 281–317, available at: www.chssp.columbia.edu/events/documents/Emirbayer.pdf (accessed 2 July 2009).

Engels, F. ([1884] 1985) *The Origin of the Family, Private Property and the State*, Harmondsworth: Penguin.

Ferguson, Y.H. and Mansbach, R.W. (1996) *Polities: Authority, Identities, and Change*, Durham, NC: University of South Carolina Press.

Franklin, S. ([1983] 2002) 'The empire of the Rhomaioi as viewed from Kievan Russia: aspects of Byzantino-Russian cultural relations', in S. Franklin, *Byzantium – Rus – Russia*, Ashgate: Variorum.

Franklin, S. and Shepard, J. (1996) *The Emergence of Rus 750–1200*, London: Longman.

Fried, M. (1967) *The Evolution of Political Society*, New York, NY: Random House.

Geanakoplos, D.J. (1976) *Interaction of the 'Sibling' Byzantine and Western Cultures in the Middle Ages and Italian Renaissance*, New Haven, CN: Yale University Press.

Golden, P.B. (2001) 'Nomads in the sedentary world: the case of pre-Chinggisid Rus' and Georgia', in A.M. Khazanov and A. Wink (eds) *Nomads in the Sedentary World*, Richmond: Curzon.

Goody, J. (1990) *The Oriental, The Ancient and the Primitive: Systems of Marriage and the Family in the Pre-Industrial Societies of Eurasia*, Cambridge: Cambridge University Press.

Grousset, R. ([1939] 1970) *The Empire of the Steppe: A History of Central Asia*, New Brunswick, NJ: Rutgers University Press.

Halperin, C.J. (1987) *Russia and the Golden Horde: The Mongol Impact on Medieval Russian History*, Bloomington, IN: Indiana University Press.

Hindess, B. (2000) 'Citizenship in the international management of populations', *American Behavioural Scientist*, 43(9): 1486–1497.

Khazanov, A.M. (2001) 'Nomads in the history of the sedentary world', in A.M. Khazanov and A. Wink (eds) *Nomads in the Sedentary World*, Richmond: Curzon.

Kobishchanow, Y.M. (1987) 'The phenomenon of gafol and its transformation', in H.J.M. Claessen and P. van de Velde (eds) *Early State Dynamics*, Leiden: Brill.

Martin, J. (2007) *Medieval Russia, 980–1585*, 2nd edn, Cambridge: Cambridge University Press.

Morgan, L.H. ([1877] 1963) *Ancient Society, or Researches in the Lines of Human Progress from Savagery through Barbarism to Civilization*, Cleveland, OH: Meridian.

Noonan, T.S. (1986) 'Why the Vikings first came to Russia', *Jahrbücher für Geschichte Osteuropas*, 34: 321–348.

Noonan, T.S. (2001) 'The Khazar Qaghanate and its impact on the early Rus' state: the translatio imperii from Itil to Kiev', in A.M. Khazanov and A. Wink (eds) *Nomads in the Sedentary World*, Richmond: Curzon.

Peregrine, P.N. (2007) 'Archaeology and world-systems theory', *Sociological Inquiry*, 60(1): 486–495.

Poppe, A. (1976) 'The political background to the baptism of Rus': Byzantine-Russian relations between 986–89', *Dumbarton Oaks Papers*, 30: 195–244.

Renfrew, C. and Cherry, J. (eds) (1986) *Peer Polity Interaction and Socio-Political Change*, Cambridge: Cambridge University Press.

Schatzky, T.R., Knorr Cetina, K. and von Savigny, E. (eds) (2001) *The Practice Turn in Contemporary Theory*, London: Routledge.

Schneider, J. (1977) 'Was there a pre-capitalist world system?', *Peasant Studies*, 6(1): 20–29.

Service, E. (1975) *Origins of the State and Civilization: The Processes of Cultural Evolution*, New York, NY: Norton.

Smith, A.T. (2003) *The Political Landscape: Constellations of Authority in Early Complex Polities*, Berkeley, CA: University of California Press.

Standen, N. (2005) 'What nomads want: raids, invasions and the Liao Conquest of 947', in R. Amitai and M. Biran (eds) *Mongols, Turks, and Others: Eurasian Nomads and the Sedentary World*, Leiden: Brill.

Stein, G. (1999) *Rethinking World Systems: Diasporas, Colonies, and Interaction in Uruk Mesopotamia*, Tucson, AZ: University of Arizona Press.

Steward, J.H. (1955) *Theory of Culture Change*, Urbana, IL: University of Illinois Press.

Vernadsky, G. (1948) *Ancient Russia. A History of Russia*, vol. 1, Cambridge, MA: Harvard University Press.

White, L. (1949) *The Science of Culture*, New York, NY: Farrar, Strauss.

6 The semantics of statebuilding and nationbuilding

Looking beyond neo-Weberian approaches

Nicolas Lemay-Hébert

Introduction: the state and its meanings

Discussed by most, defined by few, the state as a political unit is at the centre of most statebuilding debates. More often than not, these debates are based on an initial misunderstanding of what the state as a political and sociological concept actually means. As Anthony Giddens observes, there are two implicit, and often competing, concepts behind the notion of state: it sometimes means an apparatus of government or power, sometimes the overall social system subject to that government or power (1985: 17). This semantic imprecision has permeated the statebuilding literature to the extent where it is hard to distinguish what each author specifically means by state and statebuilding. Furthermore, this debate is far from being confined to aesthetics. The semantic imprecision has concrete spillover effects on other discussions related to, but not equated with the state and statebuilding. For instance, Paul Bastid acutely notes that 'the idea of legitimacy has been linked alternatively to the process of establishment of certain forms of government and, more globally, to the authority underpinning the state, to the foundations of social life' (1967: 4, my translation). Hence, whether or not one adopts a 'restrictive' conception of the state will carry specific implications for the overall analysis. This chapter will attempt to clarify the debate by associating the two conceptions of the state – as government or as social system – with distinct statebuilding approaches – institutionalism and 'social legitimacy'.

The first one, an institutional approach closely related to the Weberian conception of the state, focuses on the importance of institutional reconstruction and postulates that statebuilding activities do not necessarily require a concomitant nationbuilding effort. As this chapter claims, the Weberian approach to statehood is the starting point for a number of analyses, having attained the status of an orthodoxy in the mainstream statebuilding literature. Following the institutional approach, the state is equated with its institutions, state collapse is understood in terms of the collapse of state institutions, and statebuilding implies their reconstruction. While being portrayed as consensual and apolitical, the institutional approach to statebuilding carries specific consequences for scholarly and policy debates (Lemay-Hébert 2013).

In contrast with this approach, a second, more constructivist approach, explicitly based on the broader definition of the state and implicitly founded on a wider sociological understanding of legitimacy, coexists with the institutional approach while not getting the same amount of attention from policy circles. Influenced by other sociological strands (I draw parallels with Durkheimian sociology), this approach recognizes the need to consolidate central state institutions, but puts more emphasis on the importance of socio-political cohesion in the process. To use categories developed by Barry Buzan and Kalevi Holsti, the institutional approach focuses on the institutional and physical basis of the state, while the social legitimacy approach is more preoccupied with the social contract binding the citizens together (Buzan 1991: 64; Holsti 1996: 98). Indeed, the latter insists on the political concept of legitimacy underlying the state, and while considering the state and society as distinct in terms of 'actors', it treats the two 'semantic categories' as not strictly autonomous institutions and activities (Barker 1990: 28).

In effect, scholars adopting the social legitimacy approach approach tend to question the convenient distinctions between state and society and state and nation that have been postulated by a number of scholars. As Bernard Lacroix (1985: 471, my translation) elegantly remarks,

> by presupposing an intangible frontier separating state and civil society, by making both entities hard objects with sharp edges, and by suggesting that relations between the two have to follow the logics of solid-state physics, the semantic distinction of state and society ends up constituting the natural distinction which it intends to demonstrate.

This chapter questions head-on this 'intangible frontier' by reviving old sociological debates on the state and nation, and by linking them to contemporary statebuilding debates.

The institutional approach to statebuilding and the autonomous state perspective

Weber famously defines the state 'as a human community that successfully claims the monopoly of the legitimate use of physical force within a given territory' (Weber 1948: 78). For Weber, the formation of modern Western states relied on the constant progression of their bureaucratic foundations over time. Hence, Weber saw administration and the provision of security as benchmarks according to which each state can be judged (Badie and Birnbaum 1983). Besides security, which is certainly the central criterion of state strength for institutionalists (see for instance Doornbos *et al.* 2006), other criteria are also taken into account by various authors, all related to the capabilities of the state to secure its grip *on* the society. For Francis Fukuyama, stateness is defined by the *strength of state* – understood as 'the ability of states to plan and execute policies and to enforce laws cleanly and transparently' or its 'institutional capacity' – coupled with the *scope of state* – the different functions and goals taken on by government (2004: 7). For Robert Rotberg, it is according to the levels of the state's effective delivery of the most crucial political goods that strong states may be distinguished from weak ones. The author suggests a long list of public goods including the supply of security, a transparent and equitable political process, medical and health care, schools and education, railways, harbours, and, echoing the liberal internationalism approach (Paris 1997), even a beneficent fiscal and institutional context within which citizens can pursue personal entrepreneurial goals (2004: 2). In this context, state functions and successful service provision are generally identified as proxies of state capacity (Mcloughlin 2010: 9).

From this perspective, a weak or fragile state is a political entity that lacks the institutional capacity to implement and enforce policies. Accordingly, the process of statebuilding is conceptualized as the creation of new government institutions and the strengthening of existing ones. As Nicholas Onuf rightly points out in Chapter 2 of this book, 'institutionalists … granted functional differentiation its importance by conceptualizing the state as an institution composed of functionally related institutions'. This, inevitably, led to the perspective that 'some states were identified as strong, others weak, and talk turned to building and strengthening the state'.

Furthermore, scholars adopting this institutional approach tend to focus on the administrative capability of the state and the ability of the state apparatus to affirm its authority over the society, thus echoing the 'state autonomy' theory. For instance, Joel Migdal, a leading contributor to the state-society distinction, contends that 'the progress of statebuilding can be measured by the degree of development of certain instrumentalities whose purpose is to make the action of the state effective: bureaucracy, courts, military' (1988: 35). Thus, state capabilities include the capacities to penetrate society, regulate social relationships, extract resources, and appropriate or use resources in determined ways. Non-Western states are weak in relation to the strong societies they try to control. However, Joel Migdal (2001) came up with a different concept, the 'state-in-society' model, whereby he proposed to abandon the Weberian inspired analysis of the state due to its disconnection of theory from practice. Other examples include Alfred Stepan, who defines the state as 'the continuous administrative, legal, bureaucratic and coercive systems that attempt not only to structure relationships between civil society and public authority but also to structure many crucial relationships within civil society itself', and Evelyn Davidheiser, who offers three criteria for evaluating the strength of the state: depth of penetration of society by the state, breadth of penetration, and state autonomy, or penetration of the state by society (1992: 463).

This conception of the 'autonomous state' has long been equated with Weber's work, however, certain scholars have argued that the 'autonomous state' theory is an inaccurate interpretation of Weber's work (Hobson and Seabrooke 2001: 258). Other authors have rightly asserted that we should understand Weber's political theory in conjunction with his other sociological works (Beetham 1985: 151; Hobson 1998: 288; Palumbo and Scott 2008: 387; Weber 1958). This stems from the necessity to understand the Weberian conception of the state in conjunction with the historical context in which Weber published his major works, especially his relation with the Marxist literature on the state. Weber's work is explicitly anti-Marxist on just this issue of the autonomy of the state, rejecting Marx's determinism in that regard (Nash 2000: 10; Palumbo and Scott 2008). In any case, this division between state structures and societal forces leads, very conveniently, to a distinction between statebuilding and nationbuilding, on the premise that it is possible to conduct statebuilding operations from the outside without entering into the contested sphere of nationbuilding (Lemay-Hébert 2009; Zaum 2007: 29). In other words, it is possible to target the institutions of a given state, to strengthen state capabilities, without engaging in the dreaded realm of identity-building. Adopting a restrictive definition of the state – as state apparatus – will lead scholars to perceive statebuilding as a scientific, technical and administrative process. It is not surprising then that the statebuilding literature strikingly neglects the question of politics; what is, in fact, a highly political process becomes depoliticized through a focus on state capacity-building, where concerns of stability and regulation are discussed in a narrow technical and functionalist framework (Chandler 2006: 5–6).

As mentioned previously, discussions on the concept of state can have unexpected ramifications, on debates about legitimacy and authority for instance. If the Weberian approach to statehood has profoundly influenced the statebuilding literature, the same could be said of the Weberian legacy regarding legitimacy. While Weber is rightly regarded as one of the most influential thinkers in social science, his contribution regarding the concept of legitimacy has been deemed highly controversial, even described as 'an almost unqualified disaster' by David Beetham (1991: 8). Weber defines legitimacy as 'the prestige of being considered exemplary or binding' (Weber 1962: 72). Hence, for Weber, the claim of legitimacy is a bid for a justification of support, and its success consists not in fulfilling normative conditions but in being believed. Weber conceives legitimacy as a necessary condition and a means for a government to exercise authority over society. This could be done either by charismatic, traditional or rational-legal principles (1947: 130). In that sense, legitimacy principles are in fact principles of legitimization of the central authority. However, once again here, according to Beetham and others, the main mistake is not Weber's, but that of those social scientists, the so-called 'neo-Weberians', who have reduced the explanation of beliefs to the processes and agencies of their dissemination and internalization (Beetham 1991: 10; Hobson and Seabrooke 2001). Nevertheless, Weber's definition of legitimacy has not been exempt of criticisms of its own in the field of political sociology. Hanna Pitkin rightly points out that it was 'essentially equivalent to defining "legitimate" as "the condition of being considered legitimate," and the corresponding "normative" definition comes out as "deserving to be considered legitimate"' (1972: 281). In the field of statebuilding, Robert Rotberg's work is certainly a good example of the tendency to reduce legitimacy to a consequence of stable and effective political power. Mentioning legitimacy only as consequence of good delivery of public goods, he argues that public goods 'give content to the social contract between ruler and ruled'

(Rotberg 2004: 2–3). The author notes that 'there is no failed state without disharmonies between communities', but considers these 'disharmonies' as consequences of the failure of state institutions (Rotberg 2003: 4). Hence, legitimacy is regarded as a natural by-product of successful state institutions.

Durkheimian sociology and the social legitimacy approach

While accepting the institutional approach's focus on the security apparatus and state institutions, especially as a critical first step in statebuilding processes, the 'social legitimacy approach' adds a layer of complexity in drawing attention to the state's underlying legitimacy. In sociological terms, one could say that this approach is more influenced by a Durkheimian conception of the state than a strictly Weberian one. For Durkheim, the state 'is the very organ of social thought'; it comprises 'the sentiments, ideals, beliefs that the society has worked out collectively and with time' (Durkheim 1957: 79–80, 1964: 79, 1986a: 54). As mentioned by Iver Neumann in Chapter 5, the state for Durkheim develops from clan or lineage (mechanical solidarity) to evolve into social interactions rooted in the everyday (organic solidarity). In the process, the collective conscience becomes distinct from individual consciences. Although it is diffuse in every society, it has specific characteristics that make it a distinct reality: 'it is, in effect, independent of the particular conditions in which individuals are placed: they pass on and it remains' (Durkheim 1964: 80). For him, the division of labour and the development of organic solidarity paralleled the development of the social contract and the state. However, and contrary to Weber's conception of the state, Durkheim states that the coercive powers of the state could vary independently of the level of social development (Durkheim 1973; Horowitz 1982). The political society is primarily determined neither by possession of a fixed territorial area nor by density of population, but by the act of 'coming together', to use Durkheim's own wording (1957: 45).

The social legitimacy approach as defined here has a number of implications for statebuilding issues. Following this approach, 'state collapse' is not only solely driven by institutional collapse, but also by the collapse of the legitimacy of the central authority. Robert Dorff goes as far as to state that most of the examples of state collapse can be boiled down generally to the loss of legitimate governance (1999). The withering of legitimate governance – a process parallel to but not a by-product of institutional collapse – opens the door to 'political entrepreneurs', allowing them to mobilize the population on the basis of allegiances that displace national ones (Badie 2000). Consequently, state strength is defined as the 'capacity to command loyalty' (Holsti 1996: 82–3) in a political marketplace defined by political bargaining for loyalty (de Waal 2009). A collapsed state is one where 'authority fragments or evaporates in direct proportion to the loss of governmental legitimacy in society and its component groups. Rule – to the extent that it exists – is based on coercion, corruption or terror. It is no longer a right' (Holsti 2004: 56–7). This definition contrasts greatly with the usual Weberian or Neo-Weberian emphasis on state capacity.

Hence, the challenge of building and consolidating state institutions aside, one the most important issues is for the indigenous institutions to define, create and solidify a viable collective identity in order to provide the social bond necessary for them to be recognized as legitimate by the citizens, and, by extension, for the external actors to find efficient and unobtrusive ways to support this process. The problems faced by recently decolonised states in the 1960s are to a certain extent similar to those facing current 'weak states':

> it consists in defining, or trying to define, a collective subject to whom the actions of the state can be internally connected, in creating, or trying to create, an experiential 'we' from whose will the activities of government seem spontaneously to flow.
>
> (Geertz 1973: 238–40)

This goal can be hindered by legacies of bad governance from colonial powers in the case of decolonized states, which can then lead to neopatrimonial practices in newly created states or states striving to define their identity (Badie 2000). Hence, failure to create and nurture this 'collective subject' can lead to a wide variety of problems. Heightened self-consciousness may cause diverse solidarities and loyalties to stimulate each other by opposition, threatening the integrity of the nation-state itself if these solidarities are insufficiently represented in the politics and culture of the state (Fallers 1974).

In general, the social legitimacy approach is more sociologically or anthropologically oriented, relativising generalising assumptions and emphasising the particularities of each state and its societal context. The challenge of building and consolidating state institutions aside, one of the most important issues is for the indigenous institutions to define, create and solidify a viable collective identity in order to provide the social bond necessary for them to be recognised as legitimate by the citizens and, by extension, for the external actors to find efficient and unobtrusive ways to support this process. Rejoining the Durkheimian sociological tradition, this approach puts the emphasis on logics of social integration and solidarity and, *a contrario*, on logics of *anomie*, understood as the breakdown in moral norms which 'springs from the lack of collective forces at certain points in society' (Durkheim 1997: 382). As such, it imposes a salutary contribution to debate in the field of statebuilding.

The purpose here is certainly not to portray Durkheim's sociology of the state in an uncritical light – it is well known that Durkheim indulged in an organicist thinking prevalent in the nineteenth century and his determinism in depicting an evolutionary conception of social transformation has already been criticised many times – but rather to demonstrate the wealth of sociological approaches existing on the state and to explore an alternative approach to the institutional approach dominant in the current thinking on statebuilding. Hence, one can argue that insisting on the political concept of legitimacy allows us to concentrate our attention on the state and society as distinct in terms of 'actors', though not necessarily hermetic institutions and activities. As Alexander Wendt (1999: 199) states,

> it seems impossible to define the state apart from 'society'. States and societies seem to be conceptually interdependent in the same way that masters and slaves are, or teachers and students; the nature of each is a function of its relation to the other.

For Wendt, this interrelation creates a 'state-society complex', where the state is constituted by its relationship to society while at the same time the society is constituted by the state (1999: 210). This approach sheds light on the state and society in their mutually constitutive relationship, where legitimacy conditions state strength and is, at the same time, an element of state strength. Hence, 'a given power relationship is not legitimate because people believe in its legitimacy, but because it can be justified in terms of their beliefs' (Beetham 1991: 11). This 'two-way process' of legitimation is a central feature in Mary Kaldor's (2000: 285) conception of legitimacy, defined as

> the extent to which people consent to and even support the framework of rules within which political institutions function, either because the political institutions are seen as having gained authority through some legitimate process, and/or because they are seen to represent ideas or values widely supported.

Some see parallels here with recent developments related to the human security concept. Maybub ul Haq defines the concept of human security by setting out to redefine security in two basic ways: from an exclusive stress on territorial security to a much greater stress on people's security, and from security through armaments to security through sustainable human development. The report also identifies seven elements that comprise human security: economic security, food security, health security, environmental security, personal security, community security and finally political security (UNDP 1994). Examples abound of the interconnection between discourses on bottom-up legitimation and the broadening of the field of security. For Shahrbanou Tadjbakhsh (2007), 'mirroring the human security motto, the strength of the state is more in the eyes of the population (citizens) than in the solidity of state institutions', while for Mary Kaldor, 'human security depends on the existence of legitimate institutions that gain the trust of the population and have some enforcement capacity' (2007: 187). Major statebuilding actors, including the United Nations, endorse this normative development. However, more interestingly, it also found an echo in Washington, where the United States Army gave a central role to legitimation processes in its counterinsurgency operations. In effect, the new counterinsurgency manual states that 'the primary objective of any counterinsurgent is to foster the development of effective governance by a legitimate government' (US Army 2007: I-90), which is in itself described as a major doctrinal change by the establishment (Nagl 2007). Hence, as this example reminds us, not unlike the statebuilding parlance, one of the vulnerabilities of the human security discourse is to be shaped by powerful actors, replacing political stakes between opposing groups with non-political, 'technical' considerations (Chandler 2008).

Nationalism, Communism, Islamism and the 'realm of ideas'

As mentioned earlier, the social legitimacy approach puts a special emphasis on identity mobilisation, which in itself echoes the earlier discussion on the intertwining of the state and nation (see Lemay-Hébert *et al.*'s Chapter 1, pp. 3–5; Onuf's Chapter 2, p. 28; Kratochwil's Chapter 3, p. 46). One needs to emphasise that a nation is not a social actor per se; misrepresentations in that sense are common. For instance, Johan Galtung refers to the nation as a political actor when he says 'no nation can opt out of one state to set up another that denies the same rights to nations/peoples under their control' (2000: 205). Transferring agency to the nation is in fact commonplace in the field of political science. However, to paraphrase Leon Brunschvicg's response to Emile Durkheim, a nation is a political project that worked (1986b: 210); in other words, a nation is not a fixed concept or an 'essence'. It is subject to alteration, modification, reinterpretation, or even wholesale creation by politics. It is a mutually constitutive process where the state may well be legitimate because it is taken to express or represent concepts of collective identity, but in the process, the state also asserts its right to interpret and define them (Barker 1990: 28). The concept of nation is a social entity, a social reality, only insofar as it relates to the modern state; it is pointless to discuss nation and nationality except insofar as both relate to the state (Hobsbawm 1990: 9–10).

This intermingling between state and society in the modern age makes it problematic to understand the state in exclusively institutional terms, without questioning its ability to successfully enforce a social contract that will ensure the cohesion of the larger social entity it governs. As Philippe Braud (2004: 75–6, my translation) argues

> The acceptance of the social control exercised by the state goes hand in hand with the feeling of belonging to a community of fate which the state would constitute the political expression of; it is here that the nation steps in.

It is in that context that nationalism acquires all its meaning as a theory of political legitimacy, a 'political principle which holds that the political and the national unit should be congruent' (Gellner 1983: 1). As Carl Friedrich summarises, such is the dialectic of the political that 'the state seeks and must seek to foster the growth of a nation, indeed must posit its potential coming into being' (1963: 551; see also Kedourie 1960: 9; Kohn 2005: 19). In the process, the 'community' or the 'social contract' replaces religion or primordial allegiances in becoming the legitimating principle *par excellence*, a process identified by Durkheim: 'once a goal is pursued by a whole people, it acquires a moral supremacy which raises it far above private goals and thereby gives it a religious character' (Horowitz 1982: 364). The 'strong' state, while resting on a cohesive social order, is not as autonomous from social forces as one might think at first glance (see Elias 2000).

Nationalism as an ideology[1] only became prominent fairly recently, at the beginning of the nineteenth century more precisely (Kedourie 1960), in a process closely associated with the rise of the modern state (Breuilly 1993; Giddens 1985: 83–121; Navari 1981: 13–38). Iver Neumann is right to remind us that no process of state formation, be it 'early' or 'contemporary', ever operated *in vacuo*. If globalisation has usefully drawn our attention to the fact that no polities are close systems, as Neumann argues in Chapter 5, it has similarly led certain scholars to brush off, maybe too quickly, the centrality of nationalism in current statebuilding processes, on the very basis that we are witnessing the birth of a postmodern world. To use the Holsti/Buzan model of the state developed earlier, globalisation has induced major changes to the state's physical basis (even if the Westphalian narrative has never been the whole-encompassing narrative that a few Western scholars pretended it was) and the state's institutional foundations (see for instance Strange 1996). However, in the 'realm of ideas', nationalism is still a powerful force that profoundly shapes current statebuilding processes.

To fully grasp the centrality of nationalism – and hence in contemporary statebuilding – it is useful to contrast its development with the evolution of two competing ideologies, which came to be prevalent in the twentieth century and which also conveyed a specific vision of the interplay between politics and the state, that is Communism and Islamism. Interestingly enough, after an initial conflictual phase, both ideologies – or more precisely actors or political entrepreneurs associated with these ideologies – quickly redeployed their discourses *inside* the semantics of nationalism, henceforth reinforcing its prevalence in contemporary international relations.

At the foundation of the USSR in 1922, the dire challenges to the existence of the new state prompted an intense debate between Leon Trotsky and Joseph Stalin over the ongoing course of the revolution. Trotsky was a well-known partisan of the 'permanent revolution', hoping that the USSR would serve as a staging ground for the acceleration of the revolutionary movement in neighbouring Europe. Resolutely anti-status quo, Trotsky was suggesting a specific interpretation of Lenin's theses, based on a radical reconsidering of the international European system. The aim was to hasten the revolutionary march of events, even if that meant jumping from a feudal state straight to the dictatorship of the proletariat. In this context, Trotsky, as Lenin before him, considered nationalism as a form of Czarist backwardness (albeit Trotsky nuanced his position at the end of his life, notably in regards to Zionism). For his part, Stalin was keen to consolidate the political gains obtained following the costly civil war (1917–1922). His priority was to strengthen the USSR, of which he was the main architect after all. The rest is history: Stalin's doctrine of 'building socialism in one country' was adopted at the 14th Congress of the Russian Communist Party in 1925, which was in fact the last Congress where a genuine debate of ideas took place until Gorbachev's reforms in the 1980s.

Stalin's doctrine had a profound impact on the development of communism in the USSR and on the USSR's role in the promotion of 'national' revolutions, but it also impacted *ex post facto* statebuilding activities in the Commonwealth of Independent States (created in 1991 following the collapse of the USSR).

Stalin actually used nationalism and nationalities as building blocks in the erection of the USSR. Olivier Roy (2000) offered an insightful analysis of the creation of Central Asian nations, where languages and ethnicities were heavily manipulated by Stalin and the Russian Academy of Sciences. Yet these 'social experiments', as arbitrary and 'artificial' as some of them may have seemed, managed to create a social reality on the ground. Associating certain identities (linguistic, religious or ethnic) with distinct administrations (autonomous regions or republics inside federal republics), Stalin's institutional division, while largely symbolic in the heyday of Soviet centralism, played – and still plays – a crucial role in the emergence and persistence of conflicts in the region. Whether it is in Georgia, in Moldavia, in Armenia and Azerbaijan, in Tajikistan or in Russia, specific actors used Stalin's territorial division as a template for requesting greater autonomy or outright secession. While these administrative divisions were not necessarily accompanied with extensive executive prerogatives in the beginning, they clearly had a role in the symbolic sphere, furthering autochthonous elites and strengthening cultural bonds. That proved to be a useful resource for identity entrepreneurs, tapping into this symbolic pool to further the cause of independence in Abkhazia, Adjara, South Ossetia or Transnistria, among other cases.

A second example illustrating the continuing relevance of nationalism in statebuilding processes is the evolution associated with political Islam following the Iranian revolution. More than 30 years after the Revolution conducted by the Ayatollah Ruhollah Khomeini, we are witnessing the unravelling of the political project of reconstituting Middle Eastern societies on new foundations. Neither in Iran, nor in the Islamic Emirate of Afghanistan (1996–2001) has the Islamist project led to the birth of new society. Political Islam, like pan-Arabism, has not been able to transcend national and infranational divisions. In Afghanistan, Islamist recruiting still owes much to tribal or confessional allegiances. In Lebanon, Hezbollah, despite a soaring popularity that goes beyond the strict confessional fault lines, is de facto representing Shiite Lebanese interests in Beirut; as such, it is deeply involved in confessional politics, which is at the heart of Lebanon's state identity and functioning since the Taif Agreements in 1989. This failure to redraw the map of the Middle East has led to the splitting up of political Islam in two opposite directions. The first, probably the most influental, is born out of the transformation of Islamist movements into Islamic nationalist movements; that is to say they have renounced the original supranationalism that previously characterised their ideologies, and are now active on a national basis. They accept political pluralism and state mediation. These political parties – this is usually what they have become – have been integrated into politics and become commonplace, which in turn has led to the 'social-democratisation' of political Islam (Roy 1996: viii–ix). Examples abound, from the diverse Muslim Brotherhood movements (Egyptian, Jordanian or Lebanese), to the Turkish Justice and Development Party or the Islamic Renaissance Party of Tajikistan. The second tendency is the birth of a new fundamentalism, ideologically conservative and politically radical, Wahhabised and opposed to the so-called Western world. It is what Gilles Kepel dubs 'Salafist jihadism' (2003). The quintessence of this trend is the infamous Al Qaida network created around Osama Bin Laden from combatant networks sent into Afghanistan in the 1980s by Americans, Pakistanis and Saudis. For all the disruption that this network – and affiliated movements – has produced, this trend of political Islam has not been able to impose itself a redefinition of the Middle East, lacking a viable political project and a clear backing from Muslim populations. Salafist jihadism poses security threats – foremost for Muslim populations – and imposes societal debates in some Middle Eastern societies, yet it has hardly been able to redefine the Middle Eastern political landscape, still resolutely anchored in state-centric dynamics.

Statebuilding and nationbuilding: 'organising' states while avoiding the nation

A final consideration, that summarises to a certain extent the debate on the distinctions between the institutional and social legitimacy approaches as discussed earlier, concerns the semantic imprecision over the use of the terms statebuilding and nationbuilding in the contemporary literature. To use Durkheimian terms, it could be seen as an effort to systematically discard all preconceptions of a concept prior to defining it (1982). One central contention will be addressed here: the belief that by distinguishing statebuilding and nationbuilding, it becomes possible to 'organise states' while avoiding much-debated identity-building activities.

The first misconception is specificity linked to the theoretical debate in the American academia. The theoretical debate in the United States is blurred mainly because some scholars accept that 'nationbuilding' is the recognised term in use despite the fact that they really mean 'statebuilding', in accordance with the institutional approach defined earlier. For Simon Chesterman (2004: 114, emphasis in the text):

> the focus here is on the *state* (that is, the highest institutions of governance in a territory) rather than the *nation* (a people who share common customs, origins, history and, frequently, language) as such. 'State-building' is therefore a more precise term. Due to its prevalence in US debates on the topic, however, 'nation-building' will be used in this article.

Hence, for many American scholars, nationbuilding 'really means state-building' (von Hippel 2000: 96). This somewhat marginal semantic debate cleared out, this brings us to a second, most important, debate linked to the semantics of statebuilding. Following the statebuilding and nationbuilding distinction, it appears that the major distinguishing feature that sets apart the two concepts is the nature of international involvement: statebuilding would imply the *sole* reconstruction of the institutions of the state while nationbuilding would be a more thorough process of identity reconstruction.[2] Key in this is the belief that one can alter the state without engaging the nation. The two processes – statebuilding and nationbuilding – are separated and cleanly differentiated:

> Statebuilding: actions undertaken by international or national actors to establish, reform, or strengthen the institutions of the state and their relation to society.
>
> Nationbuilding: actions undertaken, usually by national actors, to forge a sense of common nationhood (1) to overcome ethnic, sectarian, or communal differences; 2) to counter alternate sources of identity and loyalty; and (3) to mobilize a population behind a parallel statebuilding project. (...) Confusingly, this term is often equated with either postconflict stabilization or statebuilding, especially in US policy and journalistic circles
>
> (Call 2008: 5)

Beside the (artificial) distinction between the two processes, these previous definitions of statebuilding and nationbuilding also convey the idea that statebuilding can be conducted by international actors whereas nationbuilding is 'usually undertaken by national actors'. By equating the 'state' with its institutional manifestation, and by autonomising the state from its societal moorings, externally led statebuilding processes become mainly a process of strengthening government institutions, which conveniently leave the contested realm of socio-political cohesion and identity-building for national actors to carry on (see also Tarantino 2004: 559). This approach can also take a normative expression, where 'the goal of nation-building should not be to impose common identities on deeply divided peoples' but rather 'to organize states that can administer their territories and allow people to live together despite differences' (Ottaway 2002: 17). Organising states suddenly becomes possible while leaving the identities of their populations intact. Another variation on the same theme is the recognition of the need for a more thorough statebuilding process that encompasses nationbuilding, while at the same time leaving aside the issue of legitimacy in the process. For instance, *The Beginner's Guide to Nation-Building* defines nation-building as 'the use of armed force as part of a broader effort to promote political and economic reforms with the objective of transforming a society emerging from conflict into one at peace with itself and its neighbors' (Dobbins *et al.* 2007: xvii). 'Nationbuilding' activities are therein objectivised as any other institutional expressions of the state (counting harbours, highways and so on, following Robert Rotberg's perspective).

This development has to be related with the marked tendency to abstract the tasks of statebuilding (or peacebuilding) from their historical, political and cultural contexts (Berdal 2009: 19–20). To a certain extent, this echoes what James Ferguson labelled the 'anti-politics machine': statebuilding actors generate their own form of discourse and create a structure of knowledge around the object of their intervention. Interventions are then organised on the basis of this structure of knowledge, effectively projecting a representation of economic and social life which denies politics (1994: xiv–xv). Whilst the institutional approach has been the dominant approach and has highly influenced theories and practices of statebuilding, there are alternatives to the approach, understanding the state in all its complexities and statebuilding as an inherently political process.

Conclusion

This chapter showed how academic and policy-making conceptions of the state impact on their understandings of state collapse or weakness, and therefore the policies and practices of statebuilding. It highlighted how a specific reading of Max Weber's sociology has come to dominate the statebuilding literature under the institutional approach. Defining the state by its physical and institutional basis and its strength by its institutional grasp over the society, the institutional approach equates state collapse with the collapse of state institutions, and statebuilding with institutional reconstruction. Showing that this orthodoxy can be contested, this chapter sketched an alternative approach to the institutional approach, based on Durkheimian sociology. While accepting the institutional approach's focus on the security apparatus and state institutions, especially as a critical first step in statebuilding processes, the social legitimacy approach adds a layer of complexity by looking at the nation-state as a constitutive whole, while focusing on socio-political processes of constitution – and collapse – of legitimate governance. While it is important to understand the state and the nation in a co-constitutive process – where representatives of the state gain legitimacy by representing concepts of collective identity while at the same time asserting their right to interpret them – this chapter argued against transmitting agency to the concept of nation, which could be more correctly described as a 'legitimacy pool' for identity entrepreneurs.

Building on this specific conceptual interrelation between the state and nation, and postulating, in line with the social legitimacy approach, that 'it is in the realm of ideas and sentiment that the fate of states is primarily determined' (Holsti 1996: 84), the chapter moved on to analyse the changing role of nationalism in contemporary statebuilding processes. Understood as a theory of political legitimacy – a political principle which holds that the political and the national unit should be congruent – nationalism was and still is a powerful legitimating force, for good and for bad. A testimony of the central role played by nationalism throughout the twentieth century is how political entrepreneurs associated with two main competing ideologies to nationalism – Islamism and Communism – redeployed their discourses *inside* the semantics of nationalism, acknowledging the importance of the modern nation-state in the process. Finally, the chapter took a fresh look at the contemporary literature on statebuilding, highlighting the paradoxes and pitfalls associated with the neo-Weberian 'state autonomy' theory, which has been translated into a very convenient statebuilding and nationbuilding distinction in the literature. This theoretical distinction allows scholars and policy-makers to aim at 'organising states' while pretending to avoid much-debated identity-building activities. Overall and taken together, the arguments developed in this chapter intended to shed an alternative light on the difficulties experienced by many statebuilders in fully grasping the historical, political and cultural contexts of 'targeted states', while focusing on the role of the semantics of statebuilding in the process.

Notes

1 It is useful to note here the difference between patriotism and nationalism, given that many cosmopolitan intellectuals tend to equate the two. As noted by Benedict Anderson, many scholars insist on the 'near-pathological character of nationalism', its roots in fear and hatred of the Other (1991: 141); however, nationalism is broader than this specific materialisation of the ideology.

2 It echoes to a certain extent the statebuilding versus state-formation distinction that appeared in certain strands of the sociological and anthropological literature, where statebuilding is defined as a 'conscious effort at creating an apparatus of control' and state-formation as an 'historical process whose outcome is a largely unconscious and contradictory process of conflicts, negotiations and compromises between diverse groups whose self-serving actions and trade-offs constitute the vulgarisation of power' (Berman and Lonsdale 1992: 5).

References

Anderson, B. (1991) *Imagined Communities: Reflections on the Origin and Spread of Nationalism*, London: Verso.

Badie, B. (2000) *The Imported State: The Westernization of the Political Order*, Stanford: Stanford University Press.

Badie, B. and Birnbaum, P. (1983) *The Sociology of the State*, Chicago: University of Chicago Press.

Barker, R. (1990) *Political Legitimacy and the State*, Oxford: Clarendon Press.

Bastid, P. (1967) 'L'idée de légitimité', in P. Bastid *et al.* (eds) *Annales de philosophie politique. Tome 7: L'idée de légitimité*, Paris: PUF.

Beetham, D. (1985) *Max Weber and the Theory of Modern Politics*, Cambridge: Polity Press.

Beetham, D. (1991) *The Legitimation of Power*, Basingstoke, UK: Macmillan.

Berdal, M. (2009) *Building Peace after War*, London: International Institute for Strategic Studies.

Berman, B. and Lonsdale, J. (1992) *Unhappy Valley: Conflict in Kenya and Africa. Book one: State and Class*, London: James Currey.

Braud, P. (2004) *Penser l'Etat*, Paris: Seuil.

Breuilly, J. (1993) *Nationalism and the State*, Manchester: Manchester University Press.

Buzan, B. (1991) *People, States and Fear: An Agenda for International Security Studies in the Post-Cold War Era*, New York: Harvester Wheatsheaf.

Call, C. (2008) 'Ending wars, building states', in C. Call and V. Wyeth (eds) *Building States to Build Peace*, Boulder: Lynne Rienner.

Chandler, D. (2006) *Empire in Denial: The Politics of Statebuilding*, London: Pluto Press.

Chandler, D. (2008) 'Human security: the dog that didn't bark', *Security Dialogue*, 39(4): 427–38.

Chesterman, S. (2004) 'Bush, the United Nations, and nation-building', *Survival*, 46(1): 101–16.

Davidheiser, E. (1992) 'Strong states, weak states: the role of state in revolution', *Comparative Politics*, 24(4): 463–75.

de Waal, A. (2009) 'Fixing the political marketplace: how can we make peace without functioning state institutions?', Fifteenth Christen Michelsen Lecture, Bergen, Norway, 15 October.

Dobbins, J., Jones, S.J., Crane, K. and DeGrasse, B.C (2007) *The Beginner's Guide to Nation-Building*, Santa Monica: RAND National Security Research Division.

Doornbos, M., Woodward, S. and Roque, S. (2006) *Failing States or Failed States? The Role of Development Models: Collected Works*, Madrid: FRIDE.

Dorff, R. (1999) 'Responding to the failed state: the need for strategy', *Small Wars and Insurgencies*, 10(3): 62–81.

Durkheim, E. (1957) *Professional Ethics and Civic Morals*, London, UK: Routledge.

Durkheim, E. (1964) *The Division of Labor in Society*, New York, NY: Free Press.

Durkheim, E. (1973) 'The two laws of penal evolution', *Economy and Society*, 2(3): 285–308.

Durkheim, E. (1982) *Rules of Sociological Method*, New York: The Free Press.

Durkheim, E. (1986a) 'The concept of state', in A. Giddens (ed.) *Durkheim on Politics and the State*, Cambridge: Polity Press.

Durkheim, E. (1986b) 'Patriotism and militarism', in A. Giddens (ed.) *Durkheim on Politics and the State*, Cambridge: Polity Press.

Durkheim, E. (1997) *Suicide: A Study in Sociology*, New York: Simon and Schuster.

Elias, N. (2000) *The Civilizing Process*, Oxford: Blackwell.

Fallers, L. (1974) *The Social Anthropology of the Nation-State*, Chicago: Aldine.

Ferguson, J. (1994) *The Anti-Politics Machine: Development, Depoliticization, and Bureaucratic Power in Lesotho*, Minneapolis: University of Minnesota Press.

Friedrich, C. (1963) *Man and His Government: An Empirical Theory of Politics*, New York: McGraw-Hill.

Fukuyama, F. (2004) *State-building: Governance and World Order in the 21st Century*, New York: Cornell University Press.

Galtung, J. (2000) 'The state/nation dialectic: some tentative conclusions', in J. Galtung and C. Jacobsen (eds) *Searching for Peace: The Road to TRANSCEND*, London: Pluto Press.

Geertz, C. (1973) *The Interpretation of Cultures*, New York: Basic Books.

Gellner, E. (1983) *Nations and Nationalism*, Ithaca: Cornell University Press.

Giddens, A. (1985) *The Nation-State and Violence*, Cambridge: Polity Press.

Hobsbawm, E. (1990) *Nations and Nationalism since 1780: Programme, Myth, Reality*, Cambridge: Cambridge University Press.

Hobson, J. (1998) 'Debate: the 'second wave' of Weberian historical sociology', *Review of International Political Economy*, 5(2): 284–320.

Hobson, J. and Seabrooke, L. (2001) 'Reimagining Weber: constructing international society and the social balance of power', *European Journal of International Relations*, 7(2): 239–74.

Holsti, K. (1996) *The State, War, and the State of War*, Cambridge: Cambridge University Press.

Holsti, K. (2004) *Taming the Sovereigns: Institutional Change in International Politics*, Cambridge: Cambridge University Press.

Horowitz, I. (1982) 'Socialization without politicization: Emile Durkheim's theory of the modern state', *Political Theory* 10(3): 353–77.

Kaldor, M. (2000) 'Governance, legitimacy, and security: three scenarios for the twenty-first century', in P. Wapner and E. Ruiz (eds) *Principled World Politics*, Lanham: Rowman and Littlefield.

Kaldor, M. (2007) *Human Security: Reflections on Globalization and Intervention*, Cambridge: Polity.

Kedourie, E. (1960) *Nationalism*, London: Hutchinson.

Kepel, G. (2003) *Jihad: The Trail of Political Islam*, Cambridge: Harvard University Press.

Kohn, H. (2005) *The Idea of Nationalism: A Study in its Origins and Background*, New Brunswick: Transaction Publishers.

Lacroix, B. (1985) 'Ordre politique et ordre social', in M. Grawitz and J. Leca (eds) *Traité de Science Politique, Vol. 1: La Science Politique, Science Sociale, L'Ordre Politique*, Paris: PUF.

Lemay-Hébert, N. (2009) 'Statebuilding without nation-building? Legitimacy, state failure and the limits of the institutionalist approach', *Journal of Intervention and Statebuilding*, 3(1): 21–45.

Lemay-Hébert, N. (2013) 'Rethinking Weberian approaches to statebuilding', in D. Chandler and T. Sisk (eds) *Routledge Handbook of International Statebuilding*, Abingdon: Routledge.

Mcloughlin, C. (2010) *Topic Guide on Fragile States*, Birmingham: Governance and Social Development Resource Centre.

Migdal, J. (1988) *Strong Societies and Weak States: State-Society Relations and State Capabilities in the Third World*, Princeton: Princeton University Press.

Migdal, J. (2001) *State in Society: Studying How States and Societies Constitute Each Other*, Cambridge: Cambridge University Press.

Nagl, J. (2007) 'The evolution and importance of army/marine corps field manual 3–24, counterinsurgency', *Small Wars Journal*, available at: http://smallwarsjournal.com/blog/the-evolution-and-importance-of-armymarine-corps-field-manual-3–24-counterinsurgency.

Nash, K. (2000) *Contemporary Political Sociology*, Oxford: Blackwell.

Navari, C. (1981) 'The origins of the nation-state', in L. Tivey (ed.) *The Nation-State: The Formation of Modern Politics*, New York: St Martin's Press.

Ottaway, M. (2002) 'Nation-building (think again)', *Foreign Policy*, 132: 16–22.

Palumbo, A. and Scott, A. (2008) 'Weber, Durkheim and the sociology of the modern state', in T. Ball and R. Bellamy (eds) *The Cambridge History of Twentieth-Century Political Thought*, Cambridge: Cambridge University Press.

Paris, R. (1997) 'Peacebuilding and the limits of liberal internationalism', *International Security*, 22: 54–89.

Pitkin, H. (1972) *Wittgenstein and Justice*, Berkeley: University of California Press.

Rotberg, R. (2003) 'Failed states, collapsed states, weak states: causes and indicators', in R. Rotberg (ed.) *State Failure and State Weakness in a Time of Terror*, Washington: Brookings Institution Press.

Rotberg, R. (2004) 'The failure and collapse of nation-states', in R. Rotberg (ed.) *When States Fail: Causes and Consequences*, Princeton: Princeton University Press.

Roy, O. (1996) *The Failure of Political Islam*, Cambridge: Harvard University Press.

Roy, O. (2000) *The New Central Asia: The Creation of Nations*, New York: New York University Press.

Strange, S. (1996) *The Retreat of the State: The Diffusion of Power in the World Economy*, Cambridge: Cambridge University Press.

Tadjbakhsh, S. (2007) 'Les "états fragiles" constituent-ils une menace pour la sécurité internationale?', CERI Conference, Paris, 27 March.

Tarantino, A.K. (2004) 'The two faces of nation-building: developing function and identity', *Cambridge Review of International Affairs*, 17(3): 557–75.

UNDP (United Nations Development Programme) (1994) *Human Development Report 1994*, New York: Oxford University Press.

U.S. Army (2007) *U.S. Army/Marine Corps Counterinsurgency Field Manual 3–24*, Chicago: Chicago University Press.

von Hippel, K. (2000) 'Democracy by force: a renewed commitment to nation building', *Washington Quarterly*, 23(1): 95–112.

Weber, M. (1947) *The Theory of Social and Economic Organization*, London: William Hodge.

Weber, M. (1948) 'Politics as a vocation', in H. Gerth and C.W. Mills (eds) *From Max Weber: Essays in Sociology*, New York: Oxford University Press.

Weber, M. (1958) *The Protestant Ethic and the Spirit of Capitalism*, New York: Scribner.

Weber, M. (1962) *Basic Concepts in Sociology*, New York: Citadel Press.

Wendt, A. (1999) *Social Theory of International Politics*, Cambridge: Cambridge University Press.

Zaum, D. (2007) *The Sovereignty Paradox: Norms and Politics of International Statebuilding*, Oxford: Oxford University Press.

7 Transformative statebuilding, occupation, and international law

Friends or foes?

Jan Wouters and Kenneth Chan

Introduction

In 2003, a 'Coalition of the Willing' led by the United States (US) invaded the Republic of Iraq. It quickly became clear that this offensive would not follow the typical legal agenda. The invasion, dubbed 'Operation Iraqi Freedom', was driven by a misguided (or, depending on whom one asks, dishonest) belief that Saddam Hussein had significant caches of weapons of mass destruction (WMDs) close at hand, in violation of UN Security Council Resolution 1441, which provided 'a final opportunity [for Iraq] to comply with its disarmament obligations' (UNSC 2002). However, the Security Council (UNSC or SC) had refused to provide a legal mandate for the coalition to use force against Iraq under its Chapter VII powers, rendering the military incursion illegal under international law. Indeed, there were indications that the US and its coalition partners had a more ambitious agenda than just the pursuit of WMDs, and would intervene irrespective of the lack of support from the UNSC. Thus, even though no WMDs were uncovered, the Coalition's efforts continued to gain momentum. The US and its partners swiftly shifted their rhetoric to repurpose the goals of the war, exerting (what would prove to be) long-term territorial authority over the region. This consequently brought its actions within the jurisdiction of the law of occupation, something acknowledged by the American and British governments early on in the mission (McGurk 2004–5: 452). Notably, however, the US and UK were in their rhetoric careful to place their focus on the application of international humanitarian law to the situation, thus avoiding references to themselves as 'occupying powers'. For instance, they indicated they would 'strictly abide by their obligations under international law, including those relating to the essential humanitarian needs of the people of Iraq' (UNSC 2003a).

However, the Coalition sought a far broader agenda than the mere transitional occupation permitted by international law. The Coalition emphasised in particular the importance of installing and fostering the trappings of Western democratic reform and regime change in the State (Wintour 2007), and this quickly became the fulcrum of its continued efforts for the better part of the next decade. It is hard to tell if the irony of importing such goals undemocratically into the country escaped the Coalition. Nevertheless, even as the Coalition willingly acceded to the jurisdiction of the law of occupation, it would openly defy its principal premise by pursuing the most ambitious statebuilding exercise in a generation. As both lucid focus and legal basis abandoned the intervention effort, the previously distinct role of international law, particularly international humanitarian law (IHL), had become displaced. As McGurk explains, occupation law 'explicitly prohibit[s] state-building' (McGurk 2004–5: 454). Where, then, did the Coalition's seemingly limitless authority to break down and rebuild Iraq in its westernised image come from? The law of *occupation*, a branch of IHL relating to post-conflict societies, certainly did not support such actions. Was this then the start of a new era in the laws of war governing occupation?

Following on from the changed temperament towards the role of belligerent occupation after Iraq, the purpose of this chapter is to assess the relationship between the law of occupation and the process of statebuilding. There is a clear tension between these two systems. The more conservative directives of the former explicitly prohibit the occurrence of the latter. That is, the law of occupation presupposes that an occupying power will not fundamentally alter the infrastructure of the State but, instead, will act as its trustee, facilitating post-conflict societies to engage in self-determination and reassert governance over their territories on their own terms. In this regard, occupation law permits occupiers the right to make only those changes necessary to prevent further chaos descending upon these communities and to ensure stability. How, then, can one reconcile this traditional reticence with the so-called contemporary practice of occupying powers defying such non-transformational norms – as was the case with post-Saddam Hussein Iraq? Has the law of occupation been superseded, are there new paradigms emerging that provide a clearer legal framework for transformative occupation/statebuilding to take place? In other words, is 'statebuilding' a justified extension of IHL?

In addressing these questions, this chapter will first provide some historical and thematic context by addressing the underlying tension between local ownership and external intervention that characterises the statebuilding debate. It briefly considers the evolution of state sovereignty and territorial integrity. It then examines the normative conflict between the law of occupation and statebuilding, and attempts to pinpoint its legal foundations.

Local ownership and post-conflict societies

A discussion on the modern practice of occupation should begin with colonialism. Indeed, before one can really determine the legal basis for statebuilding, it is necessary to unpack the legal issues surrounding imperialism, local ownership, and self-determination that underwrite the historical wariness of (particularly) post-colonial states towards international territorial administration.

Colonialism is understood to involve one global power extending its authority by assuming control over other peoples in territories perceived to be 'weaker'. The rise of colonial empires throughout Asia and Africa prior to the First World War was a reflection of the fundamental failure of the international community not only to recognise the rights of developing states to self-determination, but also to accept that Western cultural and political practices would not always be an ideal fit in all situations. Colonialism was marked by a belief that 'barbarians and savages' were a 'white man's burden', referring to the latter's self-assumed responsibility to civilise them (Osterhammel 2005). At the dawn of the modern age of international law, colonial practice made clear that 'civilised' powers were entitled to intervene in the internal affairs of 'less developed' countries in order to improve their quality of life – at least, from the perspective of the 'civilised' powers. However, the post-colonial period, marked by the end of the Second World War and the creation of the United Nations Special Committee on Decolonization, brought about a fairly significant shift in legal and political attitudes, because it advocated a system of sovereign equality between peers as members of the international community, where each was entitled to assume responsibility for their *own* bodily integrity without fear of outside interference. As all states were *equals*, they should not be compelled to act in ways they did not decide for themselves – irrespective of what is perceived to be 'good' for them, or is believed to make them more happy, secure, or peaceful (Bain 2003).

In 1950, a few years after its founding, the United Nations clarified the meaning of the principle of *self-determination*, which granted to all peoples and nations the right to 'freely determine their political status and freely pursue their economic, social, and cultural development' (UNGA 1950, 1952). Then, in the early 1990s, as the Cold War wound to a close, bloody and violent genocide again seized the collective imagination. Atrocities manifested in Rwanda and Yugoslavia (to name only a few instances), and the removal of central government in Somalia effectively forged the first modern example of a failed state. It was clear that the international stance of 'immutable' sovereignty would need to change again. In 1999, Kofi Annan, then Secretary-General of the UN, looked to reconceptualise the underlying norms of sovereignty, arguing that 'the Charter protects the sovereignty of peoples. It was never meant as a licence for governments to trample on human rights and human dignity. Sovereignty implies responsibility, not just power' (Annan 1999). On the tail of the new understandings of state equality in this era, 1999 saw the UN embark on the most ambitious statebuilding projects in its history – in Kosovo and in East Timor. In both instances, authority was routed directly into the hands of the UN and its officials, and the role of other international authorities moved to the margins – a strategy that clearly looked to cleave away the extraneous vestiges of 'inviolable' state sovereignty that had characterised the international legal system in the previous decades.

The intent of this brief historical reckoning of the position of international law on non-consensual interference on the soil of another State is not to recount every beat and pulse of the evolving international legal position. Rather, it seeks to highlight the genuine struggles inherent in finding a middle ground between the fundamental character of the integrity of the State and the perceived (and in many cases, genuinely held) need to refashion historically destructive local cultural, economic and/or political practices.

In recent years, it has been strongly indicated that the international community now favours a policy of 'soft'-sovereignty in the context of statebuilding. This issue, which is more fully examined in the following section, refers to a scenario where the once-unassailable sovereignty of the State can be leveraged to allow politically justified transformative process to occur in contradiction of the mostly passive role permitted by the law of occupation. However, the political and legal legitimacy of such practices are, obviously, quite different considerations. The most significant problem with this is its seeming disregard of the world's colonial history. However, to this, it could be suggested that within the context of intervention in a host State, there is a single fundamental difference between 'soft-sovereignty' driven statebuilding, and 'colonialism': while the former asserts that the State is defined by the people themselves through the exercise of self-determination, the latter never did. On the other hand, even a more benevolent form of colonialism is still colonialism. However, it is notable that sovereignty, pre-eminently the right of the State, has been increasingly equated with self-determination, traditionally understood as the quite separate rights of the *people*, under international law.

Consequently, there is a line of thought that a State's sovereignty manifests not because it can display effective control over its territory, but because it has been legitimately granted to it by the people of that territory through effective and legitimate democratic practices. This is a notion that is especially popular withtin the discipline of philosophy, though its *normative* standing is considerably less assured. Friedrich Kratochwil in Chapter 3, for instance, posits that 'the people' are understood as a community that constitutes an on-going concern for the law, and from this concern, the concept of the 'nation' is born. It is this nation, characterised not by the artificial trappings of the 'juridical' state, but by the presumed 'naturalness' of a common ancestral identity, that lends legitimacy to the 'state'. This is not the place where the positivist legal framework currently presides, but undoubtedly, as the law pursues a more effective paradigm of the state, it is certainly a possibility to consider.

This position includes the proposition that state sovereignty is bound up in the effective protection of fundamental human rights as an aspect of democratic legitimacy. In any case, statebuilding would then be based on the notion that the State had somehow failed to manifest these minimum standards of statehood and thus made it necessary for a third party to intervene in protection of the populace. Again, the stark contrast between political and legal legitimacy must be noted, as in international law neither democracy nor human rights are defining features of statehood. Rather, international law grants legal title as long as those elements codified by the 1933 Montevideo Convention on the Rights and Duties of States (further, Montevideo Convention), which lays out the custom relating to statehood, are met. These are '(a) permanent population; (b) defined territory; (c) government; and (d) capacity to enter into relations with other States'. Consequently, a justification for statebuilding following an argument of inability to meet standards of statehood would be insufficient. This must instead be found by drawing from the well of moral or political legitimacy.

Nevertheless, statebuilding policy and occupation law (which is part of international humanitarian law) draws from very similar thematic sources, and the extent of their convergence would constitute an important empirical enquiry. But as things stand, these processes are distinct and lead to different outcomes, and have not yet been entirely reconciled. Now, having briefly considered the thematic issues that dog this debate, the legal issues involved can be addressed.

The law of occupation vs the 'law of statebuilding'

The law of occupation derives from the application of principles of IHL on situations of belligerent occupation, and as such, the majority of the obligations imposed on occupants through the laws of armed conflict can be found in the Fourth Geneva Convention (GCIV), and Additional Protocol I (API) (Geneva Convention 1949; First Protocol Additional to the Geneva Conventions 1977). These focus particularly on preserving (and establishing) those rights located in, or analogous to, human rights treaties – for example, due process or fair trial entitlements for those prosecuted of criminal offences by the occupying authorities (Geneva Convention 1949: articles 64–78), or prohibiting the punishment of civilians for 'collective crimes' not directly attributable to them as in reprisals or sanctions targeted at specific groups (Geneva Convention 1949: article 33). Curiously, GCIV itself does not define the meaning of 'occupying power', instead endorsing that used in article 42 of the *Hague Regulations* with which it shares a deferential relationship (Geneva Convention 1949: article 154).

Thus, an occupation occurs when hostile armed forces have assumed effective control over a foreign territory. As explained in article 42 of the Hague Regulations of 1907, '[territory] is considered occupied when it is actually placed under the authority of the hostile army. The occupation extends only to the territory where such authority has been established and can be exercised'. This provides a factual threshold, specifying that territory is occupied 'when it is actually placed under the authority of the hostile army' (Hague Convention IV 1910: article 42). For von Glahn, the indicators of factual occupation (and therefore *legal occupation*) are the subjugation of the entire territory to the powers of the occupant, and its ability to impose its will on them (von Glahn 1957: 29). As the International Criminal Tribunal for the Former Yugoslavia (ICTY) pointed out in *Naletilic*, the law of occupation is generally triggered when a third State gains effective control of a territory without legal justification (*Prosecutor v. Naletilic* 2003: para 217). When this standard is met, the situation becomes a matter for the law of occupation, whose framework is fashioned to provide the occupying powers sufficient flexibility in installing the infrastructure necessary for its basic security, and for the peoples of the occupied territories, during a period of temporary engagement.

Whilst the human rights obligations protected by IHL are largely concordant with typical statebuilding efforts, it is the necessity of preserving existing legal and institutional infrastructure that is the hallmark of occupation law. The occupant is granted no right of title by virtue of the occupation, and is therefore obliged in law to preserve the *status quo ante*. Consequently this fundamentally prohibits the possibility of any major statebuilding effort not necessary for the immediate undertaking of regional stability. This conservationist line demands respect for the previous legal regime and political system of the State. Accordingly, article 43 of the *Hague Regulations* requires the occupier 'take all measures in his power to restore, and ensure, as far as possible, public order and safety, while respecting, unless absolutely prevented, the laws in force in the Country' (Hague Convention IV 1910: article 43). This was folded into GCIV, though article 64 provides that some changes were possible where existing infrastructure presented a threat to the security of the occupant or prohibited the effective implementation of the Convention (Geneva Convention 1949: article 64). It states that the population of the State may be subjected to provisions

> ... essential to enabling the Occupying Power to fulfil its obligations under [the fourth Geneva Convention], to maintain the orderly government of the territory and to ensure the security of the Occupying Power, of the members and property of the occupying forces or administration, and likewise of the establishment and lines of communication used by them.
>
> (Geneva Convention 1949: article 64).

In summary, where occupation law applies, it strictly binds the hand of the occupier and heavily restricts the occupier's ability to make any changes to the structure of the State – effectively only permitting changes that are necessary for humanitarian purposes. The intention of this design is to ensure that the occupier, who is *not appointed via the will of the people*, may only act in a transitional capacity until the duly appointed sovereign can assume its proper position. Consequently, the legitimacy of statebuilding efforts will *de jure* depend on whether the law of occupation was applied correctly.

Occupation law will not apply where the nature of the statebuilding intervention is not actually a case of occupation. It may, for instance, be an example of external assistance, where the factual test of occupation – a physical military presence on the territory that local authorities are subordinate to – is not present. Undoubtedly, this can only be determined by assessing the individual circumstances of each case of territorial imposition to determine the nature of the relationship between intervening and host State. However, it should be acknowledged that an initial invitation is not a permanent license for the assisting authority, and the nature of this relationship can change. In such a case, the factual threshold for an occupation should be applied to determine the applicable law.

This kind of situation does, to some degree, highlight some of the limitations of determining occupation as a factual threshold. Consider, for instance, a case where the external power effectively subordinates the inviting authority, perhaps due to institutional and governmental weakness. Thus, without necessarily requiring a physical military presence, a third party can pursue a similar statebuilding enterprise, perhaps through a proxy government or by couching its agenda in the more familiar rhetoric of regional integration, whilst avoiding the protective shield of occupation law. For instance, whilst David Chandler in Chapter 8 views EU enlargement in the Balkans as an opportunity to invest political responsibility in the 'candidate' countries whilst holding 'Western domination' or 'empire strategies' of the EU at bay, without careful management, nothing necessarily exists to prevent such a strategy taking over. This is, to some degree, a problem of the law recognising form over substance, though to some, this is not necessarily troubling at all.

In any case, if a factual occupation by an external military force has taken place, it is then necessary to determine whether there is legal justification for the interference of this third party on the receiving State. This process is easily convoluted when the occupation purports to pursue a transformative agenda well beyond the typical maintenance of status quo attributed by occupation law. Here, it is helpful to classify statebuilding in more concrete terms. The defining feature of statebuilding is its interventionist, transformational agenda. Chesterman (2004: 5) provides a useful working definition of statebuilding as:

> Extended international involvement (primarily, though not exclusively, through the United Nations) that goes beyond traditional peacekeeping and peace building mandates, and is directed at constructing or reconstructing institutions of governance capable of providing citizens with physical and economic security. This includes quasi-governmental activities such as electoral assistance, human rights and rule of law technical assistance, security sector reform, and certain forms of development assistance.

McGurk (2004–5: 454) considers the following activities as vital, but still prohibited under the law of occupation:

> Building transparent and accountable institutions; implementing power-sharing arrangements; reforming legal codes to protect human rights; reforming economic codes to foster growth and development; fostering representative capacities within formerly disenfranchised groups; and, structuring and carrying out genuine and credible multi-party elections.

This makes it clear that democracy-building and institution-transforming strategies that typify statebuilding do not find a solid basis in IHL. In fact, according to this legal regime, the purpose of post-conflict operations is strictly to tidy up after the devastation of combat. Occupying powers are intended to have a temporary presence, have no democratic basis for their authority, and should not seek to impose *long-term or permanent* changes to the functions or institutions of the State. In regards to the occupations in Kosovo, East Timor, Liberia, and Bosnia and Herzegovina, third-party actors had actual effective control of territory, but in these circumstances, the law of occupation was not specifically applied because the IHL regime was superseded by a more specific arrangement that had been established between the parties when these missions were first constructed.

The most common statebuilding scenarios are UN or UN-sanctioned missions. These typically derive their legal basis from one of two different sources – consent provides the best kind of legal justification, but Chapter VII Security Council mandates are equally valid. These justifications are largely uncontroversial, and are consequently the most desirable triggers for occupation. These kinds of occupation are likewise beneficial to the sending State/States because such arrangements considerably disperse the responsibilities and accountability that would otherwise be directly attributed to them had they intervened unlawfully (International Law Commission 2001: article 20). In the case of UN-authorised missions, the occupation will be based either on a Chapter VII mandate obliging the local government to accede to the incursion, or via a prior agreement between the UN and local authorities. Where the State has consented to the intervention, the legal basis and terms of the occupation will be strictly determined between the parties and found in the Status of Forces Agreement (SOFA) between them. In most cases, significant transformative efforts will not be permitted. These legal grounds have been engineered to present the best balance of outside and local interests.

But in what circumstances and to what extent is statebuilding permissible in these kinds of situations? Recent occupations have drawn considerable attention to occupation law's perceived failings in demanding that the status quo be held, particularly when the vanquished powers were perceived to have artificially perpetuated their authority by propagating grossly illegitimate institutions of power, based in artificial legal, political, and economic networks. Naturally, it cannot be asserted that such systems reflected the 'will of the people'. From a global governance perspective, it is undoubted that the reform of a formerly derelict State is a public good, particularly where the society itself was at risk of failing, which would have devastating international consequences.

Reflection on the legitimacy of statebuilding efforts requires, to some extent, consideration of the specific issues and methods of law-making adopted by the mission. Thus, consider the UN-authorised mission to Kosovo. The United Nations Interim Administration Mission in Kosovo (UNMIK) was created through UNSC Resolution 1244, which authorized:

> [The establishment of an] international civil presence in Kosovo in order to provide an interim administration for Kosovo under which the People of Kosovo can enjoy substantial autonomy within the Federal Republic of Yugoslavia, and which will provide transitional administration while establishing and overseeing the development of provisional democratic self-governing institutions to ensure conditions for a peaceful and normal life for all inhabitants of Kosovo.
>
> (UNSC 1999)

With the UN assuming governance responsibilities, it would not be reasonable to expect it to function effectively or responsibly without effective legislation. Whilst local laws would be *prima facie* applicable here, it was impossible to employ these wholesale because numerous existing laws generally violated the international human rights norms that formed the international *de minimis* standard. Consequently, the mission struck a balance between human rights and the decades-old domestic legal system that had been previously in place by requiring the local authorities, when applying the existing laws, to review their legitimacy and viability in light of contemporary human rights expectations. As Ambassador Hans Corell, former Under-Secretary-General for Legal Affairs and Legal Counsel of the United Nations observed:

> The Secretary-General decided that no legislation was to be promulgated in Kosovo unless it had been vetted by the UN Secretariat and, in particular, by the Department of Peacekeeping Operations and the Office of Legal Affairs … [as our] main concern was that nothing in the legislation promulgated in Kosovo could be allowed to violate international human rights standards.
>
> (Corell 2005: 33)

The process of institutional change was not without its challenges, and these on occasion have highlighted the tensions discussed in this chapter. For instance, Corell (2005: 33) points out that there were genuine tensions between the UN Secretariat and Member States when it came to the privatisation of public property. He notes that

> [it] is well known that it is difficult to create a viable economy without a proper land registry and privately owned property that can be used as collateral in financing enterprises. But privatization is a very delicate matter and has to be done properly, taking many interests into consideration.

Likewise, under UNSC Res 1244, the Secretary-General was authorised to form an international civilian presence in order to provide a transitional administration allowing Kosovars to enjoy autonomy whilst establishing a democratic self-governing authority. This group had responsibility for performing major administrative functions, including ensuring human rights protections and the maintenance of law and order, and overseeing institutions to ensure that democratic elections could be conducted effectively. The successful administration of these tasks was quintessential to augmenting the legitimacy of UNMIK. But this proved particularly challenging because of the communication issues faced by the international civilian presence with locals, and the seriousness and pervasiveness of the corruption and ethnic bias that had eaten its way through the government and judiciary.

As has been noted, the occupation of Iraq was a defining point not only in world affairs, but in the law governing occupation as well. According to Charlesworth (2007: 236), it was not until the occupation of Iraq that the IHL lens was applied to modern statebuilding enterprises because, in the past, most situations could either infer 'a form of consent to statebuilding' by the receiving

State, or were legally sanctioned via the Security Council, as in Kosovo and East Timor. The situation in Iraq was a maelstrom inside a teacup, and presented the UNSC with a *fait accompli*. Whilst most members of the Council believed that occupation was illegal and unsupportable, the occupation had already occurred *in reality*. Some may recall that there was considerable pressure on the UN at the time, when it was faced with this dilemma. Indeed, it came under heavy fire for its inability to restrain the illegal invasion of Iraq. The situation had reached a boiling point, and given the fact of occupation, there had been a clear and obvious breach of international peace and security. Thus, the Security Council had little choice but to support 'the authority' (the US-led occupation). In 2004, the Council adopted Res. 1483, which backed the occupation in ensuring the welfare of Iraqis through 'the effective administration of territory, including in particular working towards the restoration of conditions of security and stability and the creation of conditions in which the Iraqi people can freely determine their own political future' (UNSC 2003b).

Much has been made in academic circles of the 'example' set by the Coalition Authorities in Iraq. In particular, it has been argued that this situation clearly illustrates the 'inexcusable gulf between what international law clearly permits and what any successful statebuilding exercise requires' (McGurk 2004–5: 452). Independent, external occupations are generally subject to occupation law, which in the case of the Coalition in Iraq, was quickly acknowledged, albeit not particularly well followed. This of itself was somewhat surprising – typically, States are reluctant to subject themselves to the full *de jure* force of the law of occupation, because they believe 'whether or not justified, that [their] situation differs significantly from the typical case of occupation' (Scheffer 2003: 843). Thus it should not have been a surprise when the occupying powers made explicit their determination to establish a democracy in Iraq *in knowing contravention of GCIV*. Charlesworth (2007: 241) describes the 'resolution' of the tensions between occupation law and the Coalition's political agenda as:

> the Coalition sidestepping international humanitarian law's principles allowing the good to clean up after the bad ... [that is], the Coalition harked back to a pre-Congress of Vienna tradition of the rights of the conqueror, which included the power of complete domination over local populations and the capacity to alter governmental structures in a permanent way.

In these situations, the launching point for most defences of statebuilding is that the existing law is an anachronism. This contention presupposes that occupation law does not reflect modern exigencies. Indeed, the law of occupation was originally developed for a purpose long since surpassed. That is, once upon a time, territorial control was a spoil of war, and the law of occupation distinguished between *belligerent* and *benevolent* occupation. Thus, as Roberts (2006: 601) avers, 'the traditional assumption of the laws of war is that bad ... occupants are occupying a good country' (or vice versa). Even then, the law made little distinction in the obligations imposed upon different occupation situations.

Whether peaceful or belligerent, the occupiers were not democratically elected, lacked sovereign authority, and were restricted from making significant long term changes. Even if there were any practical consequences arising from this distinction, these were essentially abandoned when GCIV codified a collective shift in the practice of occupation (both belligerent and pacific) that had made the protection of the rights and entitlements of the occupied peoples the main purpose of the IHL framework. In article 47, GCIV reinforces this position, asserting that the specific protections provided to the peoples of occupied territories remain in force regardless of any changes made through occupations, regardless of their origins – whether imposed or through convivial agreement between the authorities of the occupied State and the occupiers. What seems to distinguish occupation from statebuilding, despite sharing the same focus on the interests of the occupied populations, is *how* they interpret this obligation, and particularly, how significant a role human rights law (as opposed to *humanitarian law*) has to play.

Pro-statebuilding arguments are loosely based on the grounds that substantive changes were required (or at least permitted) by international human rights law, and that in the specific situation, intervention is necessary to manifest self-determination of the peoples. There are, of course, legitimate fears that a *de rigueur* application of IHL would present a real obstacle to the efforts of forces genuinely seeking to scour a state of the remnants of its previous despotism. Roberts (2006: 619), for instance, suggests this is the case when 'transformative' occupations are considered distinct from other manifestations of statebuilding in post-conflict societies. He suggests that such forms of statebuilding are akin to those where the consent of the receiving State has been given – and should be regulated in the same way. Accordingly, he desires a rebalancing of the strictly conservative tendencies of IHL and civil and political human rights norms. This is not completely unfounded in the law. It should be noted that the International Court of Justice (ICJ) had seemingly acknowledged that occupying forces were obliged to comply with human rights obligations in its Advisory Opinion on the *Legal Consequences of the Construction of a Wall in the Occupied Palestinian Territory* (2004). Whilst the ICJ does not explicitly suggest this may permit the alterations of laws or institutions, neither does it preclude this possibility. Irrespective of the view one takes on this position, it seems clear that any major renovations of the legal or administrative situations of occupied States must be brought under close scrutiny. The occupying forces must justify their actions, presumably utilising some form of necessity and proportionality standard as is typically found in IHL. Benvenisti (2005: 31) thus argues that

> as long as the restructuring of the political process and the market are compatible with the specific obligations imposed by the law of occupation (e.g. the protection of private and public property), or by human rights law (including the collective right to internal and external self-determination), the demands of the law of occupation would seem to be fulfilled.

Concluding comments

Moving from past to future, we would like to make some broad observations about the prospects of statebuilding operations. The purpose of transformative statebuilding is specific – it is about *changing* existing architecture and not about maintaining the (usually dysfunctional) State institutions as they stand presently. International actors interfere and assume governance of States because the State has failed to some degree, and intervention is needed to rebuild and transform these structures to respond to the needs and interests of the people (Chesterman 2007). Because of this, it is sometimes impractical to install local people in vital positions in new, transitional authorities. Admittedly, how true this is will depend on the degree of transformation and intervention that is needed in each circumstance. Indeed, there is considerable merit in the position that the legal framework for statebuilding must evolve. There have been many useful offerings on the kinds of new practices that must be integrated in such a process. Yet, it is easy to forget the dangers that are inherent in such processes. Kennedy asserts, for instance, that preferential treatment towards the legitimisation of war, which had otherwise lacked a legal basis, would threaten the 'sense of personal responsibility' that should be inherent in making decisions of this kind (Kennedy 2006). Charlesworth (2007: 243) likewise points out that the calls for such changes rest uneasily on the back of the US-Iraq example, where 'humanitarianism has failed so dramatically'. She sagely points out that the process of transformational statebuilding in Iraq could not be in any way considered a resounding success. How then can one justify future efforts of this kind? In light of new statebuilding efforts on the horizon it is now a better time than ever before to reflect on the issues that surround statebuilding, not only as an academic matter, but one that has a real and genuine impact on the function of international society today.

References

Annan, K. (1999) 'Two concepts of sovereignty', *The Economist*, 18 September.

Bain, W. (2003) 'The political theory of trusteeship and the twilight of international equality', *International Relations*, 17(1): 59–77.

Benvenisti, E. (2005) 'State building i: issues of choice, creation, and legal justification: applicability of the law of occupation', *Proceedings of the Annual Meeting – American Society of International Law*, 99: 29–31.

Charlesworth, H. (2007) 'Think pieces: law after war', *Melbourne Journal of International Law*, 8(2): 233–247.

Chesterman, S. (2004) *You, The People: The United Nations, Transitional Administration, and State-Building*, Oxford: Oxford University Press.

Chesterman, S. (2007) 'Ownership in theory and in practice: transfer of authority in UN statebuilding operations', *Journal of Intervention and Statebuilding*, 1(1): 3–26.

Corell, H. (2005) 'State building i: authorization for state-building missions: legal issues related to their creation and management', *Proceedings of the Annual Meeting – American Society of International Law*, 99: 29–35.

Geneva Convention relative to the Protection of Civilian Persons in Time of War of August 12, 1949 (opened for signature 12 August 1949, entered into force 21 October 1950) 75 UNTS 287 (GCIV).

Hague Convention (IV) respecting the Laws and Customs of War on Land, Annex to the Convention, Regulations respecting the Laws and Customs of War on Land (opened for signature 18 October 1907, entered into force 26 January 1910) (1910) UKTS (Hague Regulations).

International Law Commission (2001) *Articles on State Responsibility 2001*, Article 20.

Kennedy, D. (2006) *Of War and Law*, Princeton: Princeton University Press.

Legal Consequences of the Construction of a Wall in the Occupied Palestinian Territory (2004) ICJ Rep 136, 9 July.

McGurk, B. (2004–5) 'Revisiting the law of nation-building: Iraq in transition', *Virginia Journal of International Law*, 45: 451–467.

Osterhammel, J. (2005) *Colonialism: A Theoretical Overview*, 2nd edn, Princeton: Markus Wiener.

Prosecutor v. Naletilic (Judgment of 31 March 2003).

Protocol Additional to the Geneva Conventions of 12 August 1949 and relating to the Protection of Victims of International Armed Conflicts (opened for signature 8 June 1977, entered into force 7 December 1978) 1125 UNTS 3 (API).

Roberts, A. (2006) 'Transformative military occupation: applying the laws of war and human rights', *American Journal of International Law*, 100: 580–622.

Scheffer, D. (2003) 'Beyond occupation law', *American Journal of International Law*, 97(4): 842–860.

UNGA (United Nations General Assembly) (1950) UNGA Resolution 421(V) of 4 December.

UNGA (United Nations General Assembly) (1952) UNGA Resolution 545 (VI) of 5 February.

UNSC (United Nations Security Council) (1999) UNSC Res 1244, UN Doc S/RES/1244, 10 June.

UNSC (United Nations Security Council) (2002) UNSC Res 1441 UN Doc S/RES/1441, 8 Nov.

UNSC (United Nations Security Council) (2003a) 'Letter from the permanent representative of the United Kingdom of Great Britain and Northern Ireland and the United States of America to the United Nations addressed to the President of the Security Council', UN Doc S/2003/538, 8 May.

UNSC (United Nations Security Council) (2003b) UNSC Resolution 1483, UN Doc S/RES/1483, 22 May.

von Glahn, G. (1957) *The Occupation of Enemy Territory: A Commentary on the Law and Practice of Belligerent Occupation*, Minneapolis: University of Minnesota Press.

Wintour, P. (2007) 'We were over-optimistic about regeneration, Blair Adviser says', *The Guardian*, 13 September.

8 The semantics of 'crisis management'

Simulation and EU statebuilding in the Balkans

David Chandler

Introduction: crisis is not failure

In November 2007, the European Union (EU) circulated to its member state ambassadors an Institute Note by Judy Batt asserting that: 'The eruption of the long-simmering political crisis in Bosnia-Herzegovina has painfully exposed the failure of the most intensive effort ever at internationally-supervised statebuilding' (Batt 2007). However, to read the instability and uncertainty of the political system in Bosnia as a failure for the EU would be to assume that EU intervention in the Balkans was somehow a straightforward matter of technical facilitation and assistance. This chapter suggests that understanding the EU's interaction with the Balkans through statebuilding can more fruitfully be undertaken by considering the friction inherent in the relationship and in the contradictory agendas and dynamics at work in the operation of EU foreign policy in its Balkan 'backyard'. In so doing, it seeks to highlight that the semantics of 'crisis' are not co-determinate with policy failure; in fact, it seems that crisis, and responses to and the management of crises, form the central mechanisms through which the EU legitimates itself in relation to Bosnia.

Since the Dayton agreement brought the Bosnian war to an end in November 1995 Bosnian politics seems to have operated on the basis of moving from one serious political crisis to the next, all of which make the headlines one week but are swiftly forgotten as the next crisis comes along and the process is repeated again. Dayton established a federal Bosnian state composed of two entities: the Federation of Bosnia and Herzegovina, with a population mainly of Bosnian Muslims (Bosniaks) and Croats, and the Republika Srpska (RS), with a majority Bosnian Serb population. The central state institutions were relatively weak and over the last thirteen years international actors have focused on strengthening and legitimising these institutions with mixed success.

Each political crisis has been heralded as a make or break moment for peace in Bosnia, for the enlargement strategy of the European Union, or for Balkan stability. The crisis at the end of 2007 was typical in this regard as Richard Holbrooke, the US architect of the Dayton peace agreement, warned in the *Washington Post* that the situation in the tiny state was so severe that 'Bosnia's very survival could be determined in the next few months if not the next few weeks'

(Holbrooke 2007). As will be considered in more detail later in the chapter, this stand-off between Bosnian political elites and the international administrators of the state followed a long period of crisis-driven negotiations over police reforms, which counterposed a centralising international agenda against opposition, largely from the Bosnian Serb representatives. Delays, obstructions and disagreements resulted in delays in Bosnia being offered an EU Stabilisation and Association Agreement and in attempts by the High Representative to prevent obstruction through crisis management measures of reforming the procedures of the Bosnian state institutions. In response to these institutional reforms Bosnia's Serb prime minister Nikola Špirić resigned, bringing government to a standstill before compromise was reached and the statebuilding EU enlargement process resumed.

This chapter seeks to understand why the international and EU process of statebuilding in Bosnia appears to operate only through the semantics of political crisis management. It argues that crisis management is the norm rather than the exception and that it is only through the semantics of 'crisis' and its 'management' that international statebuilding operates in a context where all the major actors in the statebuilding process lack a coherent base of social support and lack a stable set of policy-making mechanisms. In developing this analysis it argues that the case of the EU and Bosnia provides a particularly sharp example of the breakdown of political legitimacy highlighted in Baudrillard's prescient work on the 'dissolution of the political subject'. Baudrillard argued that the end of political projects of Left and Right had created a crisis of representation, making the location and operation of power no longer clear. In the hollowing out of traditional mechanisms connecting elites with the masses through electoral representation, elites were much less able to give policy-making a broader social meaning (see Baudrillard 1983a: 19, 27). In the absence of close connections to their own societies, political elites face problems in legitimising their political power and, in response, seek to simulate the existence of political capacity, for example, through external projection (for example, Baudrillard 1987).

In traditional frameworks for understanding statebuilding, recurrent crises are seen to be problematic. This is as true from a technical 'problem-solving' perspective as exemplified in the policy advice of Batt above, as it is from a more critical or realist perspective which would highlight problems as indicating the difficulties of imposing external agendas against the resistance of local elites. In both traditional pro- and anti-statebuilding intervention literature, political crises and stand-offs indicate that there is a clash of interests (legitimate or not), which indicate that the process of intervention needs to be rethought or reformed. Baudrillard's work provides some potential insights into why crisis and crisis management may be much less problematic for both EU and Bosnian policy elites. It is particularly useful in formulating a critique of EU statebuilding which highlights the fundamental question of legitimacy as an internal problem as much as an external one for statebuilding actors. It is also distinct from the critique of the critical or realist approaches which understand the projection of power under the rubric of democratisation as dissimulation, feigning 'not to have what one has', i.e. as a pretence that policy is not driven by EU self-interest or the needs of business profitability (for example, Abrahamsen 2000; Gills 2000; Smith 2000; and for application of this critique, Weber 1995; Debrix 1999: 9–15). Crisis management becomes central once there is an understanding of policy practice in terms of simulation, which, for Baudrillard, 'is to feign to have what one hasn't', i.e. the pretence that the EU is a legitimate political actor with clear instrumental interests and ideological values which are being asserted through foreign policy (Baudrillard 1983b: 5).

For Baudrillard, the framework of theoretical understanding is therefore radically distinct from dominant International Relations approaches, based on the importance, not of a presence (of interests, of representation) but of an absence (a lack of social connection between elites and society and therefore of a lack of social power). The key point that Baudrillard makes is that the framework of grasping reality as dissimulation – the critical or realist critique of claims of 'value-based' policy-making alleged to be concerned with the promotion of democracy, human rights and good governance – 'leaves the reality principle intact, the difference [between the real and the illusory] is always clear, it is only masked'. However, 'simulation threatens the difference between "true" and "false", between "real" and "imaginary"' because 'the simulator produces "true" symptoms' or effects (Baudrillard 1983b: 5).

According to Baudrillard, 'the spectre raised by simulation' is that the effects of power may exist but that 'truth, reference and objective causes have ceased to exist' (Baudrillard 1983b: 5). The EU exercises power over the Balkan states, being regulated through the mechanisms of statebuilding, but through this process the fiction of competing and clear interests between internationals (cast ideologically as operating under the technical remits of promoting democracy, the rule of law and human rights) and local resistance (cast ideologically as nationalist, sectional and self-interested) continually play out and reproduce and legitimise each other. Baudrillard suggests that while it might appear that traditional discourses of power and interests are operating, in fact, what drives policy is less political self-interest (the product of the politics of representation) but more the politics of simulation: the attempt to hide power's inability to cohere and project self-interest. Simulation is the attempt to overcome, bypass or evade political elites' lack of legitimacy and connection with their own societies.

Baudrillard worked at a level of abstraction which this chapter seeks to use to give an insight into the process of EU statebuilding in Bosnia. Before turning to the concrete use of the semantics of 'crisis' and its reproduction it will be useful to flag up that Baudrillard draws on a double technique of simulation: first, the denial of the reality of the power of elites; and, second, the exaggeration of the power of others or of events in and of themselves.

First, Baudrillard (1983b: 37) argued that: 'Every form of power, every situation speaks of itself by denial, in order to escape, by simulation of death, its real agony. Power can stage its own murder to rediscover a glimmer of existence and legitimacy.' The EU itself is a product of the crisis of legitimacy of its member states – and the fundamental centrality of foreign policy to the EU's identity is in part reflective of the difficulties its members face in clearly articulating their 'national interests' (see, for example, Heartfield 2007). The EU, by necessity, enacts, in an exaggerated form, the techniques of simulation of its member states, whose 'crisis of representation' – or inability to present and project a socially rooted 'idea of the state' or clear political project or purpose (see Buzan 1991: 69–82) – it magnifies. In effect, the EU is a gigantic simulacrum as the product of the evasion and displacement of the problem of political legitimacy through the denial of power and the reproduction of this process of denial through the politics of simulation.

Second, Baudrillard argued that power hides its incapacity through the exaggeration of the problems which it confronts, through the production of the hyperreal:

> The only weapon of power, its only strategy against [its collapse], is to reinject realness and referentiality everywhere, in order to convince us of the reality of the social, of the gravity of the economy and the finalities of production. For that purpose it prefers the discourse of crisis.
>
> (Baudrillard 1983b: 42)

He argued that 'hyperreality and simulation are deterrents of every principle and of every objective' because policy is no longer organised around objective social threats and social problems. The response to the crisis of legitimacy is the idealised view of power's disappearance produced in part in the play of simulation and in part on the reliance upon crisis, 'it [power] gambles on remanufacturing artificial, social, economic, political stakes' (Baudrillard 1983b: 43–44). It will be suggested here that the construction of the hyperreal has been central to the dynamic of legitimacy of the EU, where alleged crises in the Balkans have continually necessitated new EU activity and mandates and institutional developments on the grounds that 'European values', 'European identity', or 'European security' are at stake in these developments. The EU exaggerates the forms of simulation apparent in member states' own attempts to use foreign policy to develop 'ethical identities' (see further, Chandler 2006) – making foreign policy the centre of its ideological and institutional attempts to constitute itself as a substitute symbol of political community to the nation-state. For the EU, every external measure, from trade regulations to foreign aid, to the sending of troops abroad, comes attached with the necessity of expressing the EU's alleged shared 'identity' and 'values' in the increasingly shrill and desperate simulation of these absent factors.

This is a process with little real relationship to either the policy object (in this case, the Balkans) or the simulator (the EU) itself. This lack of coherence or social grounding in either the object or subject of policy-making is reflected in the apparent autonomy manifested by the bureaucracy of the EU itself. This autonomy of the bureaucracy, brought into sharp focus by Baudrillard's framework, reveals the 'truth' of the mechanisms of power at play, and the way in which the practice of democracy promotion in Balkans reveals the lack of 'reality' of both the EU (as a coherent strategic actor) and of the Bosnian state (as an externally constructed fiction: a simulacrum). This autonomy is particularly highlighted where the power of the EU is most overt, in the position of the EU Special Representatives (SR), which wield executive power over Bosnia and (since the 2008 declaration of independence) Kosovo.

Enlargement: the 'mission' of the EU?

The importance of Europe's 'mission' to bring democracy, peace, human rights and good governance to the Balkans reveals the difficulty which the EU has in constructing its purpose or legitimacy on a purely domestic basis, without projecting power externally. The mission to transform and save the Balkans relies on the techniques of simulation, not just the simulation of the EU itself as a legitimate political actor bearing the trappings of a sovereign state, but also the denial of the EU's power, or rather the denial of the power of the EU member states, and the construction of a hyperreality of Balkan crisis.

According to the April 2005 report of the International Commission on the Balkans, chaired by Guiliano Amato, former Italian prime minister, *The Balkans in Europe's Future*:

> If the EU does not devise a bold strategy for accession that could encompass all Balkan countries as new members within the next decade, then it will become mired instead as a neo-colonial power in places like Kosovo, Bosnia and even Macedonia. Such an anachronism would be hard to manage and would be in contradiction with the very nature of the European Union. The real choice the EU is facing in the Balkans is: Enlargement or Empire.
>
> (ICB 2005: 11)

This quote sharply sums up the dilemma facing Western Europe, or the EU, with the end of the Cold War – how to relate to and manage its new eastern 'empire'. The response of the EU has been to engage in external regulation and relationship management interventions but at the same time deny that it is exercising its authority over the region. It is entirely appropriate for the international commission to pose the EU's policy choices as 'statebuilding' or 'empire' and it is this dilemma, this denial of power, which has driven the enlargement process. This denial of the new West/East hierarchy of European power, and the EU's de facto 'empire' to the east, has taken the form of democracy-promotion and statebuilding and the rapid extension and drawing out of the enlargement process to the Balkans.

Where the international commission is slightly out of step with reality is in the assertion that the question of 'Enlargement or Empire' was one being posed in 2005. In fact, it was essentially resolved in 1999 when, with the end of the Kosovo war in April, the European Union headed the beginning of an ambitious international experiment in statebuilding and democracy promotion in the Balkan region. Statebuilding has enabled the EU to project its power in the therapeutic framework of the liberal peace, of the capacity-building and empowerment of its eastern neighbours, rather than posing the questions of political responsibility which are raised with empire. Instead of posing the question of Europe's imperial mission – in concrete terms, what Europe stands for and what Europe represents in relation to a Balkan reality – statebuilding and democracy promotion shifts the focus to the governing regime of the potential candidates.

Statebuilding through democracy promotion involves no less expenditure of resources than empire, in fact, if anything, statebuilding is more invasive and regulatory. The EU has not been hesitant to intervene, merely reluctant to assume political responsibility for intervention. The statebuilding process of EU enlargement has been able to be highly regulatory precisely on the basis that the regulatory mechanisms invest political responsibility in the candidate countries while denying the EU's domination.

In the process of enlargement, the two drives of simulation – internally, with regard to the EU's purpose and coherence, and externally, with regard to the Balkans – intervention in the hyperreal (or the creation of crisis and its management) and the denial of power (denial of the asymmetric relations of power between the EU and the Balkans) come together in a particularly forceful way. The EU's experiments in shifting the political responsibilities of power away from Brussels have been described as implying no less than the 'reforming and reinventing [of] the state in South Eastern Europe'. As the European Stability Initiative observed:

> A new consensus is emerging among both regional and international actors that the most fundamental obstacle to the advance of democracy and security in South Eastern Europe is the lack of effective and accountable state institutions. Strengthening domestic institutions is increasingly viewed as the key priority across the diverse sectors of international assistance, as relevant to human rights and social inclusion as it is to economic development and democratisation.
>
> (ESI 2001: 18)

This is argued to be the special mission of the EU; the Commission argued that its focus on exporting democracy to the region through building the capacity of state institutions and civil society development reflected not only the importance of this question and the clear needs it had identified, 'but also the comparative advantage of the European Community in providing *real added value* in this area'. It would appear that the Balkan states were fortunate in that their wealthy neighbours to the West had not only identified their central problems but also happened to have the solutions to them already at hand (EC 2001a: 9).

The result of the EU's simulation of its 'mission' is the problematisation of the Balkans, of both the states and the societies which it exercises power over. It is important to note, from the start, the artificial and somewhat forced nature of the justifications for the EU's statebuilding project. The problems identified in the governance sphere were not with the formal mechanisms of democratic government or the electoral accountability of government representatives, but were concerns that went beyond procedural questions of 'free and fair elections' to the administrative practices and policy choices of governments and the attitude, culture and participation-levels of their citizens. Regarding institution-building, the European Commission asserted that:

> The lack of effective and accountable state institutions hampers the ability of each country to co-operate with its neighbours and to move towards the goal of closer integration with the EU. Without a solid institutional framework for the exercise of public power, free and fair elections will not lead to representative or accountable government. Without strong institutions to implement the rule of law, there is little prospect that states will either provide effective protection of human and minority rights or tackle international crime and corruption.
>
> (EC 2001a: 9)

Where, only a few years previously, free and fair elections were seen to be the main indicator of representative and accountable government, institution-building was now held to be the key to democratic development. According to the Commission, strengthening state institutions was vital for 'assuring the region's future, being as relevant to human rights and social inclusion as it is to economic development and democratisation' (EC 2001a: 9). While the Balkan states met the traditional democratic criteria, necessary for the incorporation of new members, such as Spain and Portugal, into Europe-wide mechanisms in the past, they were now held to fail to meet the new, more exacting, standards which are being laid down for membership of European bodies at present (Storey 1995).

Regarding the second aspect of governance, civil society, the Commission was even more forthright in its condemnation of the aspiring members involved in the Stabilisation and Association process:

> [N]one of the countries can yet claim to have the level of vibrant and critical media and civil society that is necessary to safeguard democratic advances. For example, public and media access to information, public participation in policy debate and accountability of government and its agencies are aspects of civil society which are still largely undeveloped in all five of the countries.
>
> (EC 2001b: 10–11)

In this case, the applicant states from the Balkan region could apparently not even make a 'claim' that they could safeguard 'democracy' in their states without external assistance in the form of democracy promotion and capacity-building. In fact, the Commission was clearly concerned by society in the region as much as by government, arguing that the aim of its new programmatic development was necessarily broad in order 'to entrench a culture … which makes forward momentum towards the EU irreversible' (EC 2002: 8).

The process of constructing a Balkan hyperreality in order to construct the EU's mission and domestic legitimacy is that of simulation. The precondition for the EU's 'member state building' in the Balkans is the formal and informal subsumption and subordination of the region. The Balkans are already integrated into the EU and this is precisely the problem posed by the region: its 'real' regional subordination to the EU. It is the dependency of the Balkan states on EU policy-makers and EU policy that makes the process of 'integration' necessarily an exercise in simulation – one that is only necessary because of the EU's own perception of its lack of legitimacy and its unease with taking political responsibility for policy-making in the Balkans. The simulation of policy-making creates a hyperreality of Bosnia and Kosovo where the discursive language of choice is that of crisis (Baudrillard 1983b: 42). The EU actively seeks to deny its political subjectivity by denying its power to make policy and in so doing reveals its 'real' lack of political subjective capacity. The EU's 'inability to produce the real' is reflected in its creation of the Balkan threat – the hyperreal – simulating the EU's incapacity to take political responsibility for its power at the same time as multiplying its 'truth effects', its interventionist impact in the region.

The politics of emergency and the discourse of crisis is a simulation, but a real and necessary one. Europe's 'big challenge' in another context, where power was confident of its capacity and the legitimacy of its project, would be no challenge at all. As former international High Representative and EU Special Representative from 2002 to 2006, Paddy Ashdown argues, the Balkans are a 'relatively tiny morsel' for the EU to swallow, with their tiny populations and tiny economies (Ashdown 2007: 118). The EU has already spent €2 billion in Kosovo since 1999 and will provide a further €1.5 billion to finance its proposed office of the International Civilian Representative. The EU's formal assumption of the management of Kosovo is being described as 'the moment of Europe'. Kosovo is a re-run of Bosnia as declarations are made of Europe's mission. This is simulation, as the values and purpose of the EU are not at stake in Bosnia and Kosovo except in so far as the EU chooses to portray its relationship to the region in these terms.

In fact, this is a double simulation, first, evading where the EU's values and purpose are in question – i.e. within the member states of the EU whose populations are unlikely to be able to vote on any new version of the European Constitution – and, second, evading the 'real' political power and responsibility exercised over the Balkans and recreating the Balkans as a 'hyperreal' foreign and external challenge to the EU. Kosovo, 'crisis what crisis?' argued the Russian ambassador to the UK, Yury Fedotov, who stated that there were plenty of de facto states without de jure recognition (BBC 2007; see also Harding 2007). What is the lurking dark threat of 'inaction' over Kosovo? The EU was in a rush to give Kosovo its 'independence' to legitimise its regulation and integration of Kosovo through the process of denying its own power and simulating its 'death' as an imperial actor through Kosovo's 'emancipation' as an independent state.

Within this framework, the process of hoops of 'integration' for Balkan states to jump through, such as the Stabilization and Association process, can be seen as not so much about integrating the Balkans as attempts to distance the Balkans from the EU; in other words, attempts to avoid the questions of the capacity of the EU to represent reality, to assert real power and responsibility over the region. Bosnia is a new type of state, being built through this process of simulation. Bosnia is a powerful example of the reality of the effects of simulation, of the EU's need to simulate the exercise of power by distancing power and political responsibility.

To all intents and purposes Bosnia is a member of the European Union; in fact more than this, Bosnia is the first genuine EU state where sovereignty has in effect been transferred to Brussels (no other state is as integrated as this one). The EU provides its government; the international High Representative is an EU employee and the EU's Special Representative in Bosnia. The EU administrator has the power to directly impose legislation and to dismiss elected government officials and civil servants. EU policy and 'European Partnership' priorities are imposed directly through the European Directorate for Integration. The EU also runs the police force (having taken over from the United Nations at the end of 2002) and the military (taken over from NATO at the end of 2004) and manages Bosnia's negotiations with the World Bank. One look at the Bosnian flag – with the stars of the EU on a yellow and blue background chosen to be in exactly the same colours as used in the EU flag – demonstrates the Bosnia is more EU-orientated than any current member state.

However, the EU has distanced itself from any responsibility for the power it exercises over Bosnia; formally Bosnia is an independent state and member of the United Nations and a long way off meeting the requirements of EU membership. After thirteen years of statebuilding in Bosnia there is now a complete separation between power and accountability. This clearly suits the EU which is in a position of making policy with regard to the tiny state without either admitting it into membership of the EU or presenting its policy regime in strict terms of external conditionality. Bosnia is neither an EU member nor does it appear to be a colonial protectorate, the relationship does not appear to be one of formal equality or one of formal inequality – in fact, the relationship between the two (and their separation as separate entities) is hard to locate. Power seems to have no location, to have disappeared, through this process of denial and simulation.

Promoting 'independence' and 'democracy' in the Balkans?

The EU works best when it is in denial of its power and of political responsibility: this denial is the source of its legitimacy (as the simulated state of 'Europe' – post-sovereign, post-national, post-interest-driven) (see also Laïdi 1998: 13; Baudrillard 1987: 55). The EU needs Kosovo to have 'independence' and sovereignty (as Bosnia does), so the exercise of power can be presented as 'empowering' – as facilitation, as 'statebuilding', as capacity-building, increasing the independence, autonomy, democratic accountability, human rights, rule of law, etc. in the Balkans. But the EU has portrayed the Balkans as alien and as problematic: as hyperreal, as 'in crisis'. The export of the solutions of freedom, autonomy, democracy, self-determination only reveal the simulation involved in denying power and simulating the existence of Balkan crisis. The simulation of executive and legislative powers under EU control as 'democracy-promotion' flows from the simulation of the Balkans as alien and crisis-ridden. The mission of simulation results in the dialectic of distancing and domination.

This dialectic of simulation was revealed in the initial 1995 settlement where the Bosnian parties formally invited the external powers to develop their own mandates, creating the simulation of sovereignty rather than the 'reality' of a protectorate (see Weber 1995: 126–7). This process was reproduced with the stage-management of Kosovo's independence in early 2008 as a basis for the reproduction of the EU's administrative role in Bosnia. As Baudrillard wrote in *The Precession of Simulcra*, in terms of the external export of democracy to Bosnia:

> From now on, it is impossible to ask the famous question: 'From what position do you speak?' – 'How do you know?' – 'From where do you get the power?', without immediately getting the reply: 'But it is of (from) you that I speak' – meaning, it is you who speaks, it is you who knows, power is you.
>
> (Baudrillard 1983b: 77–8)

This process of external power imposed on the basis of the will of the Bosnian people as manifested not through representation but simulation (through the will of the EU Special Representative) was clearly articulated in EUSR Paddy Ashdown's inaugural speech of May 2002:

> I have concluded that there are two ways I can make my decisions. One is with a tape measure, measuring the precise equidistant position between three sides. The other is by doing what I think is right for the country as a whole. I prefer the second of these. So when I act, I shall seek to do so in defence of the interests of all the people of Bosnia and Herzegovina, putting their priorities first.
>
> (Ashdown 2002)

Here representation – the representation of Bosnian voters through the ballot box and expressed in the electoral support for three ethnic parties – is explicitly seen to be a problem for Bosnian society, as preventing the will of the people from being collectively manifested (see Bildt 1998: 139). In order for Bosnian people to be truly represented 'as a whole', Ashdown argued that it was necessary for him to act as their representative against the political parties (held to be unrepresentative). The Bosnian electorate and their will were simulated by Ashdown and at the same time the alien and external power of the EUSR was denied; he was not imposing his or the EU's will, but merely the will of the people.

This denial of power was taken even further in the shift (under Ashdown's rule) from the power of the Office of the High Representative to that of the EU Special Representative, which was dressed up in the emancipatory language of democratisation, away from the 'push' of the Bonn powers to the 'pull' of Brussels. Here the imposition of EU policy proposals was reposed as a voluntary choice deriving from the desire to 'join' Europe, rather than from the imposed external oversight of the Dayton settlement. This simulation now meant that Bosnian politicians were forced to 'freely' choose to implement EU programmes rather than having them imposed by edict. In 2006, Ashdown was interviewed on whether the shift from 'Bonn to Brussels' made any difference from the point of view of Bosnian representatives and citizens:

> Yes, it makes a huge difference. If it is imposed with a stick then the consequence is dependency ... It takes a great deal of strength to be able to say: 'No, we are not going to do this. You have to do it yourself.' We have to be patient enough for the country to set back a bit when this happens ... They have more independence because they are no longer supported by the use of the High Representative's powers. Europe has said that if reforms are imposed via the High Representative's powers then Bosnia cannot join...
>
> Is Europe acting in a quasi-imperialist fashion? Yes, but the difference is that it is up to people to say no if they want to. This is still persuasion, it is not coercion. I think it is perfectly legitimate for Brussels to say: 'Guys here are the rules, if you want to join the club you have to conform to the standards. If you conform to them fine, but if you do not want to you do not have to join.' It was very difficult for the Republika Srpska parliamentary assembly to agree to abolish their army and put it at the disposal of state institutions, but *they did it, not me*. It was a free vote in the Bosnian Serb parliament, I did not impose it. I may have told them it would be a good thing and that if you want to get into NATO you have to, but it was they who took the final decision.
>
> (Ashdown 2007: 113–15)

Here, Ashdown forwards a subtle distinction between direct imposition, where the EU potentially bears direct policy-responsibility, and the policy of indirect imposition, where Bosnia's elected representatives are held to be freely choosing certain policy prescriptions. The difference between these approaches may be important for the EU but makes little difference to Bosnian representatives or to the Bosnian public who are confronted with proposals drawn up by external actors. In neither framework is there any genuine debate between Bosnian parties or any role for local actors in the development of policy-making. In fact, in the case of imposition by the High Representative there is at least the clarification of power relations between the EU and the Bosnian state, even if there is the practice of simulation in the assertion that the external bureaucrat is merely ruling in the interests of the Bosnian people themselves.

Bosnia's formal international legal sovereignty gives the appearance that it is an independent entity, voluntarily engaged in hosting its state capacity-building guests. Questions of aligning domestic law with the large raft of regulations forming the EU *aquis* appear as ones of domestic politics. There is no international forum in which the contradictions between Bosnian social and economic demands and the external pressures of Brussels' policy prescriptions can be raised. However, these questions are not ones of domestic politics. The Bosnian state has no independent or autonomous existence outside of the EU 'partnership'. There are no independent structures capable of articulating alternative policies. Politicians are subordinate to international institutions through the mechanisms of governance established which give EU bureaucrats and administrators the final say over policy-making. The Bosnian state is a phantom state (a simulacra); but it is definitely not a fictional creation. The Bosnian state plays a central role in the transmission of EU policy priorities in their most intricate detail. The state here is an inversion of the sovereign state. Rather than representing a collective political expression of Bosnian interests – expressing self-government and autonomy – 'Westphalian sovereignty' in the terminology of statebuilders – the Bosnian state is an expression of an externally driven agenda.

The more Bosnia has been the subject of external statebuilding and democracy promotion, the less like a traditional state it has become. Here, the state is a mediating link between the 'inside' of domestic politics and the 'outside' of international relations, but rather than clarifying the distinction it removes the distinction completely. The imposition of an international agenda of capacity-building and good governance appears internationally as a domestic question and appears domestically as an external, international matter. Where the representative sovereign state clearly demarcated lines of policy accountability, the state without sovereignty blurs them. In fact, 'the politics of the real' – political responsibility for policy-making – disappears with the removal of sovereignty (see also Weber 1995: 127).

Democracy, in so far as it can be said to exist in the form of elections etc., has no relationship to policy-making. The simulation of representation in Bosnia and Kosovo could now be said to be complete under the reign of the EU democracy exporters and statebuilders. The EU's exercise of its power creates simulated states in its own image, where the death of representation, disappearance of power and the existence of bureaucracy isolated from society, takes its most grotesque forms.

Arbitrary power: the EU 'special representatives'

In the Balkans the EU Special Representative to Bosnia and Herzegovina, who also holds the Office of the High Representative, and the EU Special Representative in Kosovo, who has assumed the position of the International Civilian Representative, represent only arbitrary power. Their powers are arbitrary both vis-à-vis the EU and vis-à-vis Balkan society. The EU Special Representatives operate (there are nine at present, ten with the finalisation of the post-status arrangements in Kosovo) formally under the direction of the EU's 'High Representative for Common Foreign and Security Policy' (CFSP). Javier Solana, is currently the High Representative for CFSP. The post is often termed the EU's Minister of Foreign Affairs (a post which is alleged to have failed to become a 'reality' with the failure of the Constitutional treaty).

While in the realm of internal EU politics there is little clarity where political responsibility lies, whether at the level of member states or in EU forums, it seems that the further EU power stretches away from Brussels the more it appears capable of simulating itself as an independent political entity (not a composite of member nation states). It is only in the international arena that the EU comes into its own, where its representatives take on political power which is separated from the national governments comprising the EU. In fact, it is only in the international arena – where the EU is most free to simulate state-like attributes – that individuals have the authority to represent the EU as an independent political entity. They are aided in this in the Balkans by the EUSRs having the power of autonomy from the EU at the same time as 'representing' the EU; this is because they are 'double-hatted' with the ad hoc authority of the Peace Implementation Council in Bosnia and the International Steering Group with regard to Kosovo.

This means that nowhere is the power of the EU, as an independent actor standing independently and above its member governments, felt more powerfully than in the Balkans, where the High Representative and the International Civilian Representative for Kosovo have executive authority to make legislation and sack elected local political representatives. In one way, the EU's Special Representatives symbolize the end of representation. The EU is the embodiment of the rejection of sovereignty yet its 'representatives' represent sovereign power in Bosnia and Kosovo. They represent sovereign power without sovereignty. They represent neither the people of Bosnia and Kosovo nor, directly, the EU. Rather, the simulated nature of both the EU as a policy actor and the Balkan states as objects of democratisation and empowerment produces a relationship of ad hoc and arbitrary power.

This power is arbitrary in the sense of having no fixed or cohered relationship to society. This flexibility has been exemplified by the extension of the powers of the High Representative since Dayton, one incumbent explaining that his process was one which has no fixed limits: 'if you read Dayton very carefully … Annex 10 even gives me the possibility to interpret my own authorities and powers' (*Slobodna Bosna* 1997). The pattern of ad hoc and arbitrary extensions of international regulatory authority was initially set by the Peace Implementation Council (PIC) itself as it rewrote its own powers and those of the High Representative at successive meetings. The most important of these were the initial strategic six-monthly review conferences: at Florence, in June 1996; Paris, in November 1996; Sintra, in May 1997; Bonn, in December 1997; and Luxembourg, in June 1998.

In Bosnia the EUSR clearly manifests the imploding nature of the continual play of simulations, where every issue is held to manifest the 'values' of the EU and the crisis of Bosnia. In fact, the tying of reform to EU membership has made nearly every policy issue one of crisis for both parties, and has made crisis the normal form in which EU enlargement is negotiated in the interests of both parties. Crisis enables the EU to emphasise the problems of exporting its post-national and cosmopolitan values to less Europeanised states (see Zaum 2007) and enables Bosnian elites to evade responsibility for policy-making by grand-standing until the EU backs down or imposes a temporary solution. This process of crisis and swings between sweeteners and the use of coercion to keep the enlargement process on track reduces even the most political of questions to ones of bureaucratic procedure. This was clearly manifest in the regular crises over cooperation with the International Criminal Tribunal for the former Yugoslavia (ICTY), where negotiations on membership for several states were suspended over allegations of a failure to cooperate, and the bureaucratic imperative of cooperation meant that many alleged war criminals voluntarily surrendered and were waved off to The Hague with full military and political honours, seen as heroes, not so much for their role in the war, but for their willingness to sacrifice their freedom for the country's entry to the EU.

Ashdown, in particular, has been held to have overplayed his hand in seeking to use the EU (and NATO) to support his reform plans by seeking to make policy-reform a precondition for progress towards membership. This was highlighted, in particular, with the issue of police reform which dominated the last years of Ashdown's term. Ashdown wanted the abolition of entity-based police forces and the centralisation of police authority. However, he was on a very weak footing in linking his plans with EU membership, overpoliticising the issue of reform, and perpetuating the hyperreality of crisis over the reform process.

While Ashdown invoked the leverage of the 'pull of Brussels' to impose these major reform proposals, it was clear that he was acting independently of Brussels and the wishes of the European Commission. The Commission viewed Ashdown's actions as destabilising Bosnia's relations with the EU and considered the EU Special Representative to be on weak ground politically, as the Swiss, German and Belgian models, which had been specifically looked at in more detail, definitely did not follow the centralised approach intended for Bosnia. The European Commission were reluctant for Ashdown to use the issue for a political showdown and gave the Bosnian representatives evasive signals, encouraging opposition to the proposals, and were pleased to see Ashdown's radical plans eventually watered down (Muehlmann 2008).

The political reflections of this are manifest in local political 'representatives' who do not need to (and cannot) take responsibility for policy-making, knowing either that the EU will impose its will by diktat or back down and change its policy proposals so as not to risk the enlargement process. Because all that remains of the domestic political process is simulation, so-called 'policy-making' – the assent to external will – becomes a simulation exercise and therefore either a crisis in the relationship between Bosnian representatives and the Special Representative or between Bosnia and the EU. Therefore, this process is much more problematised than a 'real' exercise of political decision-making (one of representation) which necessarily involves compromise and negotiation around problems arising from and related to that society.

Conclusion

This chapter has argued that Baudrillard's concepts of simulation and hyperreality are useful to provide insights into the semantics of 'crisis' and 'crisis management' at the heart of the European Union's policy-making process with regard to democracy promotion and statebuilding in the Balkans. The use of this framework suggests that the EU lacks the internal legitimacy to coherently act as an external statebuilding actor and that, in fact, the more it attempts to find legitimacy through projecting power over the Balkans the less rational its policy processes become. It further suggests that the EU's domination of the Balkans takes the form of a denial of power and exaggeration and overpoliticisation of the relations between the EU and the Balkan potential members, through the hyperreal construction of the problems of enlargement. It further suggests that the outcome of the process of simulation is less the export of democracy than the export of power in an ad hoc and arbitrary manner and in the creation of states which are simulated – which are ciphers for external power rather than linked to their own societies.

References

Abrahamsen, R. (2000) *Disciplining Democracy: Development Discourse and Good Governance in Africa*, London: Zed Books.

Ashdown, P. (2002) 'Inaugural speech by the new High Representative for Bosnia and Herzegovina', Bosnian State Parliament, 27 May. Available at: www.ohr.int/ohr-dept/presso/presssp/default.asp?content_id=8417.

Ashdown, P. (2007) 'The European Union and statebuilding in the Western Balkans', *Journal of Intervention and Statebuilding*, 1(1): 107–118.

Batt, J. (2007) 'Bosnia and Herzegovina: politics as "war by other means" challenge to the EU's strategy for the Western Balkans', *Institute Note, Institute for Security Studies*, IESUE/COPS/INF(07)09, 19 November.

Baudrillard, J. (1983a) *In the Shadow of the Silent Majorities or, The End of the Social*, New York: Semiotext(e).

Baudrillard, J. (1983b) *Simulations*, New York: Semiotext(e).

Baudrillard, J. (1987) *Forget Foucault*, New York: Semiotext(e).

BBC (2007) *Today Programme*, BBC Radio 4, 3 April.

Bildt, C. (1998) *Peace Journey: The Struggle for Peace in Bosnia*, London: Weidenfeld and Nicolson.

Buzan, B. (1991) *People, States and Fear*, 2nd edn, Harlow: Pearson.

Chandler, D. (2006) *Empire in Denial: The Politics of State-building*, London: Pluto.

Debrix, F. (1999) *Re-Envisioning Peacekeeping: The United Nations and the Mobilization of Ideology*, Minneapolis: University of Minnesota Press.

European Commission (2001a) *The Stabilisation and Association Process and CARDS Assistance 2000 to 2006*, Brussels: European Commission.

European Commission (2001b) *Regional Strategy Chapter 2002–2006: CARDS Assistance Programme to the Western Balkans*, Brussels: European Commission.

European Commission (2002) *The Stabilisation and Association Process: First Annual Report*, Brussels: European Commission.

ESI (European Stability Initiative) (2001) *Democracy, Security and the Future of the*

Stability Pact for South Eastern Europe: A Framework for Debate, Brussels: European Stability Initiative.

Gills, B. (2000) 'American power, neo-liberal economic globalization and "low intensity democracy": an unstable trinity', in M. Cox, J.G. Ikenberry and T. Inoguchi (eds) *American Democracy Promotion: Impulses, Strategies, and Impacts*, Oxford: Oxford University Press.

Harding, L. (2007) 'The new cold war: Russia's missiles to target Europe', *Guardian*, 4 June.

Heartfield, J. (2007) 'European Union: a process without a subject', in C. Bickerton, P. Cunliffe and A. Gourevitch (eds) *Politics without Sovereignty*, London, UCL Press.

Holbrooke, R. (2007) 'Back to the brink in the Balkans', *Washington Post*, 25 November. Available at: www.washingtonpost.com/wp-dyn/content/article/2007/11/23/AR2007112301237.html.

ICB (International Commission on the Balkans) (2005) *The Balkans in Europe's Future*. Available at: www.balkan-commission.org/activities/Report.pdf.

Laïdi, Z. (1998) *A World without Meaning: The Crisis of Meaning in International Relations*, London: Routledge.

Muehlmann, T. (2008) 'Police restructuring in Bosnia-Herzegovina: problems of internationally-led security sector reform', *Journal of Intervention and Statebuilding*, 2(1): 1–22.

Slobodna Bosna (1997) 'Interview with Carlos Westendorp', *Slobodna Bosna*, 30 November.

Smith, S. (2000) 'US democracy promotion: critical questions', in M. Cox, J.G. Ikenberry and T. Inoguchi (eds) *American Democracy Promotion: Impulses, Strategies, and Impacts*, Oxford: Oxford University Press.

Storey, H. (1995) 'Human rights and the new Europe: experience and experiment', *Political Studies*, 43, Special Issue: 131–151.

Weber, C. (1995) *Simulating Sovereignty: Intervention, the State and Symbolic Exchange*, Cambridge: Cambridge University Press.

Zaum, D. (2007) *The Sovereignty Paradox: The Norms and Politics of International Statebuilding*, Oxford: Oxford University Press.

9 The semantics of contemporary statebuilding

Kosovo, Timor-Leste, and the 'empty-shell' approach

Nicolas Lemay-Hébert

Introduction

More than ten years have passed since the United Nations and the international community proceeded to set up international administrations in Kosovo and Timor-Leste: the United Nations Interim Administration Mission for Kosovo (UNMIK) and the United Nations Transitional Administration in East Timor (UNTAET). In the aftermaths of these experiences, Kosovo is still under international tutelage and Timor-Leste 'remains an underdeveloped ward of the international community' (US State Department 2009). However, despite the political, economic, and social hurdles encountered in Kosovo and Timor-Leste, the idea of direct governance of war-torn or 'dysfunctional' societies by an outside organization has retained a vast influence on certain segments of academia and policy circles. In this context, this chapter will try to demystify the statebuilding experiences of Kosovo and Timor-Leste by specifically focusing on the process that led to the establishment of nearly identical international administrations, as the process in itself could shed light on the praxis of statebuilding in other so-called fragile states. This chapter clarifies the setting up process of international administration by focusing on the concept of the 'empty shell' that came to represent the mental image practitioners shared concerning the local context following the two conflicts. As Nicholas Onuf reminds us in Chapter 2, 'any effort to characterize social relations relies on metaphors, no matter how conceptually aware the effort is'. Hence, following the Foucauldian approach that informs theoretically many contributions in this book, this chapter will try to expose the 'buried assumptions and associations' behind the international administration as a project in Kosovo and Timor-Leste.

The legitimacy gap under international administration in Kosovo and Timor-Leste

Two human-made catastrophes of gigantic proportions happened in 1999, only months apart,[1] eliciting a similar, if not practically identical, response by the international community at that time. However, everything seemed to differentiate these two territories: Timor-Leste and Kosovo. Timor-Leste and Kosovo are geographically separated by nearly 10,000 kilometers and could not be more culturally distinct. Timor-Leste's local context presented, for the most part, an ethnically and religiously homogenous society, unified behind their leader, Xanana Gusmão, and the political umbrella that carried the cause of independence during the last part of Indonesia's occupation (CNRT, National Council of Timorese Resistance), whereas Kosovo's local setting was drastically different, its society being deeply divided over ethnic, religious, and linguistic lines. Furthermore, the local Kosovar-Albanian leadership was divided between a pacifist political party led by Ibrahim Rugova, which assured a certain degree of health and education services in the Albanian language when Serbia's Milošević drastically restricted these services in the 1980s and 1990s, and Hashim Thaçi's Kosovo Liberation Army (KLA), which proclaimed itself the victor of the liberation war against the armed and paramilitary forces of the Federal Republic of Yugoslavia (FRY). Both parties established their own institutional apparatus following FRY's withdrawal from Kosovo, as did Belgrade in the northern part of Kosovo. Furthermore, in Kosovo, the final status of the territory was not clear from the outset, and there was intense international wrangling over the fate of the territory, led notably by Serbia but also by Serbia's traditional political ally and permanent Security Council member, Russia. In Timor-Leste, Security Council politics were not impeding the work of the international administration nor was the final status of the territory, which was clarified from the outset by an internationally recognized referendum. Moreover, the former occupying power, Indonesia, recognized the referendum's result, even if its armed forces and associated militias proceeded to punish the Timorese population for rejecting its proposal of autonomy.

Notwithstanding these differences, the United Nations Security Council established a full-fledged international administration encompassing executive, legislative, and judicial powers over both territories. In these two cases, the international apparatus was headed by a Special Representative of the Secretary-General (SRSG), who acted as the legal head of state of these territories, enjoying 'virtually unlimited powers' in the process (Mertus 2001: 28; Independent International Commission on Kosovo 2000: 259). The SRSG in Timor-Leste, Sergio Vieira de Mello, described his job as amounting to 'benevolent despotism' (Vieira de Mello 2000: 4). Both missions affirmed their respective authority by enacting a nearly identical decree, stating that 'all legislative and executive authority with respect to Kosovo [Timor-Leste], including the administration of the judiciary, is vested in UNMIK [UNTAET] and is exercised by the SRSG [Transitional administrator].' The similarities between the two international administrations were no coincidence. As noted by Samantha Power,

> lacking familiarity with Timor itself, UN officials in New York took the plans they had developed for the Kosovo administration and virtually transposed them onto East Timor. [...] UN staff who felt sidelined joked that SCR 1272 was a 'delete Kosovo, insert East Timor' resolution.
>
> (Power 2008: 300)

As a participant to the East Timor planning team recalled, 'the marching orders of the East Timor planning team were in short to "take the Kosovo plan and reconfigure it to fit East Timor"' (Surkhe 2001: 7). Lakhdar Brahimi, when approached to become head of the international administration in Kosovo and then a few months after in Timor-Leste, declined in both cases and made a telling comment: 'I know nothing about either Kosovo or Timor, but the one thing I am absolutely certain of is that they are not the same place' (Power 2008: 300–1).

Deprived of a peaceful and democratic outlet within the system, opposition grew outside the system in order to express its complaints. The international administration's neglect of local social processes and sources of legitimacy led certain local actors to redeploy strategies to confront the UN international administration and tap into the popular wave of discontent among the local population. The fact that these international administrations are 'exercising the sovereign prerogatives of a state' and 'functioning exactly like a government' (Blair 2002: 10, 40) has had specific repercussions on the legitimacy of the interventions. Placed in the situation of a de facto government of Kosovo and Timor-Leste, the international administrations had to face the same requirements that any legitimate government has. If political legitimacy is 'in the first place a belief, stated or implied, in the right of government to form policies' (Barker 1990: 28), or

> the extent to which people consent to and even support the framework of rules within which political institutions function, either because the political institutions are seen as having gained authority through some legitimate process, and/or because they are seen to represent ideas or values widely supported
>
> (Kaldor 2000: 285)

then the international administration will have to convince the local population of the legitimate character of its rule. In that regard, they have mostly failed in Kosovo and in Timor-Leste.

The delegitimization process pertaining to the exercise of authority by international administration is well documented in Kosovo. Indeed, thanks to the Early Warning System conducted by USAID and UNDP, one cannot fail to notice the failure of UNMIK to secure popular legitimacy among Kosovars from all communities. From the highpoint of 63.8 percent satisfaction with UNMIK's performance during the period of September–October 2002, UNMIK's ratings have steadily decreased to 20.7 percent between January and April 2004, and now stand at 23 percent according to the latest polls (UNDP and USAID 2009: 1). Indeed, if the international military campaign rode on a wave of popular sentiment (King and Mason 2006: 79) and if during the initial months of the intervention UNMIK was able to justify and legitimize its presence to a certain extent, with its honeymoon over, UNMIK had a hard time convincing the local population of the legitimate character of its rule and administration. In the words of Anthony Welch, Coordinator of the International Security Sector Review for

Kosovo, UNMIK simply failed to command the respect of the local population (Welch 2006: 225). As noted by Lesley Abdela, OSCE deputy director for democratization building in Kosovo, 'by the time I left Kosovo in December 1999, UNMIK had squandered its honeymoon period [...]. By mid-October, it had become clear that the international community was fast losing credibility' (2003: 209). The international administration quickly became the target of criticism across all communities in Kosovo. Hansjörg Strohmeyer, who played a prominent role in the UNMIK architecture, recalls the progression of the Albanian sentiment with a simple sentence:

> just before the UN moved in, the Albanians were forced to give the three-finger Serb salute. When the UN arrived, they gave us the peace sign. And then after we'd been there a week, they gave us the middle finger.
>
> (Power 2008: 280)

It is harder to get an accurate picture of the delegitimization process in Timor-Leste, mainly because the Early Warning System was not reproduced in this country. However, accounts of the delegitimization process are abundant. Not unlike Kosovo, it is generally recognized that initially the local population openly welcomed the UN (Chopra 2000: 28; Dunn 2003: 367; Martin and Mayer-Rieckh 2005: 136) and, similarly, the dissatisfaction with the international presence appeared early on in the process of administering the country. As noted by the former UNTAET official Anthony Goldstone (2004: 88):

> By April 2000, six months into the mission, voices in the East Timorese leadership were calling for the UN's prompt withdrawal, and by early 2001 a consensus seemed to be forming that the relationship was not a healthy one and should be terminated as soon as possible.

Indeed, in March 2000, there were already calls within the CNRT for civil disobedience against the UN and talk of declaring unilateral independence from what was dubbed 'another group of invaders' (Joly 2000). In May of the same year, the UN-appointed minister of Foreign Affairs, Jose Ramos-Horta, in a meeting with Annan, asked for the removal of all district administrators by August and their replacement with local leaders, as well as a fixed date for the UN's departure. He notably said in a public statement, 'I told the Secretary-General there is a growing level of frustration and disillusionment with the UN in East Timor, particularly among the young' (Riley 2000; Corcoran 2000). James Dunn reported 'considerable discontent and criticism' among local population directed towards UNTAET in October 2000 (Dunn 2000), while members of the National Council, an organization created in July 2000 to advise the Transitional administrator,[2] clearly stated in the middle of the 'Timorization' process that 'the UN transitional phase had been going on for too long, was neither efficient nor popular, and should be terminated quickly' (Dodd 2000). In 2001, some of the violence was turned directly against the UN. For instance, when Portuguese riot police roughed up a Dili taxi driver in February 2001, a crowd quickly gathered to pelt the police with stones, and only dispersed when shots were fired in the air (Murphy 2001). In March, a mob surrounded and stoned Jordanian peacekeepers in Baucau, the second biggest city in Timor-Leste (Suara Timor Lorosae 2001).

The empty-shell approach: picturing the local context as a *tabula rasa*

The unprecedented powers devoted to the world organization in Kosovo and in Timor-Leste were directly related to the perception of these war-torn territories following the dramatic events in 1999. The state of the material and institutional destruction in Kosovo[3] and in Timor-Leste[4] led commentators and experts at the UN and elsewhere to see the political situation in these countries figuratively as a black hole. As the UN official Hansjörg Strohmeyer noted in an interview to James Traub, 'UN officials in Kosovo used to refer to the bombed-out territory they administered as the "empty shell"' (Traub 2000: 74). He explained the meaning of the expression elsewhere, stating that

> one of the consequences of the violence was that practically overnight, both territories were stripped of their entire administrative and executive superstructures. (…) It was in this situation that the 'empty shell' metaphor later used so often to describe Kosovo and East Timor obtained its meaning.
>
> (Strohmeyer 2001b: 109)

It was also a phrasing used by Kofi Annan himself to legitimize the UN's role in Timor-Leste (Crossette 1999). Along the same line, Simon Chesterman, like others, remarked that many of the expatriates working for the UN and non-governmental organizations tended to treat the political system as a *tabula rasa* or *terra nullius* (Chesterman 2001: 26; Surkhe 2001: 13). Hence, the common view at the time was that the challenge of these missions could be described as taking these territories 'from virtually nothing to practically everything in the next few years' (Priest and Graham 1999), given that these territories have 'to be invented from scratch' (ABC 1999).

Thus, an implication of the empty-shell approach is the implicit prescription that 'more is better' in terms of statebuilding, where 'the more intrusive the intervention is, the more successful the outcome would be' (Zuercher 2006: 2; Lemay-Hébert 2011a: 1825–6). Basically, the idea is 'the deeper the hostility, the more the destruction of local capacities, the more one needs international assistance to succeed in establishing a stable peace' (Doyle and Sambanis 2006: 4). In that perspective, the term 'collapsed state' becomes 'a prescriptive term that is employed in connection with the contemplation and execution of international involvement' (Jackson 2004: 22). The concept of 'empty shell' legitimizes the means of international intervention.

One could argue, along with Caroline Hughes and Vanessa Pupavac (2005: 873), that the notion of failed states, and *a fortiori* the notion of empty shell, 'fixes culpability for war on the societies in question, rendering the domestic populations dysfunctional while casting international rescue interventions as functional'. As Jarat Chopra (2002: 979–81) astutely observes, 'perceptions of a power vacuum [. . .] have drawn the world community in an ever more intensive role in the exercise of transitional political authority. [. . .] The project [global governorship] assumed a state-centric *terra nullius* and an open season on institutional invention.' Thus, it served additionally as a convenient legitimization basis for the setting up of international administrations in these territories. Indeed, one of the assumptions made by advocates of direct international administrations was that the extent of destruction on the ground required the international community to take charge of the process of governance. Once the reconstruction process began to take hold, the international community would start a progressive withdrawal from the territory as the state infrastructure grew firmer and stronger. If there was 'nearly nothing' in these countries for the UN to build on, as Sergio Vieira de Mello posited, then, in his own words, 'nearly everything had to be brought in' (UN 2000b; Surkhe 2001: 14). UNTAET specifically was resting on the assumptions that Timor in 1999 represented a 'blank slate as far as governance was concerned' and that, because of this purported absence of pre-existing structures, 'Timor represented almost laboratory conditions in which to experiment with state-building' (Hughes 2009: 222–3). However, as asserted by Chopra (2002: 980), this approach 'missed the fact that population continues to exist, that market forces of whatever kind are always at work, and that the social structures of indigenous communities invariably generate sources of political legitimacy according to their own paradigm.'

When looking more closely at the debate surrounding the international interventions in 1999, it is clear that this particular institutional focus – which leads to a neglect of other social structures – actually appeared months before the adoption of the Security Council Resolutions on establishing the international administrations. For instance, as expressed by the International Crisis Group one month before the adoption of Resolution 1244, there was a general feeling that 'conditions in Kosovo are right for a protectorate-style model of administration' (ICG 1999a: ii). The research group continues (ICG 1999a: 21), stating that

> given the scope of depopulation and destruction, and the difficulty of identifying local interlocutors who are neither too weak (Rugova) nor potentially too strong (Kosovo Liberation Army leaders), this may be the ideal time to try the Protectorate or Mandate model.

Similarly, in May 1999, *The Guardian* boasted that 'we have argued from the start [. . .] for a land war to capture Kosovo and turn it into an international protectorate' (*The Guardian* 1999). The International Crisis Group stated more bluntly in a later report that 'the role of the international administration will be to govern the country, in the *absence of indigenous authorities*, while at the same time developing indigenous structures which will in due course be capable of providing self-government' (ICG 1999b: 2, italics added).

In the specific mention of the 'absence of indigenous authorities' resides the main legitimizing criterion for the international administrations in Kosovo and Timor-Leste. Joel Beauvais also summarizes this general assumption by a rhetorical question that 'most UN officials asked themselves': 'how does one get from such a situation, in which there is virtually no administrative class, organized civil society, or history of self-rule, to a viable, independent, and democratic state?' (Beauvais 2001: 1104). Although this point of view was generally consensual, certain organizations thought to dissent. For instance, the World Bank's Joint Assessment Mission (1999: para. 15) reported that 20–25 percent of the civil servants had left Timor-Leste in the aftermath of the elections, which, from a strictly administrative standpoint, presented a slightly different assessment of the situation on the ground than the tenants of the empty shell perspective. The fact that the World Bank was using Timorese to conduct its Assessment Mission was in itself a rebuttal of the empty shell perspective (Surkhe 2001: 16). Furthermore, the UNDP stated clearly in 1999 that 'East Timor should not be considered *terra nullis* insofar as the emerging UN Administration is concerned' (UNDP 1999: 5). The authors of the report argue that 'this entails adopting a very cautious attitude to applying any "state of the art" type systems and facilities, as these will simply break down in the absence of significant foreign capital and skills input.' Furthermore, forecasting the local resistance and contestation that will take place, the authors remark:

> for the people of East Timor there is not likely to be endless patience for yet another foreign administrative class managing their affairs. This should be seen against the background that this would be the fourth such group in the past 60 years. *This suggests most strongly that the UN Administration's prime objective in East Timor must be to make itself redundant as soon as possible.*
>
> (UNDP 1999: 6, emphasis in text)

The UNDP report never got a hearing, according to Astri Surkhe (2001: 16).

The limits of the empty shell approach: the difficulties of creating from scratch a system of justice in Timor-Leste

Hansjörg Strohmeyer, who was the acting principal legal adviser to the transitional administrator in Timor-Leste, noted how hard it was to build a system of justice when not 'a single lawyer' was present in Timor-Leste (Strohmeyer 2001b: 114). He also saw his tasks as 'a complete re-creation of the judiciary' and asks aloud the question 'how can a justice system be administered when there is no system left to be administered?' (Strohmeyer 2001a: 47–8). This 'ground zero' approach, as Strohmeyer dubbed it, was also shared to a certain extent by certain academics or by the media (Chesterman 2002: 6; Kaminski 1999). A different perspective, nevertheless leading to the same policy prescription, was focusing on the democratization challenges and the need to completely restart and change the legal system. For instance, Jürgen Friedrich (2005: 241–2) notes how

> promoting human rights as well as completely rebuilding and democratising a society which had up to that point been dominated by a discriminatory and suppressive legal system requires extensive legal reform. For similar reasons, the justice system and the executive had to be completely restarted and changed. In other words, the objectives could not be pursued in practice without possessing full governmental powers.

One of the first acts of the Transitional Administrator was to create a Transitional Judicial Service Commission, composed of three Timorese and two international experts. Its primary function was to recommend to the Transitional Administrator candidates for provisional judicial or prosecutorial offices. At the same time, the International Force in East Timor (INTERFET) volunteered to drop leaflets from airplanes throughout the territory, calling for legally qualified East Timorese to contact any UNTAET or INTERFET office or outpost (Strohmeyer 2001a: 54). It took more than a year for the UN to officially acknowledge the presence of the local systems of justice,[5] although it appears that there was some amount of knowledge of the traditional system among officers in the political affairs or national security departments, as well as the Civpol or the Office of the Principal Legal Adviser (Mearns 2001: 6). What is believed to be the first report emanating from UNTAET that included references to the local systems of justice concluded that international police officials were acting pragmatically at the village level by encouraging some (often most) situations to be resolved through the village chief and a village council, conceding that the local justice system was operating and appeared to be the preferred system in many cases. Furthermore, both local people and international police officials recognized that the formal system of law was and will remain too remote, too expensive, and too slow to resolve disputes at the local level (Mearns 2001: 7; Kerr and Mobekk 2007: 151). This was also the conclusion of the *Report on the National Constitutional Consultation in East Timor*, which noted around the same time a strong desire of the people to retain the system of traditional justice at the local level to overcome the problems caused by local disputes and crimes (Mearns 2001: 6).

Initially, UNTAET tried to build from scratch a Western model of governance. In that regard, the UN simply followed the global trend in post-conflict reconstruction – where 80 percent of the worldwide development assistance in the area of justice goes to the development of an institutional justice sector, while traditional and customary systems resolve around 90 percent of the conflicts (UNDP 2004: 8–9). Early on, UNTAET officials declared that 'judicial authority in East Timor shall be exclusively vested in courts that are established by law and composed of judges who are appointed to these courts' (UN 2000a: section 1). In this Regulation, the UN made no mention of local systems of justice. However, the UN's attempt to build a Westernized system of justice never gained any legitimacy in the eyes of the population. As Tanja Hohe and Rod Nixon (2003: 2) state:

> There was not even tension between the two systems – as they both operated in different universes. The international community never paid attention to the nature and relevance of local systems in the determination of strategies. It was taken for granted that new systems would be readily accepted by societies, though they do not match with local concepts and despite the negative experiences with the former Indonesian justice sector.

Hence, in a report mandated by the World Bank and UNTAET, Sofi Ospina and Tanja Hohe noted that despite the overt attempt to engineer a new local democratic basis for social development, customary leaders and the elders of the villages still retained considerable authority and influence (Ospina and Hohe 2001: 8–9). Furthermore, a survey conducted in 2003 indicated an overwhelming support for traditional systems of justice: 84 percent considered the local systems as easier to understand than the court system, 86 percent considered them cheaper and requiring less traveling, 78 percent considered them as contributing more effectively to reconciliation, and 75 percent considered the local systems faster and more efficient than the courts (USAID 2004: 55). This trend was also confirmed by subsequent reports (Asia Foundation 2008). Moreover, confronted with a backlog of more than 4,000 cases, the formal system is in many ways simply not able to cope with local expectations, leading many to engage informal and customary practices (Butt *et al.* 2009: 7). Hence, for a substantial proportion of Timor-Leste's population, there is simply no alternative – traditional law is the sole acknowledged recourse (Marriott 2012: 55).

In that context, UNTAET was forced to gradually change its position. For instance, a couple of months before handing over governmental authority to local institutions, UNTAET adopted the Regulation on the 'establishment of a commission for reception, truth and reconciliation in East Timor,' which allowed the new Commission to facilitate 'community reconciliation processes' in relation to criminal or noncriminal acts committed within the context of the Indonesian occupation of Timor-Leste, thus more in accordance with local traditional structures (Babo-Soares 2004: 30–1). In doing so, UNTAET was recognizing a process that was already taking place at the local level. However, it proved a belated attempt to bring legitimacy to public institutions. The hybrid tribunals, involving international and local judges to prosecute serious crimes committed under Indonesian rule, were already seriously inefficient. The Public Prosecutor's Office was so underfunded and inexperienced that it did not call a single witness at any of its first 14 trials, leaving David Cohen (2002: 1) to ask if 'a minimally credible tribunal is better than none.'

Taking into account local systems of political, social, and justice systems is not in itself a panacea for all the problems encountered by international administrations. Many reasons could be invoked to explain the international neglect of these social structures. In Timor-Leste, the traditional system of justice was perceived as going against certain basic human rights principles, especially concerning women's rights, whereas in Kosovo, the ethnic, linguistic, and religious cleavages and political rivalries forced the UN to be cautious concerning the local role in governance. However, one could argue that to ignore the local mechanisms, such as in Timor-Leste, does not make them disappear.

Conclusion

One of the lessons learned from the experience of the UN administration of Kosovo, according to an internal UNMIK document, is that 'the Mission demonstrated a lack of cultural sensitivity and an insufficient understanding of the dynamics of the society, in terms both of power structures and of negotiations' (UN 2008). For Vieira de Mello, 'if there is one lesson to be learned from the United Nations' previous attempts at nation-building [in Kosovo and Timor-Leste], it is to include national political figures and parties. Be as inclusive as circumstances permit.' If not, the risk is that 'those who have come to help will come to be seen as invading interlopers' (Vieira de Mello 2001). Indeed, in line with Vieira de Mello's own lecture of the lessons learned in Kosovo and Timor-Leste, this chapter has analyzed the legitimacy crisis that followed the setting up of international administrations in Kosovo and Timor-Leste. It has linked this legitimacy crisis with the actual setting up process of the international administrations by focusing on the concept of 'empty shell' that came to represent the metaphor practitioners shared concerning the local context following the two conflicts. Unveiling practices associated with this discursive field allowed us to enter the realm of governance – and legitimization of governance – as portrayed from the United Nations perspective. Finally, this chapter has zeroed in on the (re)construction of the system of justice in Timor-Leste as a specific example of these practices. This example also shows clearly the limits of state-centric conceptions of statebuilding, as well as the vitality of social actors acting sometimes outside the classical structures of the state.

As the UNMIK internal document quoted earlier attests, there are many calls for more 'local ownership' in contemporary statebuilding contexts. Certainly, cultural sensitivity, along with robust accountability mechanisms and a greater local ownership of the process can help certain peacebuilding mission garner a certain degree of legitimacy. However, as Simon Chesterman (2004: 237) states,

> political structures created for foreign control (benevolent or not) tend to be unsuited to local rule. The reason for this, in part, is that the 'limited goals' of foreign control (benevolent or not) are generally determined with limited regard to local circumstances.

'Participatory intervention' (Chopra and Hohe 2004), 'local ownership' or 'indigenous empowerment' (Lederach 1995: 212) do not fit neatly with direct governance by an international administration, at least not following the perspective which led to the establishment of UNMIK and UNTAET. Concretely, it means at the very least a substantive normative shift in the conduct of statebuilding. First, local actors have to be recognized as true partners in the statebuilding process rather than mere recipients of foreign aid. Hence, the empty shell perspective is antithetical to local ownership. Second, the 'participatory intervention' framework also seems at odd with the 'more is better' perspective, which theoretically supported the establishment of the international administrations in Kosovo and Timor-Leste. If one wants to allow space for local actors in a participatory framework, authority can hardly be monopolized by the international actors (Lemay-Hébert 2012). One of the lessons identified in the Timor-Leste and Kosovo experiments is that a certain restraint in the exercise of authority on the part of external actors in the statebuilding process can be positive and can contribute to an increase of legitimacy of the mission while allowing the local population 'to learn from their experience and prevent the administrative equivalent of aid dependency' (Salamun 2005: 59; Stahn 2005: 24). Kofi Annan also identified this point as a general lesson to be drawn from past experiences. For him, 'the role of the United Nations and the international community should be solidarity, not substitution' (UN 2004: para. 17). Hardly any society experiences a complete 'social void,' even following traumatizing experiences, and infrastructural destruction following disasters or conflict should not prevent international actors from looking at social processes beyond the Weberian state. Actually, ignoring these actors and processes will only make international action irrelevant at best, while contributing to further delegitimize the internationally led statebuilding project at worst.

Notes

1 The armed conflict between the Kosovo Liberation Army (KLA) and the Federal Republic of Yugoslavia (FRY) that took off in February 1998 proved to be the second main challenge posed to Western Europe and the United States in less than a decade. With the Rambouillet Agreement of March 18, 1999 being rejected by the Serbian leadership, military response took over from diplomacy in the Balkans and the NATO Operation *Allied Force* followed on March 22, 1999, with the aim of expelling the Federal Republic of Yugoslavia's forces from Kosovo. In response, the Serb military and paramilitaries stepped up their campaign against Kosovo Albanians. At the end of June 1999, more than 10,000 casualties were attributed to Serb forces in Kosovo, while in the meantime more than 1.5 million Kosovo Albanians were forcibly expelled from their homes, which represented some 90 percent of the estimated 1998 Kosovar Albanian population.

In Timor-Leste, Indonesia agreed on a consultation process whereby the population of East Timor would vote to accept or reject the idea of autonomy within Indonesia. Despite Indonesia's overt pressure on the Timorese, the result was overwhelming clear. The vote on August 30, 1999 showed that 78.5 percent of East Timorese voters, in a 98 percent turnout, rejected the option of autonomy within Indonesia in favor of independence. However, following the vote, certain elements of the Indonesian armed forces, in collaboration with local militias, waged an operation called *Operation Clean Sweep*, a three-week campaign of scorched earth meant to punish the East Timorese for their decision. The operation, in which an estimated 1,500 to 2,000 East Timorese were killed, led to the displacement of three-quarters of the total population of 890,000, including the exodus of 250,000 persons.

2 The National Council, consisting of 33 members and later 36, was to constitute a sort of legislative forum, in order to provide a separation of power that Timor-Leste had never experienced up till then. The NC had the competence to initiate, modify, and recommend draft regulations, as well as to amend existing regulations. The Transitional Administrator nevertheless retained final decision-making authority.

3 According to the UNMIK, 'preliminary results of an UNHCR-led survey of 141 villages show 64 percent of homes to be severely damaged or destroyed.' See UNMIK website: www.unmikonline.org/chrono.htm (accessed June 1, 2009). Furthermore, 'UNICEF estimates that 40 to 50 percent of schools have been damaged' (Kifner 1999).

4 The World Bank estimated that about 70 percent of the territory's infrastructure and all governmental functions were destroyed in 1999 (*The Straits Times* 2000).

5 According to a former UNTAET official, when the UN mission started to talk about the traditional system of justice, it was mainly to know 'how to codify it' and 'who were the representants.' Interview with former UNTAET official, July 20, 2008, Dili, Timor-Leste.

References

ABC [Transcript] (1999) 'World Bank releases plan for rebuilding East Timor', November 18.

Abdela, L. (2003) 'Kosovo: missed opportunities, lessons for the future', *Development in Practice*, 13(2–3): 208–16.

Asia Foundation (2008) *Law and Justice in East Timor: A Survey of Citizen Awareness and Attitudes Regarding Law and Justice in East Timor*, Dili, Timor-Leste.

Babo-Soares, D. (2004) 'Nahe biti: the philosophy and process of grassroots reconciliation (and justice) in East Timor', *Asia Pacific Journal of Anthropology*, 5(1): 15–33.

Barker, R. (1990) *Political Legitimacy and the State*, Oxford: Clarendon Press.

Beauvais, J. (2001) 'Benevolent despotism: a critique of UN state-building in East Timor', *New York University Journal of International Law and Politics*, 33: 1101–78.

Blair, S. (2002) *Weaving the Strands of the Rope*, Dalhousie: Centre for Foreign Policy Studies.

Butt, S., David, N., and Laws, N. (2009) 'Looking forward: local dispute resolution mechanisms in Timor Leste', Legal Studies Research Paper 09/33, University of Sydney.

Chesterman, S. (2001) 'A nation waits', *The World Today*, 57(5): 25–7.

Chesterman, S. (2002) *Justice under International Administration: Kosovo, East Timor and Afghanistan*, New York: International Peace Academy Report.

Chesterman, S. (2004) *You, the People: The United Nations, Transitional Administration, and State-building*, Oxford: Oxford University Press.

Chopra, J. (2000) 'The UN's kingdom of East Timor', *Survival*, 42(3): 27–39.

Chopra, J. (2002) 'Building state failure in East Timor', *Development and Change*, 33(5): 979–1000.

Chopra, J. and Hohe, T. (2004) 'Participatory intervention', *Global Governance*, 10(3): 289–305.

Cohen, D. (2002) 'Seeking justice on the cheap: is the East Timorese tribunal really a model for the future?', *Asia Pacific Issues*, 61: 1–8.

Corcoran, B. (2000) 'Temperature rises in East Timor as UN digs in', *The Sunday Tribune*, June 18.

Crossette, B. (1999) 'Annan says UN must take over East Timor rule', *The New York Times*, October 6.

Dodd, M. (2000) 'East Timor gets ready for tricky birth', *Sydney Morning Herald*, December 13.

Doyle, M. and Sambanis, N. (2006) *Making War and Building Peace: United Nations Peace Operations*, Princeton: Princeton University Press.

Dunn, J. (2000) 'UNTAET after nine months', *Asian Analysis*, available at: www.aseanfocus.com/asiananalysis/article.cfm?articleID=308 (accessed June 8, 2009).

Dunn, J. (2003) *East Timor: A Rough Passage to Independence*. New South Wales: Longueville.

Friedrich, J. (2005) 'UNMIK in Kosovo: struggling with uncertainty', *Max Planck Yearbook of United Nations Law*, 9: 225–93.

Goldstone, A. (2004) 'UNTAET with hindsight: the peculiarities of politics in an incomplete state', *Global Governance*, 10(1): 83–98.

The Guardian (1999) 'A choice that cannot wait: NATO must settle its view on a ground war', May 7, available at: www.guardian.co.uk/world/1999/may/07/balkans6.

Hohe, T. and Nixon, R. (2003) *Reconciling Justice: 'Traditional' Law and State Judiciary in East Timor*, Report prepared for the United States Institute of Peace (on file with authors).

Hughes, C. (2009) 'We just take what they offer: community empowerment in post-war Timor-Leste', in E. Newman, R. Paris, and O. Richmond (eds) *New Perspectives on Liberal Peacebuilding*, Tokyo: United Nations University Press.

Hughes, C. and Pupavac, V. (2005) 'Framing post-conflict societies: international pathologisation of Cambodia and the post-Yugoslav states', *Third World Quarterly*, 26(6): 873–89.

Independent International Commission on Kosovo (2000) *Kosovo Report: Conflict, International Response, Lessons Learned*, Oxford: Oxford University Press.

ICG (International Crisis Group) (1999a) 'Kosovo: let's learn from Bosnia: models and methods of international administration', Balkans Report No. 66, May 17.

ICG (International Crisis Group) (1999b) 'The new Kosovo protectorate', Balkans Report No. 69, June 20.

Jackson, R. (2004) 'International engagement in war-torn countries', *Global Governance*, 10(1): 21–36.

Joly, J. (2000) 'Respect for UN mission is falling, warns local adviser', *South China Morning Post*, March 15.

Kaldor, M. (2000) 'Governance, legitimacy, and security: three scenarios for the twenty-first century', in P. Wapner and E. Ruiz (eds) *Principled World Politics*, Lanham: Rowman and Littlefield.

Kaminski, M. (1999) 'UN struggles with a legal vacuum in Kosovo: team improvises in effort to build a civil structure', *Wall Street Journal*, August 4.

Kerr, R. and Mobekk, E. (2007) *Peace and Justice: Seeking Accountability after War*, London: Polity.

Kifner, J. (1999) 'Laying claim to govern in the ruins of Kosovo', *The New York Times*, July 16.

King, I. and Mason, W. (2006) *Peace at Any Price: How the World Failed Kosovo*, Ithaca: Cornell University Press.

Lederach, J.P. (1995) *Preparing for Peace: Conflict Transformation across Cultures*, New York: Syracuse University Press.

Lemay-Hébert, N. (2011a) 'The bifurcation of the two worlds: assessing the gap between the internationals and locals in state-building processes', *Third World Quarterly*, 32(10): 1823–41.

Lemay-Hébert, N. (2011b) 'The "empty-shell" approach: the setup process of international administrations in Timor-Leste and Kosovo, its consequences and lessons', *International Studies Perspectives*, 12(2): 190–211.

Lemay-Hébert, N. (2012) 'Coerced transitions in Timor-Leste and Kosovo: managing competing objectives of institution-building and local empowerment', *Democratization* 19(3): 465–85.

Marriott, A. (2012) 'Justice sector dynamics in Timor-Leste: institutions and individuals', *Asian Politics and Policy*, 4(1): 53–71.

Martin, I. and Mayer-Rieckh, A. (2005) 'The United Nations and East Timor: from self-determination to state-building', *International Peacekeeping*, 12(1): 125–45.

Mearns, D. (2001) 'Variations on a theme: coalitions of authority in East Timor. A report on the local and national justice systems as a basis for dispute resolution', Report for Australian Legal Resources International with the assistance of the Australian Agency for International Development.

Mertus, J. (2001) 'The impact of intervention on local human rights culture: a Kosovo case study', *Global Review of Ethnopolitics*, 1(2): 21–36.

Murphy, D. (2001) 'UN makes feeble Timor midwife', *Christian Science Monitor*, February 14.

Ospina, S. and Hohe, T. (2001) 'Traditional power structures and the community empowerment and local governance project', Final Report Presented to CEP/PMU, ETTA/UNTAET and the World Bank.

Power, S. (2008) *Chasing the Flame: Sergio Vieira de Mello and the Fight to Save the World*, New York: Penguin Press.

Priest, D. and Graham, B. (1999) 'NATO faces daunting task of governing Kosovo', *The Washington Post*, June 19.

Riley, M. (2000) 'Time for UN to go: Timor leaders', *Sydney Morning Herald*, May 24.

Salamun, M. (2005) *Democratic Governance in International Territorial Administration*, Baden-Baden: Nomos Verlagsgesellschaft.

Stahn, C. (2005) 'Accountability and legitimacy in practice: lawmaking by transitional administrations', Paper presented at the European Society of International Law Research Forum, Geneva, May 26–28.

The Straits Times (2000) 'Dawn of a new nation: difficult birth for East Timor', February 13.

Strohmeyer, H. (2001a) 'Collapse and reconstruction of a judicial system: the United Nations missions in Kosovo and East Timor', *American Journal of International Law*, 95(1): 46–63.

Strohmeyer, H. (2001b) 'Making multilateral intervention work: the UN and the creation of transitional justice systems in Kosovo and East Timor', *Fletcher Forum of World Affairs*, 25(2): 107–28.

Suara Timor Lorosae (2001) 'Violence in Baucau: one mosque burnt, UN vehicles stoned', March 9.

Surkhe, A. (2001) 'Peacekeepers as nation-builders: dilemmas of the UN in East Timor', *International Peacekeeping*, 8(4): 1–20.

Traub, J. (2000) 'Inventing East Timor', *Foreign Affairs*, 79(4): 74–89.

UN (United Nations) (1999) 'Conceptual framework for reconstruction, recovery and development of East Timor (draft)', available at: atpascal.iseg.utl.pt/~cesa/concept_paper_east_timor.pdf (accessed March 21, 2010).

UN (United Nations) (2000a) *UNTAET Regulation 2000/11: On the Organization of Courts in East Timor*, UN Doc. UNTAET/REG/2000/11, March 6.

UN (United Nations) (2000b) 'Security Council briefed by Sergio Vieira de Mello, Special Representative for East Timor', UN Doc. SC/6882, June 27.

UN (United Nations) (2004) 'Report of the Secretary-General on the rule of law and transitional justice in conflict and post-conflict societies', UN Doc. S/2004/616, August 23.

UN (United Nations) (2008) 'Civil aministration in Kosovo 1999–2007: achievements, challenges and lessons learned', UN internal document (on file with author).

UNDP (United Nations Development Program) (2004) 'Access to justice', Practice Note, March 9.

UNDP (United Nations Development Program) and USAID (United States Agency for International Development) (2009) 'Early warning report 26: November 2009', available at www.ks.undp.org/repository/docs/Fast_Facts_26_English.pdf (accessed March 21, 2010).

United States Agency for International Development (USAID) (2004) 'Report on research findings and policy recommendations for a legal framework for land dispute mediation', Timor-Leste Land Law Program.

United States State Department (2009) 'Timor-Leste at ten years: to the brink and back', Unclassified Cable, US Embassy in Dili, August 21.

Vieira de Mello, S. (2000) 'How not to run a country: lessons from the UN in Kosovo and Timor-Leste', Unpublished manuscript.

Vieira de Mello, S. (2001) 'How to put the pieces together', *Newsweek*, December 17.

Welch, A. (2006) 'Achieving human security after intra-state conflict: the lessons of Kosovo', *Journal of Contemporary European Studies*, 14(2): 221–39.

World Bank (1999) 'Report of the joint assessment mission to East Timor', December 8.

Zuercher, C. (2006) 'Is more better? evaluating external-led state building after 1989', CDDRL Working Paper number 54, Stanford University, April.

10 The 'crisis of capitalism' and the state – more powerful, less responsible, invariably legitimate

Albena Azmanova

From the crisis of capitalism to its metamorphosis

On the alleged crisis of capitalism

In the midst of the global financial meltdown, pronouncements on the terminal crisis of capitalism abound: French President Nicolas Sarkozy's rebuke of finance capitalism (with Marx's *Das Kapital* in hand) has chimed with the admonitions advanced by the radical sociologist David Harvey.[1] Despite the global spread of popular protest against capitalism (which originated with the Occupy Wall Street movement in September 2011 in New York), the system's legitimacy is hardly in crisis. If democratic elections are any indicator of prevailing preferences in our societies, the most recent round of elections in the mature democracies of Europe suggests that neoliberal capitalism has considerable popular support, as the democratic vote has gone persistently to the economically liberal center-right parties advocating the very economic model that caused the economic meltdown of 2008–2011.[2]

By all evidence, there is no broad, cross-ideological coalition of forces mobilizing to protect society from the disembedded market, in the style of the countermovement against free markets that Karl Polanyi had observed taking shape in the early twentieth century. At the time, European Conservatism and Socialism came to a consensus on the need to constrain markets – a consensus which enabled the construction of the post-war welfare states. Instead, we now have governments, irrespective of their ideological allegiance, running to the rescue of financial capital and big business, and implementing austerity programs to reassure capital markets – at the social cost of increased poverty and insecurity – while society bears this with relative equanimity. Social frustration is, instead, being channeled into xenophobia.

While we have been busy debating the crisis of capitalism, as I will ascertain in what follows, capitalism has metamorphized itself into a new form, which the most recent economic crisis has helped consolidate, but certainly did not trigger. In order to understand why our societies are not making an effort to protect themselves, to comprehend the social pathology associated with this complacency, as well as to discern a perspective of emancipation, we need to understand the nature of this new, post-neoliberal capitalism, which I will name *aggregative* capitalism (because of the way it aggregates risks and opportunities among a new set of winners and losers, as I shall explain later on). The novel features concern three dimensions in the structuring of the socio-economic order: (1) the organization of the political economy (state-market relations), (2) the legitimation of political power within the semantics of a new social contract between public authority and citizens, and (3) the type of power public authority is entitled to exercise. Before I proceed to adumbrate the contours of this new modality of democratic capitalism, let me briefly review the three configurations of capitalism that the new one sublimates.

The 'repertoire' of capitalism and its first three configurations

Capitalism as a particular socio-economic order has not only been institutionalized in a variety of national models that have co-existed synchronically,[3] but has also undergone a linear, diachronic, transformation – from its initial, liberal (entrepreneurial) modality that was consolidated in the early nineteenth century, to its current state. I do not propose to see these diachronic modalities as distinct 'epochs' but rather, in the style in which both Nicholas Onuf and Friedrich Kratochwil discuss social change in this volume, these should be seen as overlapping blueprints, reconfigurations of a repertoire.

The 'repertoire' of capitalism is composed of its operative logic – the pursuit of 'forever renewed profit by means of continuous, rational, capitalistic enterprise' (Weber 1930/1992: 17), together with its ethos[4] – a set of worldviews orienting behaviour and giving it the meaning of rational enterprise under individual initiative (ibid.: 25). This repertoire emerged as early as the seventeenth century in Europe, within varied institutional frameworks – from those of monarchical absolutism to the free merchant Hansa towns, and consolidated as a distinct socio-economic order in the nineteenth century. The process of consolidation, as Polanyi (1944/1957: 3) reminds us, took place within the institutional framework of the liberal state – itself a creation of the self-regulating market.

The connection between, on the one hand, economic action and, on the other, a political-institutional framework – a connection that engenders the particular symbiosis between capitalism as a system of economic interactions and the modern liberal state – rests on a matrix of shared norms shaping the legitimacy relationship between public authority and citizens. This relationship is, in turn, articulated in the form of what Claus Offe has called 'the legitimate and legitimacy-conferring functions of the state.'[5] These are functions (e.g. protection of private property, defence of territorial integrity, safeguarding order) that citizens expect from public authority, and therefore condition their obedience on the effective exercise of such functions. It is important to note that what are deemed to be legitimate functions of the state are neither simply embodiments of interests, nor of functional needs of the system. The functions of public authority are articulated within a symbolic fabric of perceptions within which they are socially constructed as being 'legitimate and legitimacy conferring.' These legitimating perceptions are akin to ideology understood as mental representations specific to a given era – 'a set of shared beliefs, inscribed in institutions, bound up with actions, and hence anchored in reality' (Boltanski and Chiapello 1999/2005: 3). The legitimacy relationship between public authority and citizens, in turn, determines the thematic scope of the agenda of public debate: which social practices get politicized and thus become an object of contestation and which ones are accepted as a matter of course and therefore remain unchallenged.

The first modality of capitalism, the nineteenth-century entrepreneurial form, developed within a unique political framework – that of the liberal constitutional state committed to ensuring institutional autonomy for the individual. This institutional autonomy was the foundation for the freedom of economic enterprise (laissez-faire) via the freedom of contract vested in law.[6] The emergence of the legal system of the modern liberal state cannot be simply attributed to capitalistic interests, although such interests, as Weber writes, have 'undoubtedly also helped, but by no means alone and nor even principally' (Weber 1930/1992: 25). The form of capitalism that Weber deemed to be unique for the modern West – the rational capitalistic organization of (formally) free labour (ibid.: 21) – is correlated with the institutional set-up of liberal constitutionalism via a particular mindset Weber calls 'Occidental rationalism' – 'the ability and disposition of men to adopt certain types of practical rational conduct' (ibid.: 26). Worldviews valorizing (and motivating) rational enterprise under individual initiative are a key component of this mindset. Thus, economic liberalism, in this first modality of capitalism, was not simply a norm governing the realm of economic action. It was rather a spiritual mindset, a Zeitgeist, and as such it assumed the status of 'the organizing principle of a society engaged in creating a market system' (Polanyi 1944/1957: 135). At the dawn of the nineteenth century, Wilhelm von Humboldt gave expression to this entrepreneurial Zeitgeist when, writing against the interventionist, 'positive' state, he exclaimed: 'But what human beings are after, and should be after, is diversity and activity ... surely we human beings have not sunk so low that we actually prefer welfare and happiness to greatness for ourselves, as individuals.'[7]

The separation of economics and politics that is a constitutive feature of the liberal state, together with its typical institutional paraphernalia (e.g. the separation of powers, the legal safeguards against unlawful interference with the rights of privacy and property) thus provided the political setting for entrepreneurial capitalism; it became 'the irrefragable condition of the existing system of society' (Polanyi 1944/1957: 225). In this first modality of Occidental capitalism, the behavior-orienting value of individual entrepreneurial action moulds the semantics of collective social and political existence. The correlation between risk and opportunity (rewarding entrepreneurial risk with affluence) is one of the key legitimating resources of liberal capitalism, and maintaining that correlation is among the liberal state's key legitimacy-conferring functions – namely, to enact and safeguard the free market.

After the Second World War, nineteenth-century entrepreneurial capitalism was replaced by a new modality – what Scott Lash and John Urry (1987) named 'organised capitalism.' This second enunciation of the repertoire of capitalism developed within the institutional format of the welfare state.

The catalyst for the birth of the second modality of capitalism was the broad societal movement against the economic dogma of the self-regulating market – a movement that emerged already at the waning of the nineteenth century. The collectivist countermovement, Polanyi (1944/1957: 145) notes, was a broad societal endeavour, which 'was not due to any preference for socialism or nationalism on the part of concerted interests, but exclusively to the broader range of the vital social interests affected by the expanding market mechanism.' This consensus was brought about not by the threat the market economy represented to the interests of a particular social group, but because the market, disembedded from society, 'became a threat to the human and natural components of the social fabric' (ibid.: 150).[8] The matrix of state-society relations thus came to be built on broadly shared worldviews converging on the novel, for the early twentieth century, value of social rights whose raison d'être is the protection of society from the market. As citizenship came to incorporate the social right to a decent standard of living, the normative scope of the legitimacy of modern democracies thus expanded to include the concept of social justice (i.e. the equitable distribution of social risk), alongside the political and civil liberties and the value of economic entrepreneurship that had been political cornerstones of the liberal constitutional state. The legitimate and legitimacy-conferring functions of the state came to include a redistributive one, together with its corollary – the *social* responsibility of public authority.

The social partnership among organized capital, organized labor, and a democratic state that marked this new socio-political constellation was institutionalized in a variety of models of democratic capitalism. This variation is captured along the 'varieties of capitalism' and 'varieties of welfare regimes' taxonomies, which I will refrain from reviewing here.[9] Instead, I will refer generally to 'organized,' or 'welfare' capitalism as an over-arching modality that was consolidated in the course of the three post-war decades. Welfare capitalism was characterized by an organized and institutionalized political collectivism that existed on two levels: within the realm of political economy – as corporatism; and within the realm of political competition – as mass, class-based parties competing along a left-right axis of ideological orientation and forming the large political families of the Left and the Right.

Since the 1970s, 'organized' (welfare) capitalism came to be subjected to policy pressures for economic liberalization and deregulation. These transformative dynamics have been broadly described as 'dis-organization' of capitalism – a breakdown of the mechanisms that had previously ensured, through mediation, a dynamic balance between social power and political authority (Offe 1985/1989: 6). This disorganization is often cast in the terms of liberalization and deregulation of coordinated market economies for the sake of enhancing market efficiency, 'a trend in the political economy away from centralized authoritative coordination and control towards dispersed competition, individual instead of collective action, and spontaneous, market-like aggregation of preferences and decisions' (Streeck 2009: 149). Eventually, the hierarchical Fordist work structure that had emerged in the early twentieth century, and had been predominant in the period of 'organized capitalism,' was dissolved into a new, flexible, network-based form of organization.[10]

The matrix of legitimacy-conferring worldviews in this third enunciation of the capitalist repertoire is shaped by the 'new spirit of capitalism' (Boltanski and Chiapello) – not so much the entrepreneurial individualism that anchored the first modality, but an ethos that celebrates more largely initiative and autonomy, co-opting the libertarian currents (including the environmental political consciousness)[11] of the late 1960s for the purposes of endless capital accumulation.

The fourth modality: 'aggregative' capitalism

Already before the current economic crisis, capitalism had begun its transformation into a new modality, which I have described elsewhere as 'reorganized capitalism' (Azmanova 2010), to set it apart from the previous, neoliberal form Offe, Lash and Urry had named 'disorganized capitalism.' Neither Offe nor I see these modalities as perfectly articulated, distinct ones: we have in mind tendencies and dominant features. 'Reorganized capitalism' preserved many of the features of the neoliberal form that preceded it, as 'disorganized capitalism' in its turn had preserved many of the features of the welfare state it dismantled. Most importantly, all these modalities preserve the essential characteristics of the 'repertoire of capitalism' – namely its *operative logic* (the unlimited pursuit of profit by means of the rational capitalistic organization of formally free labor) and its *ethos* (of rational enterprise under individual initiative). I will now only discuss those transformative dynamics that concern the formation of a new matrix of state-society relations as they affect the semantics of state-building.

Recasting state-market relations: from economic growth to global competitiveness, from social safety to societal resilience

Post-industrial societies have undergone a transformation in the late twentieth century under the influence of the new economy of open borders and information technology that, in turn, has altered the parameters of the relationship between public authority and citizens. Late modernity is marked not simply by the proliferation of *risk*, as Ulrich Beck (1992) has claimed, but also the proliferation of *opportunity*, while the distribution of both risk and opportunity has become strongly stratified, with the state shifting its role from countering social stratification (via compensatory social protection) to fostering it. Let me trace the logic of this shift more carefully.

The starting point of this movement is the redefinition of state-market relations at the close of the twentieth century. The policy agenda at that time came to be centered not simply on enhancing market efficiency in order to increase growth (as in the formula of neoliberal capitalism of the 1980s and 1990s), but on achieving increased competitiveness in the global economy. Growth became strongly predicated on competitiveness. Democratic governments across the left-right political spectrum undertook liberalization and deregulation of the economy as part of national strategies for international competitiveness.[12] This shift has been explicit in the EU policy agenda since the turn of the century, as the stress on global competitiveness has become more acute in the transition from the *Lisbon Strategy* of 2000[13] to its revised version adopted in 2006, to the current *Agenda 2020*. The objective of global competitiveness has generated a trans-ideological policy consensus, embraced by capital and labor, and enforced by public authority both at the level of European Union institutions as well as at the level of member states. Tellingly, even trade-union activity has changed its nature, as labor-market liberalization, accepted under the threat of losing jobs, became a central object of agreement.[14] Within this new corporatism, access to the labor market (obtaining and keeping a job) is the key element around which the value-matrix of social rights is being reconfigured. Thus, notions of social justice have shifted from the original concerns with decent working conditions and standards of living towards preoccupations with one's employability and capacity to retain a job – in the spirit of what Julian Reid describes in Chapter 11 as a shift from 'security' to 'resilience'.

The extreme marketization of the economy (under the imperatives of global competitiveness) resulted not only in the proliferation of risk, but also in the asymmetrical distribution of economic opportunity and risk among economic actors. In an (idealized) market society risks and opportunities are evenly mixed for every participant – thus, in a liberal economy, capital's opportunity for wealth-creation is offset by the investment risks it assumes. This correlation between opportunities and risks supplied much of the legitimation resource for both liberal (entrepreneurial) capitalism and its neo-liberal reincarnation. Recently, however, risks and opportunities have become disentangled and even polarized. Indeed, a plethora of recent studies have observed the emergence of 'losers' and 'winners' (a new precariat) among advanced industrial democracies as a result of globalization.[15] I have argued that risks and opportunities are asymmetrically allocated according to an actor's ability to benefit from the two vectors of globalization – open borders and information technology (Azmanova 2011: 393). Moreover, the privatization of sectors of the economy that cannot be properly exposed to competition (such as energy infrastructure, rail transport) has given their owners the privileged status of rentiers – a status marked by reduced risk (due to low exposure to competition) and high earnings.

If the proliferation of risk is a definitional feature of what Zygmunt Bauman has called our 'liquid modernity,' a definitional feature of the emergent new modality of capitalism is that investment risk becomes a fictitious commodity (like previously land, labor, money and knowledge). What we might call the 'commodification of risk' consists in the packaging of leveraged financial products and selling them as profit-creating goods – a situation in which the risk contained in the package is the primary entity generating profit. The commodification of risk is most apparent in the case of credit default swaps (CDS).[16] In contrast to standard insurance, which one takes on a property one owns (a life, a house),

CDS allow one to insure what one does not own – namely the risk of someone else's loan defaulting. In this context risk is not just an externality, but a product created for market exchange.

The 'teen-age', 'nanny', 'step-mother' and 'rich uncle' states

In the course of the transformative dynamics of state-market and state-society relations since the emergence of democratic capitalism in the late eighteenth century, the semantics of statehood regarding the social role of the state have undergone considerable alteration. The institutional matrix of the liberal state under nineteenth-century entrepreneurial capitalism ensured the autonomy of the individual (constrained, of course, by labour commodification) in a modus we can call 'the teen-age state'. The trans-ideological consensus between European Socialism and European Conservatism on the need to safeguard society from market forces supplied the political grammar of the post-World War II welfare state: the 'nanny state.' During the third, neo-liberal stage, the matrix of state-society relations was what Giandomenico Majone (1990) has described as the 'regulatory state' – a state that gives priority to the use of legal authority and regulation over other tools of stabilization and redistribution. A peculiarity of this style of regulation is that it is individual-based. Regulatory policy under what the French call *l'état social actif* was conducted in a style of policy-making that consisted in transferring responsibilities for wellbeing from public authority to citizens. Thus, 'the nanny state' of welfare capitalism was replaced by 'the stepmother state' of the neo-liberal 1980s and 1990s – a state that used legal authority to enforce individual self-reliance.

The role of the state has been further altered in recent years to allow it to actively manage the distribution of opportunities and risks via a new type of intervention: action aiming to lend support to specific economic actors. We all witnessed the massive bailout of failing banks, but also the special support states provided to specific companies (especially in the automotive industry) during the economic crisis. This aligns with a practice, preceding the crisis, of setting up so called 'national champions' – private companies receiving large financial support from the state, in defiance of EU competition rules, on the grounds of their being strategically important for the competitiveness of national economies. Even before their bailout, 'mega-banks' enjoyed lower funding costs not simply because of their economies of scale but due to a market perception that financial groups were guaranteed by the government. The entrenched practice of the state to absorb companies' risk and pass it on to society has most recently produced the phenomenon of the 'zombie' companies: during the post-2008 financial meltdown the state placed ailing companies on life-support in the form of cheap bank loans backed by the government, which helped these companies refinance their old debt at much lower interest rates, thus saving them from bankruptcy. However, these companies spend all their revenue servicing debt rather than investing in growth. At the same time, the state is forcing society to absorb the risk thus generated by implementing austerity policies (cutting down spending on essential social services). This redistribution of funds from taxpayers to particular businesses or sectors of the economy amounts to saving capitalists, rather than salvaging capitalism.

However, it is not only corporate capital that has profited from privileged treatment by the state; so have groups of workers. Illustrative of this development, for instance, was the manner in which the French government attempted to alleviate the social pain of the austerity measures it had introduced in early 2011. Alarmed by stagnating and dropping incomes (and a drop in purchasing power), the French government introduced in April 2011 a one-off payment of 1000 euros per salaried worker. However, the beneficiaries of this seemingly generous provision were select: only workers in the largest publicly listed corporations on the French stock-exchange (the CAC 40). Left out were those working in small and medium companies, public sector employers, and those on minimum wage (the so called *smicards*). Thus, the state renewed its redistributive function but directed it differently – not towards those most at risk of impoverishment (as in the times of welfare capitalism), but instead towards those in the best position to enhance the competitiveness of the national economy in the global market.

As Claus Offe has observed, the tendency for the state to help those who have a competitive advantage is exacerbated by the transformation from the 'taxing' to the 'borrowing' state: 'The taxing state diminishes the disposable income of the well-to-do through (progressive) taxation, while the borrowing state increases that income by paying interest on what the well-to-do can afford to loan the state' (Offe 2013: 74, my translation).

By force of these newly assumed redistributive functions of public authority that came into existence well before the economic crisis, we have entered into a new matrix of state-society relations. The overly protective 'nanny state' of post-war welfare capitalism, and the 'step-mother state' of the neoliberal late twentieth century (a state which keeps its distance from society), have been replaced by the 'rich uncle' state – one that readily intervenes to help select actors for the sake of competitiveness in the global economy.

In the liberal modality of capitalism the state plays a market-constitutive function; in the modality of organized capitalism within the framework of post-World War II welfare capitalism, it plays a remedying function (using regulation and redistribution to remedy social risk). In the third, neoliberal form, the state lets the market assume more governing functions. In the fourth modality, it actively intervenes in order to enhance the global competitiveness of national economies. Be it inadvertently, this amounts to the state's playing an active role in social stratification by way of *aggregating* risks and opportunities for specific social groups, rather than distributing risks and opportunities evenly among citizens. (In this sense, I prefer to refer to the fourth modality of capitalism as 'aggregative' rather than 'reorganized').

Furthermore, as I have discussed in previously published research, as a result of the new distributional functions of the state, the polarization of life chances in the new context is no longer determined by class position (labor vs. capital), but by *institutionalized* access to security and opportunity (Azmanova 2004), increasingly managed via public intervention or implicit state guarantees of the sort discussed above. As a result, a new configuration of winners and losers has formed, beyond the traditional divide between capital and labor.

This in turn is forging a new ideological divide, cutting across the left-right axis of ideological opposition that had been the basis of political competition throughout the twentieth century. I have described this new ideological and political division as one running between an 'opportunity' and a 'risk' pole of preference aggregation: depending on citizens' perceptions of the social effect of globalization (Azmanova 2011). This entails not simply the dissolution of the left-right ideological divide (a tendency under 'disorganized' capitalism), but its reconfiguration in accordance with the novel ethos of post-neoliberal, 'aggregative' capitalism, and the novel semantics of state-citizen relations. Let me now trace how the novel redistributive functions of the state under aggregative capitalism find their legitimation within the semantics of the social contract.

The state: more powerful, less responsible, unfailingly legitimate

As we noted, public authority (at all levels of governance) has been undertaking ever more policy action to enhance market efficiency and intensify the production of wealth (including via regulations enabling the commodification of risk and rentierism), but less and less action to redistribute it. This has entailed a dramatic increase in social risk, while the responsibility for the generated risk has been diffused. Rather than a retrenchment of the state, we have the new phenomenon of an increase in the *power* of governing bodies (and their capacity to inflict social harm), while their *responsibility* for the social consequences of policy action is decreasing. As I have observed, this discrepancy between power and responsibility is harmful to democracy, as the exercise of power becomes ever more autocratic, even as the rituals of democratic politics are dutifully enacted (Azmanova 2013).

The discrepancy between power and responsibility should be eroding the authority of states, as Richard Sennett (2006) has claimed, and could be expected to trigger a legitimation crisis of the system. Yet, no such crisis ensues. This is the case because in the meantime, the *legitimacy relationship* between citizens and public authority has altered in such a way as to absolve the state from social responsibility.

The shedding of the state's responsibility for social protection, the individual responsibilization of citizens for their wellbeing (within the discourse of *resilience*, rather than social security), the privileging of specific economic actors for the sake of global competitiveness, and the resulting formation of a new precariat of those who are marginalized, all combine to alter the parameters of the socio-economic and political order in our societies. This new order is marked by a particular state of the legitimacy relationship between public authority and citizens – a condition that appears to be pathological from the point of view of standard notions of democratic legitimacy.[17]

I have proposed to conceptualize the connection between, on the one hand, economic interactions and, on the other, their political-institutional settings, via the notion of a matrix of shared norms shaping the legitimacy relationship between public authority and citizens (itself embedded within an ethos, in a Weberian sense). This relationship is, in turn, articulated as what citizens perceive to be legitimate and legitimacy-conferring functions of the state. In the course of the institutionalized practices of individual responsibilization to which I referred above, the very legitimacy relationship between public authority and citizens has been altered to exclude distributional issues from the range of political responsibility. This is evidenced, for instance, in analyses establishing that globalization weakens the connection between the national economy and citizens' political choice – economic openness reduces voter tendencies to hold incumbent policy makers responsible for economic performance and, by default, for the social consequences of economic policies.[18] Such absolution of the state from its social responsibility is asserted even via measures explicitly and deliberately intended to enhance social protection. Thus, the Council of Europe's *Charter on Shared Social Responsibilities* that was proposed for public consultation in the spring of 2011 justifies the novel concept of sharing responsibilities among various social actors with the assertion that states are, allegedly, 'less able to fulfil their role of ensuring access to social protection' (Council of Europe 2011: 3). Justifying neo-liberal economic policy with the imperatives of globalization, itself presented as a natural phenomenon (rather than engineered by specific policies), public authority has thereby effectively managed to redefine its relationship with citizens: market-regulative functions linked to the provision of social rights (such as wealth redistribution and guaranteed employment) have exited the matrix of this relationship.

There is no legitimacy crisis even at the nadir of the economic meltdown in advanced liberal democracies because the very legitimacy relationship has been altered to exclude issues of social safety from the range of public authority's responsibility. Public authority can cause social harm for which it does not assume responsibility since the very publics who are suffering the effects of economic policy have absolved public authority of the responsibility for the social consequences of that policy. This deficiency of responsibility cannot be easily remedied with the tools of representative, participatory or deliberative democracy. To the extent that democratic politics is a matter of an institutionally mediated expression of largely shared preferences, democratic politics takes place on the terrain of an existing legitimacy relationship between public authority and citizens. Whatever is not part of that relationship cannot be politicized and challenged. Therefore, if this relationship excludes social injustice and thus precludes the formulation of certain social grievances addressed to the political authority, the common instruments of democratic politics are unlikely to be of much use. A readjustment of the pathological legitimacy relationship between public authority and citizens would require that the state again assume responsibility for the social effect of its economic policy. Failing that, the pledges of high-tech, flexible, neo-liberal capitalism for a life of autonomy and re-invention (borrowed unabashedly from the Enlightenment) would but degenerate into social exasperation. What we must fear is not the revolt of the masses, but their silent escape from freedom – their resignation to the dogma 'there is no alternative.'[19]

Conclusion

Appropriating Polanyi's pronouncement on the fate of the nineteenth century, we might say that twentieth-century civilization has collapsed. I have here attempted to trace one particular trajectory of this collapse: the recasting of the legitimacy relationship between public authority and citizens, which, throughout the past century, had been anchored on a broadly shared notion of social justice and the state's responsibility for the social consequences of economic policy. I argued that we are witnessing, since the turn of the new century, a novel modality of capitalism which, although preserving capitalism's operational principle and ethos, has changed the semantics of state power – as it has changed the framework within which public authority and citizens mutually relate. My sketch here of the emergence of post-neoliberal, 'aggregative capitalism' is but the prolegomena of a broader investigation which should account for the formation of new political ideologies and public expectations, as well as provide a more elaborate account of the hermeneutics of political responsibility in relation to the notion of ethos adumbrated here. Echoing the way Weber brought to closure his *The Protestant Ethic and the Spirit of Capitalism*, let me end by saying that if this inquiry should serve as a conclusion of an investigation, rather than as its preparation, it is bound to accomplish little.

Notes

1 Harvey's Marxian critique of contemporary capitalism has gained spectacular popularity; the animated video recording of his lecture titled 'Crises of Capitalism' has been viewed by millions (Harvey 2010a, 2010b).

2 Elections in 2010 and 2011 brought to power the center-right in Spain, Portugal, Switzerland, Finland, Andorra, Ireland, Italy, Denmark, Britain, and the Netherlands – to consider only the 'mature' democracies of Europe. In that period the majority of the vote went to the center-left only in Sweden, where the Social Democrats scored only 0.6 percentage points higher than the economically liberal Moderate Rally Party (the vote for the former dropped by 4 percentage points since the last election, while the vote for the latter rose by 4 percentage points).

3 As discussed in the 'varieties of capitalism' literature, generated by the pioneering work of Peter Hall and David Soskise. The variation typically extends from 'liberal market economies' (such as the United States and Britain) to 'coordinated market economies' (such as Japan, Germany and the northern European states), passing through the 'mixed' type we find in southern European countries such as France, Italy, Spain and Portugal. (See Hall and Soskise 2001).

4 Max Weber defines ethos in terms of ethical ideals of duty having important formative influences on conduct; in this sense he talks about the ethos, or the 'economic spirit,' of an economic system (Weber 1930/1992: 27).

5 This concerns 'the state capacity to manage and distribute societal resources in ways that contribute to the achievement of prevailing notions of justice' (Offe 1985/1989: 5).

6 The freedom of contract in time generated the economic constraints to the institutional autonomy of the individual, constraints known as labour commodification.

7 Wilhelm von Humboldt, 'Ideas for a Proposed definition of the Limits and the Legality of the State' (1792), in Sidorsky (1970: 72).

8 Polanyi goes to great lengths to emphasize that the countermovement against the free market was not driven by particular interests or a given ideological agenda: 'Precisely because not the economic but the social interests of different cross sections of the population were threatened by the market, persons belonging to various economic strata unconsciously joined forces to meet the danger' (Polanyi 1944/1957: 154–5).

9 The first taxonomy captures variation in the degree to which the political economy is coordinated – as already noted, here variation typically extends from 'liberal market economies' to 'coordinated market economies.' The second taxonomy, introduced by Gosta Esping-Andersen, captures variation in the nature and generosity of social benefits provision. Within it, national varieties are clustered into 'liberal,' 'conservative' and 'social-democratic' types of welfare regimes.

10 This process is detailed in Boltanski and Chiapello (1999/2005).

11 As Julian Reid discusses in Chapter 11, neoliberalism has found in the ecological discourse of sustainable development a new reasoning to exert its economic logic and achieve legitimacy.

12 For a wealth of empirical evidence on this, see Rueda (2007).

13 Which pledged to make the EU, by 2010, 'the most competitive and dynamic knowledge-based economy in the world' (European Council 2000).

14 On this, see Streeck (1984) and Rhodes (2001).

15 The groups of winners and losers are often cast in terms of the growing income gap between low-skilled and highly skilled workers in industries exposed to globalization (Geishecker and Gorg 2007; Kapstein 2000).

16 Credit default swaps have existed since the early 1990s, but their use was rapidly increased between 2003 and 2007.

17 The analysis that follows builds on my discussion of the altered authority of the state in Azmanova (2013).

18 On this, see, for instance, the comprehensive analysis of elections in 75 countries in Hellwig and Samuels (2007).

19 Introduced by Herbert Spencer in the nineteenth century, the phrase 'there is no alternative' (abbreviated as TINA), was endorsed by Margaret Thatcher as a dictum that spurred the neoliberal turn in the 1980s.

References

Azmanova, A. (2004) 'The mobilisation of the European left in the early 21st century,' *European Journal of Sociology*, 45(2): 273–306.

Azmanova, A. (2010) 'Capitalism reorganized: social justice after neo-liberalism,' *Constellations: An International Journal of Critical and Democratic Theory*, 17(3): 390–406.

Azmanova, A. (2011) 'After the left-right (dis)continuum: globalization and the remaking of Europe's ideological geography,' *International Political Sociology*, 5(4): 384–407.

Azmanova, A. (2013) 'The crisis of Europe: democratic deficit and eroding sovereignty – not guilty,' *Law and Critique*, 24(1): 23–38.

Beck, U. (1992) *Risk Society: Towards a New Modernity*, London: Sage.

Boltanski, L. and Chiapello, E. ([1999] 2005) *The New Spirit of Capitalism*, London and New York: Verso.

Council of Europe (2011) Draft recommendation of the Committee of the Ministers to Member States on the Council of Europe's Charter on Shared Social Responsibilities, DGII/DCS (2011) 09.

Esping-Andersen, G. (1990) *The Three Worlds of Welfare Capitalism*, Princeton: Princeton University Press.

European Council (2000) 'The Lisbon Special European Council (March 2000): towards a Europe of innovation and knowledge (Presidency conclusions),' available at: www.europarl.europa.eu/summits/lis1_en.htm (accessed December 20, 2011).

Geishecker, I. and Görg, H. (2007) 'Winners and losers: a micro-level analysis of international outsourcing and wages,' Discussion Paper 6484, Centre for Economic Policy Research, London.

Hall, P. and Soskise, D. (eds) (2001) *Varieties of Capitalism: The Institutional Foundations of Comparative Advantage*, Oxford: Oxford University Press.

Harvey, D. (2010a) *The Enigma of Capital and the Crisis of Capitalism*, London: Profile Books.

Harvey, D. (2010b) 'The crisis of capitalism. Lecture at the Royal Society for the Encouragement of Arts, Manufactures and Commerce,' London, April 26, available at: www.youtube.com/watch?v=qOP2V_np2c0 (accessed December 25, 2011).

Kapstein, E.B. (2000) 'Winners and losers in the global economy,' *International Organization*, 54(2): 359–84.

Hellwig, T. and Samuels, D. (2007) 'Voting in open economies: the electoral consequences of globalisation,' *Comparative Political Studies*, 40(3): 283–306.

Lash, S. and Urry, J. (1987) *The End of Organized Capitalism*, Oxford: Polity Press.

Majone, G. (1990) *Deregulation or Re-regulation? Regulatory Reform in Europe and the United States*, London: Francis Pinter.

Offe, C. ([1985] 1989) *Disorganised Capitalism*, ed. J. Keane, Cambridge, Mass: MIT Press.

Offe, C. (2013) 'Europa in der Falle,' *Eurozine – Blätter für deutsche und internationale Politik*, 1/2013: 68–80.

Polanyi, K. ([1944] 1957) *The Great Transformation*, Boston: Beacon Press.

Rhodes, M. (2001) 'The political economy of social pacts: competitive corporatism and European welfare reform,' in P. Pierson (ed.) *The New Politics of the Welfare State*, Oxford: Oxford University Press.

Rueda, D. (2007) *Social Democracy Inside Out: Partisanship and Labour-Market Policy in Industrialised Democracies*, Oxford: Oxford University Press.

Sennett, R. (2006) *The Culture of the New Capitalism*, New Haven and London: Yale University Press.

Sidorsky, D. (ed.) (1970) *The Liberal Tradition in European Thought*, New York: G.P. Putnam.

Streeck, W. (1984) 'Neo-corporatist industrial relations and the economic crisis in West Germany,' in J.H. Goldthorpe (ed.) *Order and Conflict in Contemporary Capitalism*, Oxford: Clarendon.

Streeck, W. (2009) *Re-Forming Capitalism: Institutional Change in the German Political Economy*, Oxford: Oxford University Press.

Weber, M. ([1930] 1992) *The Protestant Ethic and the Spirit of Capitalism*, trans. T. Parsons, London and New York: Routledge.

11 The neoliberal biopolitics of resilience and the spectre of the ecofascist state

Julian Reid

There is an ecology of bad ideas, just as there is an ecology of weeds.
Gregory Bateson

There is no such thing as 'the state' but only rationalities of power and governance through which statehood is mediated. Rather, then, than make assumptions concerning the nature of the state, or presuppose the possibility of a theory of the state that might be propounded in universal terms, it befalls us to conduct an empirical examination of hegemonic assumptions concerning what is the difference between a right and a wrong way of governing, and the function of such assumptions in shaping the exercise of state power domestically and internationally. In the modern age the rationalities in accordance with which statehood has been mediated have tended to derive their authority from assumptions concerning the necessity to promote the biological welfare of human populations, the improvement of their wealth and health, and the increase of their life. Such was the hypothesis suggested by and explored exhaustively by Michel Foucault, and more recently, his followers, under the rubrics of the studies of liberal governmentality and biopolitics. But how true does this approach to the neoliberal governmentalization of the state remain? In this chapter I will argue that making sense of the rationalities of statehood contemporarily requires drawing out and exploring the paradigm shift in the account of the 'bio' underpinning the biopolitics of the neoliberal governmentalization of the state as distinct from more historical forms of liberal regimes. The entrenchment of liberalism in rationalities claiming to protect life itself has only become deeper over the course of liberal modernity, and the pathologization of subjects and dispositions defined by their supposed antipathy to life itself has only become more vicious. But when we examine specifically neoliberal regimes of power we see that the terms of their legitimacy have changed in accordance with a much altered account of the life that is said to be at stake. The legitimacy of neoliberal regimes, in contrast with the forms of liberal regime that Foucault examined historically, depends on claims as to their abilities to protect the life not so much of human populations, but of the biosphere. Neoliberalism has broken from earlier liberalisms in that it correlates claims for its legitimacy not simply with practices for the development of the species life of humanity, as Foucault directed us to recognize, but with biospheric life. These correlations of governance, development and biospheric life in and among neoliberal regimes of practice and representation increasingly comprise the foundation of its biopolitics. I have argued time and again in previous works that we cannot understand how liberalism functions, most especially how it has gained the global hegemony that it has, without addressing how systematically the category of life has organized the correlation of its various practices of governance. But this contemporary and ongoing shift in the very locus of the life that is at stake for liberal governance, from the human to the non-human, seems to me profoundly important for anyone concerned with resistance to liberalism. Looking at how this shift is impacting the life of peoples worldwide, this chapter will show that it is 'the poor' who are being systematically targeted, on account of their being said to be the greatest threat to the security of biospheric life. Alleviating threats to the biosphere requires targeting the poor because it is precisely the poor who are said to be the most 'ecologically ignorant' and, thus, most prone to live in non-sustainable ways. Thus does protecting the life of the biosphere require targeting the poor and relieving them of their ecological ignorance. The means to that removal is argued to reside not only in building neoliberal frameworks of economy, governance, but building neoliberal forms of subjectivity, and within the poor it is most often women who are the principal target population for such strategies of subjectification.

What I will do, therefore, in this chapter, is to chart how the discourse of resilience has been articulated, first through the emergence of the doctrine of sustainable development, and the allied rise in political influence of ecology, which can itself be attributed partly to the success of the environmental movement in reshaping the agenda of liberal governance, by shifting the locus of concern from the issue of the security of merely human life to that of the biosphere; but this must also be understood as an aspect of the ways in which neoliberalism, as distinct from classical liberalism, is grounded in a posthuman understanding of the nature of life itself. Whereas resilience was originally conceived by proponents of sustainable development as a property that distinguishes the extra-economic 'life-support systems' that humans require to live well, gradually it has become reconceived as a property which humanity intrinsically possesses just like all other living systems. But as a property of human populations its growth is said to be dependent on their interpellation within markets, their diversity as economic subjects, and their subjection to systems of governance able to ensure that they continue to use natural resources in sustainable ways. Thus, as we will see, did a doctrine which started out as a critique of neoliberal policy prescriptions for development transform into an imperative discourse which legitimates a neoliberal model of development based upon the constitution of markets and the interpellation of subjects within markets. In this sense, I concur with much of the analysis of Albena Azmanova in the previous chapter as to the ways in which neoliberalism has only become more powerful, while wanting to underscore the importance of the biopolitics of liberal legitimacy. Attention to the function of the discourse of resilience is necessary, especially, if we are to understand why it is that there is no legitimacy crisis for neoliberalism in the context of this era of economic crisis and exposure of peoples to endemic insecurity. Legitimacy, as argued in the Introduction to this volume, does not derive simply from the delivery of public goods but from the interpellation of a subject commanded to recognize its regime as legitimate on account of the ways in which it is called upon to perceive itself. Comprehending the biopolitical techniques of subjectivization by which neoliberalism reproduces itself is central to this question of neoliberal legitimacy (see also Reid 2011).

Every imperative discourse, regardless of how life affirmative it may be, runs the risk of turning fascistic. Indeed it seems to me that the problem of fascism today can no longer be construed in terms of the question of how to prevent the return of a despotic form of state, but how to resist the despotic nature of the ecological discourses which already underpin the exercise of liberal state power. The spectre of the ecofascist state is contemporarily haunting liberal international relations. Preaching that sustainable development will follow only when peoples give up on specifically human development, as well as attendant political ideals of progress and security, and learn to practice the virtue of resilience, so the ecofascist state renders life for human beings a finite game of mere survival. The making of resilient subjects and societies fit for neoliberalism by agencies of sustainable development is based upon a degradation of the political capacities of human beings far more subtle than that achieved in Auschwitz and Buchenwald. But the enthusiasm with which ideologues of sustainable development are turning resilience into an 'imperative' is nevertheless comparable with that of the SS guards who also aimed to speed up the processes of adaptive learning among those Jews and other populations in their charge by convincing them of the futility of resistance.

The sustainable development-resilience nexus

Following the end of the Cold War, development and security came to be conceived in the words of the former British Secretary of State for International Development, Hilary Benn, as something of a 'shared challenge' (Benn 2004). Development was said to make 'a critical contribution to global security by reducing poverty, inequality and the root causes of conflict' while 'global prosperity, everyone's prosperity, depends on security against threats to human development' (Benn 2004). 'The truth is', as Benn declared in a now classic speech, that 'development without security is not possible; security without development is only temporary' (Benn 2004). At least three different axioms were at work in Benn's formulation of the interrelation between development and security; what became referred to in International Relations as the 'development-security nexus' (Duffield 2008, 2001; Chandler 2007). First, the development of the developing world was said to depend on its security; security conceived as a prerequisite of development. Second, development of the developing world became conceptualized itself as a means towards the security of developing societies;

security conceived also, therefore, as the end towards which development was aimed. And third. no security of the developed world was said to be possible without increasing the development of undeveloped states and societies; thus the ultimate subject of both development and security proved to be not the developing world at all, but the developed. This trinity of axioms underlay not just British development policy, but those of most western national governments, as well as international organizations concerned with development, significantly the United Nations, as well as a wide range of NGOs, and their academic proxies. In the United States, Senator John Kerry, chairman of the Senate Foreign Relations Committee, was to be heard calling for development to 'rank alongside defense at the heart of America's foreign policy' (Staats 2009).

While the development-security nexus would appear to have become evermore tightly woven in international relations, semantic shifts in the conceptualization of both development and security are occurring. Demands for development are increasingly tied not simply to demands for 'security' but to a discursively new object of 'resilience'. And this shift from security to resilience is tied likewise to a reconceptualization of development as 'sustainable development'. The axioms that flow from this discursive shift in the development-security nexus obey the same trinitarian structure as those noted above. First, the sustainable development of the developing world is said to depend on the developing world achieving resilience; resilience conceived thus as a prerequisite of sustainable development. Second, sustainable development must be aimed, it is said, at increasing the resilience of the developing world; resilience conceived thus as the end to which sustainable development is driven. And third, the resilience of the developed world is said to be inextricably intertwined with the task of making developing peoples into resilient ones; the subject of both sustainable development and resilience is thus revealed in actuality as the developed world. Are these, then, merely semantic shifts, or do they signify changes in the rationalities that have shaped both development and security policies during the post-Cold War period? Are the rationalities that distinguish resilience different to those underpinning demands for security? And are those of 'sustainable development' different to what was once known simply as 'development'? Does the weaving of a nexus of relations between 'sustainable development' and 'resilience' represent a departure from the 'development-security nexus' in some way? And, if so, what explains that shift and what are its political implications?

Choosing life over economy?

Sustainable development is proclaimed by its proponents to offer a more progressive way of framing the development problematic to that propagated previously by Western states and international organizations. In contestation of the economic rationalities that shaped the development policies of the West during much of the Cold War, and especially in protest at the implications of the reification of the economic development of societies for their environments, sustainable development seeks to secure the 'life-support systems' which peoples otherwise require in order to live well and prosper (Khagram *et al.* 2003; Gladwin *et al.* 1995; Barbier and Markandya 1990; Folke and Kautsky 1989). By privileging the security of the biosphere over and against the imperative to secure economies, 'life' is thus offered as an obstacle to 'economy' by the doctrine of sustainable development. Sustainable development was always vulnerable to a re-appropriation by the economic rationalities of Western governments, I argue however, because of the interface between its 'alternative' rationality of security and that of specifically neoliberal doctrines of economy. While sustainable development deploys ecological reason to argue for the need to secure the life of the biosphere, neoliberalism prescribes economy as the very means of that security. Economic reason is conceived within neoliberalism as a servant of ecological reason; claiming paradoxically to secure life from economy through a promotion of the capacities of life for economy. This is the paradoxical foundation on which neoliberalism constructs its appropriation of sustainable development. Sustainable development and neoliberalism are not the same, nor is the former simply a proxy of the latter, but they do come into contact powerfully on the terrains of their rationalities of security. This surface of contact ought to make for a tense and political field of contestation, but has instead made largely for a strategically manipulable relation between the two doctrines.

In recent years we can see, at the very least, how vulnerable the ecological reasoning that underpins sustainable development has been to the economic reasoning of neoliberalism. Indeed I argue that the ongoing disarticulation of the concept of security in development doctrine and correlate emergence of the concept of resilience is an expression of this. Neoliberalism is able to appropriate the doctrine of sustainable development on account of its claims not to the 'security' but 'resilience' of specifically neoliberal institutions (significantly markets), systems of governance and conditions of subjectivity. Resilience is defined by the United Nations as 'the capacity of a system, community or society potentially exposed to hazard, to adapt by resisting or changing in order to reach and maintain an acceptable level of functioning and structure' (UN 2004: Ch. 1, s. 1, 17). Academics concerned with correlating the promotion of 'sustainable development' with that of resilience define it as 'the capacity to buffer change, learn and develop – as a framework for understanding how to sustain and enhance adaptive capacity in a complex world of rapid transformations' (Folke *et al.* 2002: 437). The concept of resilience arose not as a direct product of neoliberal doctrines but as an element of the critique of neoliberalism which sustainable development itself pertained to be at its origin. This should not surprise us. Neoliberalism is not a homogeneous doctrine, nor are its particular forms of dogmatism homeostatic. Its powers of persuasion and discursive prosperity depends on its own capacity to adapt to the hazards of critique. It is, you might well say, a paragon of the resilience that sustainable development demands of its subjects. The current prosperity of the doctrine of sustainable development is also a vexed expression of the resilience of neoliberalism. It is on account of this power to absorb and align itself with the very sources of its critique that what I call the 'sustainable-development-resilience nexus' is becoming to twenty-first-century liberal governance what the development-security nexus was to its earlier post-Cold War forms. If 'security' functioned during the first two decades of post-Cold War international relations as a rationality for the subjection of development to Western states, their governance practices, institutions and conditions for subjectivity, then the rationality which governs that subjection is increasingly going to be 'resilience'. Voices from within International Relations calling for the dismantling of the sign of security because it is 'the supreme concept of bourgeois society and the fundamental thematic of liberalism' (Neocleous 2008: 186) miss the point. Calling for a new politics to take us 'beyond security' does little to solve the problem; indeed it obfuscates the very nature of the problem, which is that liberalism itself is outgrowing its long-standing correlation with security, and locating new discursive foundations – principally that of resilience.

Beyond showing how the discourse of resilience legitimates neoliberal systems of governance and institutions, it is also necessary to attend to the forms of subjectivity it attempts to bring into being. The account of the world envisaged and constituted by development agencies concerned with building resilient subjects is one that presupposes the disastrousness of the world, and likewise one which interpellates a subject that is permanently called upon to bear the disaster. A subject for whom bearing the disaster is a required practice without which he or she cannot grow and prosper in the world. This may be what is most at stake in the discourse of resilience. The resilient subject is a subject which must permanently struggle to accommodate itself to the world: not a subject which can conceive of changing the world, its structure and conditions of possibility, but a subject which accepts the disastrousness of the world it lives in as a condition for partaking of that world and which accepts the necessity of the injunction to change itself in correspondence with the threats and dangers now presupposed as endemic. Building resilient subjects involves the deliberate disabling of the political habits, tendencies and capacities of peoples and replacing them with adaptive ones. Resilient subjects are subjects that have accepted the imperative not to resist or secure themselves from the difficulties they are faced with but instead adapt to its enabling conditions via the embrace of neoliberalism. Resisting neoliberalism in the present may thus require rejecting the seductive claims to 'alternative futures' offered by seemingly contrary doctrines of sustainable development and their political promises of resilience. A reinvestment in an account of political subjectivity is needed, and a rearticulation of the more classical concept of security may be useful for such a purpose.

The political genealogy of sustainable development

The ideas that shaped the doctrine of 'sustainable development' became influential in the 1970s but they only took concrete form with the 1987 publication of the Bruntland Commission report *Our Common Future* (WCED 1987). On the surface of things sustainable development appeared to operate as the foundation for a powerful indictment of hitherto dominant theories and practices of development. Development policies were classically aimed at increasing the production, consumption and wealth of societies. What 'sustainable development' did was to pose the problem of the implications of such economy-centered policies for the 'life support systems' on which societies otherwise depend for their welfare (Khagram *et al.* 2003: 296–7). The doctrine of sustainable development that emerged from *Our Common Future* and which culminated in the 2002 World Summit on Sustainable Development in Johannesburg was based upon the seemingly contrary axiom that economic development had to be subordinated to the need to ensure the sustainable use of natural resources, healthy environments, ecosystems and biodiversity. Here, the utility and value of 'life' in all of its complexities was offered by the doctrine of sustainable development as an obstacle to economy. Committed to securing life from the dangers posed to it by unfettered economic reason, the doctrine of sustainable development appeared to emerge in direct conflict with the governmental doctrine of neoliberalism which, during the 1980s, had become increasingly hegemonic, and which would have the opportunity to go global with the end of the Cold War in 1989. The kinds of 'pure liberalism' championed by Thatcherites and Reaganites, said to reify the economy at all costs as both means and ends of development, was subject to an apparently new line of questioning, not on account of its equally questionable implications for the economic welfare of peoples, but on account of the threats it posed to something outside of the order of economy: life. Proponents of sustainable development did not claim to question the value of economic development in and of itself, but they did aspire to offer a framework for the re-regulation of the economy in alignment with the needs and interests of the biosphere. And indeed its effects were palpable during the 1990s, a decade in which a Senior Vice President of the World Bank, Joseph Stiglitz, was to be heard making savage indictments of the implications of liberal policy prescriptions, and in which the advice of environmentalists was increasingly taken into account by governments and international economic institutions (O'Brien *et al.* 2000: 109–58).

But the relationship between the emergence of sustainable development and the crisis in liberal reason which began to trouble governments in the 1980s and 1990s is highly complex. Mark Duffield has shown how the shift from strategies of development preaching modernization to sustainable development owed much to a specifically neoliberal framing of the problematic of development (Duffield 2008: 67–70). As Duffield argues, sustainable development emerged as part of a neoliberal counter-critique of modernization strategies of development which, rather than undermining the authority of liberal reason, gave it a new and even more powerful footing. While recognizing the function of ecological reason in shaping the doctrine of sustainable development and its critique of modernization strategies, Duffield draws attention to the neoliberal rationalities which have nevertheless defined it. For one, the strength of its challenge to traditional models of development owed much to its alignment with the neoliberal critique of the state (Duffield 2008: 67). Preaching that sustainable development would only follow once peoples gave up on state-led modernization strategies and learnt to practise the virtue of 'community-based self-reliance', so sustainable development reflected a neoliberal political agenda that shifts the burden of security from states to people (Duffield 2008: 69). Sustainable development functions in extension of neoliberal principles of economy, Duffield argues, by disciplining poor and underdeveloped peoples to give up on states as sources for the protection and improvement of their well-being, and instead practice the virtue of securing themselves. Thus does sustainable development engage in the active promotion of a neoliberal model of society and subjectivity in which everyone is demanded to 'prove themselves by bettering their individual and collective self reliance' (Duffield 2008: 69). In African states such as Mozambique, for example, it has provided 'a virtually free social security system offering the possibilities of adaptation and strengthening in order to manage the risks of market integration' (Duffield 2008: 93).

Revealing the convergences between sustainable development and the neoliberal critique of the model of society and subjectivity it proposes as solutions to the problem of the state, and the economic pay-offs that follow, Duffield offers a powerful riposte to those narrative accounts of sustainable development as arising simply from the empowerment of ecological over economic reason. But how then should we understand the nature of the relation between sustainable development and neoliberalism? Is ecological reason just a proxy of the neoliberal rationalities which Duffield argues has shaped the agenda of sustainable development? If we understand sustainable development as a servant of neoliberalism then what should we make of those voices arising from environmental movements, and the many other ways in which ecological reason has been mobilized, to critique economy-based strategies of development in the interests of sustaining life? Answering these questions requires grappling further with the fundamental and complex correlations of economy, politics and security with life in neoliberal doctrine; what Duffield rightly names its biopolitics (2008: 4–8). Neoliberalism is widely understood as a 'theory of political economic practices proposing that human well-being can best be advanced by the maximization of entrepreneurial freedoms within an institutional framework characterized by private property rights, individual liberty, unencumbered markets, and free trade' (Harvey 2007: 22). Less understood, however, is how its claims to be able to increase wealth and freedom are correlated with ways to increase the prosperity and security of life itself. Its capacities to correlate practices for the increase of economic profit and prosperity with those dedicated to increasing the profitability and prosperity of the biosphere are precisely why the doctrine of sustainable development is so compatible with it.

In the first instance this is a problem of the neglect of the complexities of economic doctrines per se. If we examine the origins of economics we find that it was from its earliest usage conceptualized as a domain of knowledge concerned with the prosperity not just of human communities, families and subjects, but a knowledge which seeks to increase that prosperity in alignment with the needs of nature in its entirety. For Aristotle, economics, it was said, 'must conform to nature … in as much as nature has already distributed roles and duties within the species themselves' (Mondzain 2005: 19) 'Implicit', therefore, 'within the economy is the notion of an organic objective and functional harmony . . . a providential and natural order to be respected while acting in the service of the greatest cohesion of utility and well-being' (Mondzain 2005: 19). As Michel Foucault's historical analyses have shown, with the birth of the modern discipline of political economy so 'nature' lost its status as the major correlate of economy and thus did 'life' began to play that role (Foucault 1997). For political economists of the modern age, however, the life which economy had to respect was specifically that of the human species; the question of the prosperity and security of human populations became conceived as limiting conditions for the exercise of economic reason and practices. Neoliberalism breaks from earlier liberalisms and traditions of political economy in so far as its legitimacy rests on its capacities to correlate practices for the increase of economic profitability and prosperity not just with practices for the securing of the human species, but with the life of the biosphere. These correlations of economy, well-being, freedom, security and biospheric life in and among neoliberal regimes of practice and representation comprise some of the foundations of what have been named its biopolitics (Dillon and Reid 2009; Duffield 2008; Cooper 2008; Reid 2006). And if there is anything 'fundamental' to liberalism then it is this; one cannot understand how liberalism functions, most especially how it has gained the global hegemony that it has, without addressing how systematically the category of life has organized the correlation of its various practices of governance, as well as how important the shift in the very understanding of life, from the human to the biospheric, has been for changes in those practices.

Examining neoliberalism biopolitically means we can understand better how it is that ecological reasoning has enabled the growth of strategies for the promotion of market-based entrepreneurial capitalism in and among developing societies. Of particular importance here are the ways in which the very account of security deployed by neoliberal states and their development agencies has began to alter through its correlation with ecological reason. Crucial to this story is the relatively recent emergence of the discourse of resilience. When neoliberals preach the necessity of peoples becoming 'resilient' they are, as I will show, arguing in effect for the entrepreneurial practices of self and subjectivity which Duffield calls 'self reliance'. 'Resilient' peoples do not look to states or other entities to secure and improve their well-being because they have been disciplined into believing in the necessity to secure and improve it for themselves. Indeed so convinced are they are of the worth of such capabilities that they proclaim it to be a fundamental 'freedom' (UNEP 2004). But the emergence of this discourse of resilience within the doctrine of neoliberalism owes massively, I argue, to the power of ecological reason in shaping the very rationality of security which otherwise defines it. In other words comprehending how a neoliberal rationality of security functions in shaping the agenda of sustainable development requires us to examine the constitutive function of ecological reason in shaping both. Far from being a proxy of the neoliberal rationalities shaping sustainable development, ecological reason has been formative of them.

From security to resilience

The strategic function of sustainable development in the global expansion of neoliberalism has been to naturalize neoliberal frameworks of governance; the institutions, practices and forms of subjectivity which it demands are brought into being on account of the desire for increase of the economic profitability and prosperity of human communities. But how is it that neoliberal ways of governing came to be conceived as an answer to the problem of sustainability? Some of the answer to this question can be given, I believe, by looking closely at the emergence and discursive expansion of the concept of 'resilience'. Because that is the concept against which all such institutions, practices and subjectivities are increasingly legitimized. It is no accident that the concept of resilience derives directly from ecology, referring to the 'buffer capacities' of living systems; their ability to 'absorb perturbations' or the 'magnitude of disturbance that can be absorbed before a living system changes its structure by changing the variables and processes that control behaviour' (Adger 2000: 349). Living systems are said by ecologists to develop not on account of their ability to secure themselves prophylactically from threats, but through their adaptation to them. Exposure to threats is a constitutive process in the development of living systems, and thus the problem for them is never simply how to secure themselves but how to adapt to them. Such capacities for adaptation to threats are precisely what ecologists argue determines the 'resilience' of any living system. Sustainable development started out by preaching that the economic development of societies must be regulated so that it contributes not just to the security of states and their human populations, but so that it increases the resilience of all living systems; shifting the object of concern from that of human life to that of the biosphere, incorporating every known species, as well as habitats of all kinds, vulnerable to the destructions wrought by economic development. Life not economy, it said, must provide the rationalities according to which peoples are entitled to increasing their prosperity. The emergence of such a doctrine had to have significant implications for the ways in which not only the problem but the very nature of security was conceived in developmental circles. Once the referent object of development became the life of the biosphere rather than simply states and their human populations so the account of security to which development is allied was required to transform. Security, with its connotations of state and governmental reason, territoriality, military capacities, economic prosperity, human resources and population assets became less fashionable and gradually gave way to the new concept and value of 'resilience'. Resilience is a useful concept, the proponents of sustainable development argued, precisely because it is not a capacity of states, nor merely of human populations and their various political, social and economic practices, but a capacity of life itself. Thus did resilience emerge within the doctrine of sustainable development as a way of positing a different kind of policy problematic to those formulated in the security doctrines of neoliberal states and their more conventional development agencies: one which would privilege the life of the biosphere in all its dimensions over and against the human focus which shaped the 'development-security nexus'. If one aspect of the subordination of rationalities of economy to rationalities of life in developmental discourse has been the shift from doctrines of economic development to sustainable development, then a correlate shift has been that from security to resilience.

Allied to this shift, then, the doctrine of sustainable development brought into being a new guiding axiom, one which created a surface of friction with the rationalities of economic development pursued by Western states and development agencies up until the 1980s. And this in turn, during the 1990s, gradually brought into being a 'sustainable development-resilience nexus' to rival the development-security nexus woven by previous regimes. By the time of the 2002 World Summit on Sustainable Development in Johannesburg, however, a summit which is widely recognized as the coming of age party of 'sustainable development', new ways of thinking about resilience were coming into view. A major report prepared on behalf of the Environmental Advisory Council to the Swedish Government as input to the process of the World Summit described how resilience is a property associated not just with the diversity 'of species', but also 'of human opportunity', and especially 'of economic options – that maintain and encourage both adaptation and learning' among human populations (Folke *et al.* 2002: 438). In an adroit reformulation of the problematic, neoliberal economic development, in which the function of markets as generators of economic diversity is basic, became itself a core constituent of the resilience which sustainable development had to be aimed at increasing. Thus was it that, post-Johannesburg, the correlation of sustainable development with resilience started to produce explicitly neoliberal prescriptions for institutional reform. 'Ecological ignorance' began to be conceptualized as a threat, not just to the resilience of the biosphere, but to humanity (Folke *et al.* 2002: 438). Resilience began to be conceived not simply as an inherent property of the biosphere, in need of protection from the economic development of humanity, but a property within human populations which now needed promoting through the increase of their 'economic options.' As remarkably, the biosphere itself began to be conceived not as an extra-economic domain, distinct from and vulnerable to the economic practices of human populations, but an economy of 'services' which 'humanity receives' (Folke *et al.* 2002: 437).

There is a double and correlated shift at work, here, then, in the elaboration of the sustainable-development-resilience nexus post-Johannesburg. In one move 'resilience' has shifted from being a property of the biosphere to being a property of humanity, while in a second move 'service' has shifted from being an element of economy to being a capacity of the biosphere. Crucified on the cross that this double shift carves are 'the poor'. For they are the segment of population of which resilience is now demanded and simultaneously the population said to threaten the degradation of 'ecosystem services.' Increasing the 'resiliency' of the poor has become a defining goal, for example, of the United Nations Environment Programme (UNEP) in the years post-Johannesburg (UNEP 2004: 39). Alleviating threats to the biosphere requires improving the resilience of the poor, especially, because it is precisely the poor that are most 'ecologically ignorant' and thus most prone to using 'ecosystem services' in non-sustainable ways. Thus does ensuring the resilience of the biosphere require making the poor into more resilient kinds of subjects, and making the poor into more resilient subjects requires relieving them of their ecological ignorance, and the means to that removal is argued to reside in building neoliberal frameworks of economy, governance and subjectivity. Developing the resilience of the poor is said to require, for example, a social context of 'flexible and open institutions and multi-level governance systems' (Folke *et al.* 2002: 439). 'The absence of markets and price signals' in ecological services is a major threat to resilience, UNEP argues, because it means that 'changes in their conditions have gone unnoticed' (UNEP 2004: 13). Property rights regimes have to be extended so that they incorporate ecosystem services and so that markets can function in them (UNEP 2004: 15). 'Markets', it is argued, 'have proven to be among the most resilient institutions, being able to recover quickly and to function in the absence of government' (Pingali *et al.* 2005: S18). When and where the market fails to recover, development policies for increasing resilience have to be aimed at 'ensuring access to markets' (Pingali *et al.* 2005: 518). Ensuring the resilience of the poor also requires the building of neoliberal systems of governance which will monitor their use of ecological services to ensure they are sustainably managed (UNEP 2004: 39). The poor, in order to be the agents of their own change, have to be subjectivized so that they are 'able to make sustainable management decisions that respect natural resources and enable the achievement of a sustainable income stream' (UNEP 2004: 5). 'Over-harvesting, over-use, misuse or excessive conversion of ecosystems into human or artificial systems damages the regulation service which in turn reduces the flow of the provisioning service provided by ecosystems' (UNEP 2004: 20). Within 'the poor' itself women are the principal target population. 'I will transform my lifestyle in the way I farm and think' has become the mantra that poor women farmers in the Caribbean region are demanded, for example, to repeat like Orwellian farm animals in order to receive European Union funding (Tandon 2007: 12–14).

This double shift is integral, I argue, to the strategy by which neoliberalism has absorbed the critique of sustainable development. Whereas resilience was originally conceived by proponents of sustainable development as a property that distinguishes the extra-economic 'life-support systems' which humans require to live well, it has become reconceived post-Johannesburg as a property which humanity intrinsically possesses, is capable of developing further, and which it can never have too much of. As a property of human populations it is dependent moreover on their interpellation within markets, their diversity as economic subjects, and their subjection to systems of governance able to ensure that they continue to use natural resources in sustainable ways. Thus did a doctrine which started out as a critique of neoliberal policy prescriptions for development transform into a doctrine which legitimates a neoliberal model of development based upon the constitution of markets and the interpellation of subjects within markets.

The disastrous and politically debased subject of resilience

Having established how sustainable development, via its propagation of the concept of resilience, naturalizes neoliberal systems of governance and institutions, I want to consider how it functions to constitute subjects amenable to neoliberal governance. Every regime of governance invokes its own particular subject of governance. Producing subjects the liberal way has long since been a game of producing self-securing subjects. Subjects that are capable of securing themselves are less of a threat to themselves and in being so are not a threat to the governance capacities of their states nor to the governance of the global order either. And in this sense the correlation of development with security feeds upon the political imaginary of liberalism predicated as it became upon the belief that a global order of self-securing subjects would in turn deliver a more secure form of world order (Rosenau 2008, 2002, 1992). What, then, does the shift in the correlation of development with security to resilience tell us about the nature of the subject which development is now aimed at producing? What differences are entailed in being a resilient subject as opposed to a merely secure subject? Is the emergence of this new object of development just an extension of the liberal rationalities of governance that feed upon what is otherwise described as the development-security nexus?

There is, in fact, a considerable shift here. The major condition of possibility for the subject of sustainable development is that it sacrifices its capacity and desire for security. Security, here, is less that which liberalism demands of its subjects than what it forbids them. The resilient subject of sustainable development is, by definition, not a secure but an adaptive subject; adaptive in so far as it is capable of making those adjustments to itself which enable it to survive the hazards encountered in its exposure to the world. In this sense the resilient subject is a subject which must permanently struggle to accommodate itself to the world: not a political subject which can conceive of changing the world, its structure and conditions of possibility, with a view to securing itself from the world, but a subject which accepts the disastrousness of the world it lives in as a condition for partaking of that world and which accepts the necessity of the injunction to change itself in correspondence with the threats and dangers now presupposed as endemic. One can see readily how this plays out in relation to debates, for example, over climate change. One enthusiast for resilience as an answer to the problem writes:

> What is vital to understand is not the degree of climate change that we should expect, nor necessarily the impact that we might anticipate on water resource management, coastal defence, food security, species survival, etc. What is important to grasp is that we do have the abilities to adapt and adjust to the changes that climate change will bring.
>
> (Tandon 2007: 12)

Sustainable development is no longer conceived, thus, as a state of being on account of which a human is capable of securing itself from the world, and via which he or she becomes a subject in the world. Once development is said to follow ecological laws of change and transformation, and thus once exposure to hazard becomes a condition of possibility for development, so the ecofascistic demand which sustainable development makes on the communities and individuals subject to it is: can you survive in the world without securing yourself from the world?

This is precisely why resilience has become so intimately tied in the policy, practice and theory of sustainable development not just to neoliberalism but to disaster management. Indeed the latter is also crucial in legitimating the former. The ability to manage exposure to hazard in and among developing societies is dependent, the UN says, on their maintenance of a healthy and diverse ecological system that is productive and life sustaining, but it also demands a healthy and diverse economy that adapts to change and recognizes social and ecological limits (UN 2004: Ch. 1, s. 2, 18). It requires 'capturing opportunities for social change during the "window of opportunity" following disasters, for example by utilizing the skills of women and men equally during reconstruction' (UN 2004: Ch. 1, s. 2, 20). As fundamentally it requires making societies 'aware of the importance of disaster reduction for their own well-being' (UN 2004: Ch. 3, s. 4, 1), because 'it is crucial for people to understand that they have a responsibility towards their own survival and not simply wait for governments to find and provide solutions' (2004: Ch. 3, s. 4, 20). Disasters, thus construed, are not threats to the development of human beings from which they might aspire to secure themselves. They are events of profound 'opportunity' for societies to transform themselves economically and politically. They are events which do not merely expose communities to dangers from which they must be saved in order that they might be set back onto the path of development, but, rather, where communities, in their exposure, are able to undergo novel processes of developmental change in reconstitution of themselves as neoliberal societies. Exposure to disaster, in this context, is conceptualized in positive terms as constitutive of the possibility for the development of neoliberal systems of governance. But the working of this rationality depends on a subject that will submit to it. Sustainable development requires subjects, the UN report insists in a remarkable passage, to understand the 'nature' of hazards. The passage of societies to such knowledge must in turn involve, it states

> a consideration of almost every physical phenomenon on the planet. The slow movements in the earth's mantle – the convection cells that drive the movement of continents and the manufacture of ocean floors – are the starting and also the sticking point. They lift mountains and shape landscapes. They also build volcanoes and trigger potentially catastrophic earthquakes. Like those other invisible movements that take place on a vast scale through the atmospheric medium – the carbon cycle and the water cycle and the nitrogen cycle – volcanoes and earthquakes, along with technological advancements, provide the bedrock of strong nations, rich industries and great cities. They do, of course, also have the potential to destroy them.
>
> (UN 2004: Ch. 2, S. 1, 4)

The account of the world envisaged and constituted by development agencies concerned with building resilient societies is one that presupposes the disastrousness of the world, and likewise one which interpellates a subject that is permanently called upon to bear the disaster, a subject for whom bearing the disaster is a required practice without which he or she cannot grow and prosper in the world. This is precisely what is at stake in the discourse of resilience. The resilient subject is a subject which must permanently struggle to accommodate itself to the world: not a subject which can conceive of changing the world, its structure and conditions of possibility, but a subject which accepts the disastrousness of the world it lives in as a condition for partaking of that world, which will not question the reasons why he or she suffers, but which accepts the necessity of the injunction to change itself in correspondence with the suffering now presupposed as endemic.

The human here is conceived as resilient in so far as it adapts to rather than resists the conditions of its suffering in the world. To be resilient is to forego the very power of resistance. 'The imperative of adaptation rather than resistance to change will increase inexorably' two ideologues of sustainable development claim (Handmer and Dovers 1996). In their enthusiasm for the 'inexorable increase' of this 'imperative' theorists of sustainable development engage in some vivid discursive representations of the human. 'As a species, humanity is immensely adaptable – a weed species. We are also capable of considerable adaptability as individuals, and also as households (variously defined) – the latter being the perennial and universal human social unit' (Handmer and Dovers 1996). The combination of the imperative of humanity to adapt with the representation of humanity as a 'weed species' recalls the discursive currency of similar combinations within the concentration camps of Nazi Germany during the Second World War. Those camps were, as Barrington Moore has demonstrated in a still brilliant and wide ranging historical study, sites for the constitution of precisely such resilient subjects and the honing of precisely such adaptive capacities. The inhabitants of such extreme spaces of suffering often failed to exhibit any sign of resistance, seeking to survive through the development of complex and ultimately failed strategies of 'adaptation' to the conditions of their suffering (Moore 1978: 66). The 'conquest' of the perception of inevitability and necessity of circumstances is 'essential', Moore argues on the other hand, 'to the development of politically effective moral outrage' (1978: 459). The making of resilient subjects and societies fit for neoliberalism by agencies of sustainable development is based upon a degradation of the political capacities of human beings far more subtle than that achieved in Auschwitz and Buchenwald. But the enthusiasm with which ideologues of sustainable development are turning resilience into an 'imperative' is nevertheless comparable with that of the SS guards who also aimed 'to speed up the processes of adaptive learning' among those Jews and other populations in their charge by convincing them of the futility of resistance (Moore 1978: 66).

Development contra neoliberalism?

Can the doctrine of sustainable development be retrieved from the grip which neoliberalism seems to have achieved on it? My intention here has not been to argue against claims as to the necessity of concern for the state of the biosphere, but to raise the problem of the surface of contact between such an ecological mode of reasoning and a mode of economic reason complicit with the degradation of the biosphere. While sustainable development deploys ecological reason to argue for the need to secure the life of the biosphere, neoliberalism prescribes economy as the very means of that security. Economic reason is conceived within neoliberalism as a servant of ecological reason; claiming paradoxically to secure life from economy through a promotion of the capacities of life for economy. If, then, sustainable development is to escape its appropriation it would seem imperative that it contest the nexus of relations on which claims as to the necessity of neoliberal frameworks for the sustainability of life are based. For a start this has to mean rethinking the ways in which it engages with the concept of resilience. The problem here is less the demands to improve the resilience of ecosystems which distinguished the agenda of sustainable development in its early years than it is the post-Johannesburg shift to propagating resilience as a fundamental property and capacity of the human. The ecological imaginary is colonizing the social and political imaginaries of theorists and practitioners of development in ways that are providing fertile ground for the application of neoliberalism as a solution to the problem of sustainability. Understanding how that is possible requires understanding the biopolitics of neoliberalism; how its claims to be able to increase wealth and freedom are correlated with ways to increase the prosperity and security of life itself. For its capacities to correlate practices for the increase of economic profit and prosperity with those dedicated to increasing the profitability and prosperity of the biosphere are precisely why the doctrine of sustainable development is so compatible with it.

What is needed is a policy and practice of sustainable development reflexive enough to provide space for a 'speaking back' to the forms of neoliberalism that are currently being pushed by Western states and international organizations as answers to the problem of sustainability. A policy and practice that will cut the poor and underdeveloped some slack when it comes to issues of environmental degradation, climate change, and struggles for and over natural resources. A policy and practice that will, while taking into account the grave nature of these problems, take seriously the degradations of capacities for the development of political subjectivity that occur when adaptation rather than resistance to the conditions of worldly suffering becomes a governing imperative. We have enough voices, now, calling within the chorus of development for the saving of the planet. But where are the voices that will call for the saving of the political? For sustainable development to reinvent itself it needs to master the ecological reason from out which it emerged and forge newly political paradigms of thought and practice. Why is it that the conception of ecology at work in sustainable development is so limited that it permits neoliberalism to proliferate, like a poison species, taking over entire states and societies in the wake of their disasters, utilizing their suffering, as conditions for its spread, installing markets, commodifying anything it can lay its hands on, monetizing the value of everything, driving peoples from countryside into cities, generating displacement, homelessness and deprivation? Isn't this an ecological problematique? Why is this ecofascistic death and suffering producing machine tolerated in the name of sustainability? It is not only living species and habitats that are today threatened with extinction, and for which we ought to mobilize our care, but the words and gestures of human solidarity on which resistance to such biopolitical regimes of governance depends (Guattari 1995). A sense of responsibility for the survival of the life of the biosphere is not a sufficient condition for the development of a political subject capable of speaking back to neoliberalism. Nor a sense of responsibility for the life of humanity. What is required is a subject responsible for securing incorporeal species, chiefly that of the political, currently threatened with extinction, on account of the overwrought fascination with life that has colonized the developmental as well as every other biopoliticized imaginary of the modern age.

References

Adger, W.N. (2000) 'Social and ecological resilience: are they related?', *Progress in Human Geography*, 24(3): 347–64.

Barbier, E.B. and Markandya, A. (1990) 'The conditions for achieving environmentally sustainable development', *European Economic Review*, 34(2–3): 659–69.

Benn, H. (2004) 'A shared challenge: promoting development and human security in weak states', Center for Global Development, Washington, 23 June, available at: www.dfid.gov.uk/Documents/pdf_misc/sp-weakstatesbenn.pdf.

Chandler, D. (2007) 'The security-development nexus and the rise of "anti-foreign policy" ', *Journal of International Relations and Development*, 10(4): 362–86.

Cooper, M. (2008) *Life as Surplus: Biotechnology and Capitalism in the Neoliberal Era*, Seattle: Washington University Press.

Dillon, M. (2007) 'Governing terror: the state of emergency of biopolitical emergence', *International Political Sociology*, 1(1): 7–28.

Dillon, M. and Reid, J. (2009) *The Liberal Way of War: Killing to Make Life Live*, London and New York: Routledge.

Duffield, M. (2001) *Global Governance and the New Wars: The Merging of Development and Security*, London and New York: Zed Books.

Duffield, M. (2008) *Development, Security and Unending War: Governing the World of Peoples*, Cambridge: Polity.

Folke, C. and Kautsky, N. (1989) 'The role of ecosystems for a sustainable development of aquaculture', *Ambio*, 18(4): 234–43.

Folke, C., Carpenter, S., Elmqvist. T., Gunderson, L., Holling, C.S. and Walker, B. (2002) 'Resilience and sustainable development: building adaptive capacity in a world of transformations', *Ambio*, 31(5): 437–40.

Foucault, M. (1997) *The Order of Things*, London: Routledge.

Gladwin, T.N., Kennelly, J.J. and Krause, T.S. (1995) 'Shifting paradigms for sustainable development: implications for management theory and research', *The Academy of Management Review*, 20(4): 874–907.

Guattari, F. (1995) *Chaosmosis*, Indiana: Indiana University Press.

Handmer, J.W. and Dovers, S.R. (1996) 'A typology of resilience: rethinking institutions for sustainable development', *Organization and Environment*, 9(4): 482–511.

Harvey, D. (2007) 'Neoliberalism as creative destruction', *The ANNALS of the American Academy of Political and Social Science*, 610(1): 22–44.

Khagram, S., Clark, W.C. and Raad, D.F. (2003) 'From the environment and human security to sustainable security and development', *Journal of Human Development*, 4(2): 289–313.

Mondzain, M-J. (2005) *Image, Icon, Economy: The Byzantine Origins of the Contemporary Imaginary*, Stanford: Stanford University Press.

Moore, B. (1978) *The Social Basis of Obedience and Revolt*, Plains, NY: M.E. Sharpe.

Neocleous, M. (2008) *Critique of Security*, Edinburgh: Edinburgh University Press.

O'Brien, R., Goetz, A.M., Scholte, J.A. and Williams, M. (2000) *Contesting Global Governance: Multilateral Economic Institutions and Social Movements*, Cambridge: Cambridge University Press.

Pingali, P., Alinovi, L. and Sutton, J. (2005) 'Food security in complex emergencies: enhancing food system resilience', *Disasters*, 29(s1): S5–S24.

Reid, J. (2006) *Biopolitics of the War on Terror: Life Struggles, Liberal Modernity and the Defence of Logistical Societies*, Manchester and New York: Manchester University Press.

Reid, J. (2011) 'The vulnerable subject of liberal war', *South Atlantic Quarterly*, 110(3): 770–9.

Rosenau, J. (1992) 'Citizenship in a changing global order', in J. Rosenau and E. Czempiel (eds) *Governance without Government: Order and Change in World Politics*, Cambridge: Cambridge University Press.

Rosenau, J. (2002) 'Information technologies and the skills, networks and structures that sustain world affairs', in J. Rosenau and J.P. Singh (eds) *Information Technologies and Global Politics: The Changing Scope of Power and Governance*, Albany: SUNY Press.

Rosenau, J. (2008) *People Count! Networked Individuals in Global Politics*, Boulder and London: Paradigm Press.

Staats, S.J. (2009) 'Sen. Kerry champions development in knock-out speech', Center for Global Development, available at: http://blogs.cgdev.org/globaldevelopment/2009/05/sen-kerry-champions-development-in-knock-out-speech.php.

Tandon, N. (2007) 'Biopolitics, climate change and water security: impact, vulnerability and adaptation issues for women', *Agenda*, 73: 4–20.

UN (United Nations) (2004) *Living with Risk: A Global Review of Disaster Reduction Initiatives*, New York: United Nations Publications.

UNEP (United Nations Environment Programme) (2004) *Exploring the Links: Human Well-Being, Poverty and Ecosystem Services*, Nairobi: United Nations Publications.

WCED (World Commission on Environment and Development) (1987) *Our Common Future*, Oxford: Oxford University Press.

Index